MEXICO IN REVOLUTION, 1912–1920

OTHER TITLES IN THIS SERIES

Also Available

CONTRIBUTING ADVISORS

Benjamin Harris
Trent Wolf

REACTING TO THE PAST

MEXICO IN REVOLUTION, 1912–1920

Jonathan Truitt, Central Michigan University

Stephany Slaughter, Alma College

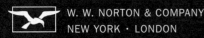

W. W. NORTON & COMPANY
NEW YORK · LONDON

BARNARD
REACTING TO THE PAST

W. W. Norton & Company has been independent since its founding in 1923, when William Warder Norton and Mary D. Herter Norton first published lectures delivered at the People's Institute, the adult education division of New York City's Cooper Union. The firm soon expanded its program beyond the Institute, publishing books by celebrated academics from America and abroad. By midcentury, the two major pillars of Norton's publishing program—trade books and college texts—were firmly established. In the 1950s, the Norton family transferred control of the company to its employees, and today—with a staff of four hundred and a comparable number of trade, college, and professional titles published each year—W. W. Norton & Company stands as the largest and oldest publishing house owned wholly by its employees.

Editor: Justin Cahill
Project Editor: Caitlin Moran
Editorial Assistant: Funto Omojola
Managing Editor, College: Marian Johnson
Production Manager: Jeremy Burton
Marketing Manager, History: Sarah England Bartley
Design Director: Rubina Yeh
Book Design: Alexandra Charitan
Director of College Permissions: Megan Schindel
Permissions Clearance: Patricia Wong
Composition: Six Red Marbles
Illustrations: Mapping Specialists
Manufacturing: Sheridan Books

Library of Congress Cataloging-in-Publication Data

Names: Truitt, Jonathan G., 1977- author. | Slaughter, Stephany, author.
Title: Mexico in revolution, 1912–1920 / Jonathan Truitt, Central Michigan
    University ; Stephany Slaughter, Alma College.
Description: First edition. | New York : W. W. Norton & Company, [2020] |
    Series: Reacting to the past | Includes bibliographical references.
Identifiers: LCCN 2019026486 | ISBN 9780393690392 (paperback)
Subjects: LCSH: Mexico—History—Revolution, 1910–1920—Study and
    teaching—Activity programs. | Role playing.
Classification: LCC F1234 .T875 2020 | DDC 972.08/16—dc23
LC record available at https://lccn.loc.gov/2019026486

W. W. Norton & Company, Inc., 500 Fifth Avenue, New York, NY 10110
W. W. Norton & Company Ltd., 15 Carlisle Street, London W1D 3BS

DEDICATION

Dedicated to Braeden and Kai and Ana Sofia and Alexa, who have diligently reminded us that making a game requires us to stop working and play from time to time.

ABOUT THE AUTHORS

Dr. Stephany Slaughter is an associate professor of Spanish and chair of the World Languages and Cultures Department at Alma College, where she teaches courses related to language, literature, and culture of Latin America. She pursues research in gender studies; cultural studies; Latin American (especially Mexican) film, theater, performance; borders and immigration; and representations of the Mexican Revolution. Interest in the intersections of gender, memory, and the Mexican Revolution began during doctoral study at the Ohio State University with her dissertation, "Performing the Mexican Revolution in Neoliberal Times: Reinventing Iconographies, Nation, and Gender." Other publications related to the Mexican Revolution include "Transnational Zapata: From the Ejército Zapatista de Liberación Nacional to Immigrant Marches" (*Journal of Transnational American Studies*, Dec 2012); "Queering the Memory of the Mexican Revolution: Cabaret as a Space for Contesting National Memory" (Summer 2011 *Letras Femeninas*); and the book chapter "Adelitas y coronelas: un panorama de las representaciones clásicas de la soldadera en el cine de la Revolución mexicana" in *La luz y la guerra: el cine de la Revolución Mexicana* (CONACULTA, 2010). In 2010 she won an Emmy for her work as a field producer on the Oscar nominated and Emmy Award winning documentary *Which Way Home* (directed by Rebecca Cammisa, 2009), an experience that has inspired her more recent work focusing on immigration, as well as other film projects.

Dr. Jonathan Truitt is Professor of Latin American History and Chair of the Center for Learning through Games and Simulations at Central Michigan University. He is the author of *Sustaining the Divine in Mexico Tenochtitlan: Nahuas and Catholicism, 1523–1700* and co-editor of *Native Wills from the Colonial Americas: Dead Giveaways in a New World*. His research interests focus on the religious interactions of Nahuas and Spaniards in Colonial Mexico City and the use of games as a pedagogical tool, in the past and the present. At Central Michigan University he teaches courses on Latin American History, World History, and Game Design. When not working, he spends his time exploring the world with his family.

CONTENTS

PART 1: INTRODUCTION

PART 2: HISTORICAL BACKGROUND

PART 3: THE GAME

PART 4: ROLES AND FACTIONS

PART 5: CORE TEXTS

PART 1: INTRODUCTION

BRIEF OVERVIEW OF THE GAME

The year is 1912. Francisco Madero is president of Mexico. Just last year he and his top general, Pascual Orozco, ousted the long-standing president (some say dictator) Porfirio Díaz, who is now in exile. But the country is far from stable. Madero has been president of the United States of Mexico for four months and has moved too slowly on his reforms for some of his allies, but too quickly for his critics. General Orozco and General Emiliano Zapata, one-time allies, have risen in revolt against the Madero government. A basic cultural rift between the elite and the poor of the country portends a sequence of tumbling revolts.

Students play characters that are charged with stabilizing their country and preventing further civil war. The goal is to reform Mexico to make it a better nation for all of its inhabitants. The hope, by some, is that President Madero will be able to regain control of events before they spin out of control. Many fear, however, that Porfirio Díaz's parting words, "Madero has unleashed a tiger, now let us see if he can control it," may be accurate. Mexicans and foreigners worry that without a firm hand, Mexico might indeed be a wild tiger recently released from captivity. The characters in the game will work to reform Mexico and keep the prophetic tiger in the cage.

At the beginning of the game students are divided into one of four groups: Maderistas (supporters of President Francisco Madero), Felicistas (supporters of his main political opponent, Félix Díaz), Zapatistas (the followers of indigenous revolutionary and one-time Madero ally Emiliano Zapata), and Indeterminates (a collection of characters who are unaligned with one of the three main groups). For each session of the game students consult contemporary sources (such as political plans, manifestos, the constitution, corridos, and artworks) to reform the constitution of 1857 by passing laws related to a key topic. As each law is passed, it becomes clear that what works for one group does not work for another. At a time when people continually feel betrayed, can peace and stability be achieved? Can it be sustained?

PROLOGUE IN FOUR PERSPECTIVES

I. Wealthy Elite

*W*hen, for the first time in Mexico's history, the streets were festive after the announcement of a new leader, when there were no troops—organized, ragtag, or otherwise—marching toward the capital, when there was no gunfire, no bloodshed, when there were no bodies to collect and quietly bury, you were scared. You knew something inevitable, when deferred, returns with a greater fury, as if it were angry for having been pigeonholed. Amid all this, something even worse gnawed at you: that everything was changing, and changing fast, and for the first time that anyone could remember, your life was no longer sacrosanct. Your class was no longer untouchable.

Porfirio Díaz had held power for years; a benevolent dictator to people like you, because anyone in his good graces could rely on security and prosperity. There were sacrifices to be made for this prosperity, of course: the press was tightly controlled, elections were rigged, dissidents were jailed, but this was a small trade for the real stake. Mexico, for the first time, enjoyed decades of uninterrupted peace.

There was the occasional native uprising, the occasional critical opinion column, of course, but Don Porfirio had built an elaborate state apparatus for dealing with these things. Mexico City's secret police were competent and quick and made easy work of those who were stupid enough to ramble on about the injustices of the government.

Félix Díaz, Don Porfirio's own nephew, was once the head of this police unit, but he also languished in Chile as the consul general for disappointing his uncle. Don Porfirio soon brought him back, though, because the president was good to his own. And that was how it worked. As long as you were good to Don Porfirio, Don Porfirio was good to you.

Some say you were lucky, privileged, but what did they know? You went to school, worked hard, and earned what you made. Now there is criticism of too many foreigners making their money in Mexico, but you did what you had to do. What was lucky was that the president allowed it to happen. He once remarked, "Poor Mexico. So far from God, so close to the United States," but he was more pragmatist than idealist, more practical than proud. He knew that letting in the oilmen, like the American Edward Doheny and the British Weetman Dickinson Pearson, and allowing them to own land and export Mexico's oil may have seemed to some like an imperialist invasion. But these foreigners put Mexicans to work and built much needed infrastructure like railroads. Oil was flowing out of Mexico, but foreign money was pouring in. If anyone faulted you for riding that wave, for taking a little off the top, they were just jealous. Maybe people were being displaced from marginal farmland, but schools were being built, and it was only a matter of time before the poor would be lifted up out of their poverty, along with the rest of Mexico. What right had they to complain?

Now all of that is ruined. The populist Francisco Madero, in what he is calling "free elections," has won the vote, mostly from people who should not have been allowed to cast a ballot in the first place. Of course, when he started making stump speeches and declaring his bid for the presidency, nobody took him seriously. This turned out to be a mistake. But he has made some serious missteps of his own. He might have won a peaceful election, but he overthrew Don Porfirio with violence. He wanted a revolution, and got one; he's foolish to think that the violence will stop now that he is in power. He has ruined the tenuous peace that prevailed over the previous decades, and he will likely destroy Mexico's chance at becoming a modernized, industrial nation. Despite the veneer of democracy, he assumed power using force, and it is with force that he will be overthrown. Nobody is safe. For the first time in your life, the protection you enjoyed as an elite cannot save you. It is not the time for business lunches and vacations. You must fight or assimilate with the Maderistas. You must try to seize power or flee. Whatever happens, you have to do something. Mexico can't stay the way it is now for very much longer.

II. A Female Perspective

Your struggle has always been a losing one, a perpetual uphill battle in the face of condescension and minced words. Growing up you thought that maybe it was just you and the people who lived around you, but as you came of age you found that so many other women had similar experiences. "Politics, business, these things are for men," you were always told. "The household, the family, that is where your focus should lie." But you always wanted something more.

While the men decide the fate of their companies and, more importantly, of the country—and by consequence your fate as well—you are expected to do nothing but prepare dinner and look after the children. Granted, these duties are sacred and necessary—you understand that—but it is so frustrating to lack choice and power. Professional fields like medicine and law are virtually closed to you. If you were only given a chance, you know you could make your mark.

Other women you have met since you defied your family and moved to Mexico City have convinced you that the only way to get your chance is to snatch it from the hands of the men holding on so tightly. You know you need the vote, the opportunity to formally voice your opinion, because power starts with the vote. Suffrage is not easily won, however, and you are frustrated that few women are fighting for it. The longer you study and discuss it, the more convinced you are that the right to cast a vote is not something that can be peacefully acquired. Other women who publish radical tracts find themselves the target of fierce government investigations and oppression. If you are so strong, you need to prove it.

The conservatives[1] of Mexico will not step quietly aside. The Church, that bastion of culture and tradition, is too influential and divides even the radical women you know. The Catholic Church can never accept divorce, for example, but the right of women to file for divorce is essential to your cause. The ability to leave a marriage, a legal and religious arrangement the woman may have never agreed to in the first place, conveys untold influence both within and outside the household. For women to truly have the chances they deserve, they cannot be totally under the control of men. In resisting a woman's right to file for divorce, the Church is hindering the cause of all women.

The Church is so deeply ingrained in Mexican life and culture that most people you know could never, would never, go without it. Abandoning the Church, for most people, is not even a possibility. How can you, as a woman, reconcile the needs of your culture and your religion with your needs as an individual? How can you break with tradition and yet stay true to your faith? This is the question that you and so many others wrestle with.

You realize now that you are an exceptional woman who stands out among the other women of Mexico. Your ideas are unpopular with both sexes. While a small group of women seeks changes relating to labor reform and education, those women still believe they should perform jobs that no man will accept or those that support the men in their life. They do not seek political or civil equality like you do. The one thing you know more than anything else, though, is that you are finished stifling your dreams while men are allowed to pursue whatever lives and careers they wish. You're through staying silent while men make the important decisions. You know that your voice matters. Lately, there has been a lot of talk and fighting among the men about who should govern Mexico. Your opinion, of course, is that men and women should both be in charge. Some of the revolutionaries, especially Francisco Madero, have expressed sympathies for women. He promises change, but how much? In what form? And can you trust him?

III. Northern Laborer

ne person can take only so much. You were raised in a small, dusty town near the American border, and it was the only home you'd ever known. Then, abruptly, your family was kicked off their small farm. You and your family had to move to Cananea, another town near the border because the only work was in the mines there. Farmwork is hard, but mine work is something else altogether. Instead of baking in the sun, you toil in the dark.

The entire family—you, your mother, father, grandmother, and two brothers—stay in a single room, eating, sleeping, and cooking. So many people in a small space is cramped, but mostly you aren't there: six days out of the week, sixteen hours a day, you are underground, inhaling lung-blackening dust. Before dawn you descend, and after dusk you resurface, having missed the sun.

Despite the low pay, your family manages to sustain itself, and everything has become rote: work, eat, work, eat, work, sleep, and start again the next day. You're still young, not even married yet, but you've seen how the harshness of your job wears on people. Skin hardens like minerals, and every frequent cough summons a black lump of sputum.

The Consolidated Copper Company, an American company, owns the mine where you work, and they freely and openly favor Americans over Mexicans. They treat you and your people as if you were totally expendable. The grueling hours and low pay are nothing if not insulting. You must endure them simply for being a Mexican. The Americans with whom you work are more than just arrogant. They are paid almost double what you are paid. Worse, the Americans are quickly promoted, and always over Mexicans. Mexicans are never promoted. They tell you that toiling underground is all you'll ever be good for. As if those profiteers who scurry across the river to pillage would know more about anything than a person whose first steps were among the mustard-colored dust of Mexico.

Long had there been talk in the mines of doing something. And things had been done. There had been strikes. But that was at a time when the Mexican government had no problem favoring the rights of foreigners over those of the native people. Oppression was met with action, and action with violence. You witnessed people being returned to the dust from which they were made: it always started with a command, and then insults. A shovel connected with someone's cheek, a pickaxe driven into a shoulder, maybe, and then it was all over. Amid a few knocked-out teeth, bodies and bullet casings littered the ground.

The biggest strike was in 1906, when things got so bad that everybody stopped working and marched. The strikers demanded that three-quarters of the jobs go to Mexicans, that Mexicans be promoted equally based on skill and, of course, receive equal pay. As the strikers marched, some Americans fired into the crowd and killed three people. That was the start of it. The strikers set the Americans on fire and began rioting. Unsurprisingly, rangers from Arizona came across the border and squashed the uprising. Strikers lay dead, and everyone went back to work without any concessions from the management.

Especially infuriating about this was that the Mexican government allowed foreigners to handle a dispute on Mexican land. Had a posse of armed Mexicans gone across the border and killed striking Americans, you and others said over dinner some nights, the Americans would have countered by declaring war. The U.S. government would not have tolerated foreigners entering their territory and killing its citizens, then why did Mexico?

It seemed only natural when a struggle to depose the Díaz dictatorship broke out that you and other miners would support it. The new leader, Francisco Madero, is a large landowner, though he professes to be in support of the working people. The anarchists, whom you know to be sympathetic to your cause, are on board with this revolution, too, but you can't help but be a little wary. All you ask is a fair wage and working conditions that aren't so harsh. Can you trust this new revolution, or will it use you up and kick you aside, like everyone and everything else has done?

IV. Indigenous Campesino

hey call you a *campesino*. The term literally means someone from the *campo* (country) but is often used to refer to someone who works the land—in other words, a person of low socioeconomic status, a peasant.

The biggest affront to your family after the passage of the Ley Lerdo[2] in 1856 wasn't that the community where you lived had to give up the land it had lived on and farmed for countless generations. It wasn't even that, after the forfeiture, so many rich landowners swooped in to purchase outright the lands your family and village had held communally, as if these rich vultures had been waiting all along until you lost your grip. No, the biggest insult of all was that they forced you to work on your former lands, now aggregated into a rich man's *hacienda* (a large estate), where you were paid a measly sum for your labor and did not get to keep what you grew.

This new law, it was said, was supposed to weaken the power of the Church by forcing it to sell lands not used in daily operations. But nobody in your family ever understood why the Church needed to be weakened. The government seemed to change every six months, but the Church was a constant, something to rely on. That the Mexico City elite wanted to weaken its power angered a great many people. The politicians said they hoped people like you would buy the holdings, but who would commit the heresy of purchasing lands the Church was forced to forfeit? Let alone have the funds to do so? And then, as an unintended consequence of the very general law, the civil corporation managing your and your village's land was forced to sell as well, and again you had no money to buy it back.

Here in the south, in Morelos, land had been held the same way, communally for the village, for longer than anyone can remember—long before the Spaniards arrived with their ideas about landownership. Your people, who are indigenous, have communal customs stretching much further back than Mexico itself. You were here in Morelos before the first Spaniards crossed the ocean, and you had planned to be around long after they left. The problem is that they never left, and now it looks like they never will.

You still live with your family all in the same house, where you eat, sleep, and rest together. But before, you had to provide only for yourselves. You went to sleep when you got tired; you woke up when you were done sleeping. Now there are cruel taskmasters to please, and they call you awake at dawn and make you work for degrading pay every day until dusk. While the owners sit in their mansions and get rich, you work out in the blistering heat on land you can no longer call your own. The village has stayed together instead of dispersing, and the sense of community has not evaporated. But now all anybody does is grumble. Generations of tradition have been wiped out by this so-called modernism, at great expense to the people who had an original claim.

It is impossible—even laughable—to think that the village could ever earn enough money to buy back the land. The owners, prejudiced and fat, would surely never agree to part with their lands at any price you could pay, even if the village pooled all its money over a long period of time. Your ancestral lands were ripped from you by the simple passing of a law by the rich and empowered. You can take the lands back only by force. You have heard much talk, talk that is no longer secret, of one named Emiliano Zapata leading the charge. Although you do not know this man personally, you have heard of him as a rising figure in his village. Because of his obvious charisma and penchant for leadership, you know that it was not difficult to convince the others to take up arms. People have been complaining louder and louder, no longer in fear of losing their jobs or their livelihood. You've heard that they are stockpiling weapons, training for a fight. You have a family to feed, but under the current conditions you can barely afford to do so. When Zapata comes knocking and asks you to join him—what choice will you really have?

HOW TO REACT

Reacting to the Past is a series of historical role-playing games. Students are given elaborate game books that place them in moments of historical controversy and intellectual ferment. The class becomes a public body of some sort; students, in role, become particular persons from the period, often as members of a faction. Their purpose is to advance a policy agenda and achieve their victory objectives. To do so, they will undertake research and write speeches and position papers; and they will also give formal speeches, participate in informal debates and negotiations, and otherwise work to win the game. After a few preparatory lectures, the game begins, and the players are in charge; the instructor serves as adviser, or "game-master." Outcomes sometimes differ from the actual history; a postmortem session at the end of the game sets the record straight.

The following is an outline of what you will encounter in Reacting and what you will be expected to do. While these elements are typical of every Reacting game, it is important to remember that every game has its own special quirks.

Game Setup

Your instructor will spend some time before the beginning of the game helping you understand the historical background. During the set-up period, you will read several different kinds of materials, including:

- The game book (from which you are reading now), which contains historical information, rules and elements of the game, and essential documents

- Your role sheet, which describes the historical person you will play in the game

You may also be required to read primary and secondary sources outside the game book (perhaps including one or more accompanying books), which provide additional information and arguments for use during the game. Often you will be expected to conduct research to bolster your papers and speeches.

Read all of this contextual material and all of these documents and sources before the game begins. And just as important, go back and reread these materials throughout the game. A second reading while *in role* will deepen your understanding and alter your perspective: ideas take on a different aspect when seen through the eyes of a partisan actor.

Players who have carefully read the materials and who know the rules of the game will invariably do better than those who rely on general impressions and uncertain recollections.

Game Play

Once the game begins, certain players preside over the class sessions. These presiding officers may be elected or appointed. Your instructor then becomes the gamemaster (GM) and takes a seat in the back of the room. While not in control, the GM may do any of the following:

- Pass notes to spur players to action.

- Announce the effects of actions taken inside the game on outside parties (e.g., neighboring countries) or the effects of outside events on game actions (e.g., a declaration of war.)

- Interrupt and redirect proceedings that have gone off track.

Presiding officers may act in a partisan fashion, speaking in support of particular interests, but they must observe basic standards of fairness. As a failsafe device, most Reacting games employ the "Podium Rule," which allows a player who has not been recognized to approach the podium and wait for a chance to speak. Once at the podium, the player has the floor and must be heard.

To achieve your objectives (outlined in your role sheet) you must persuade others to support you. You must speak with others, because never will a role sheet contain all that you need to know and never will one faction have the strength to prevail without allies. Collaboration and coalition building are at the heart of every game.

Most role descriptions contain secret information that you are expected to guard. Exercise caution when discussing your role with others. You may be a member of a faction, which gives you allies who are generally safe and reliable, but even they may not always be in total agreement with you.

In games where factions are tight-knit groups with fixed objectives, finding a persuadable ally can be difficult. Fortunately, every game includes roles that are undecided (or "indeterminate") about certain issues. Everyone is predisposed on certain issues, but most players can be persuaded to support particular positions. Cultivating these players is in your interest. (By contrast, if you are assigned an "indeterminate" role, you will likely have considerable freedom to choose one or another side in the game; but often, indeterminates have special interests of their own.)

Make friends and find supporters. Before you speak at the podium, arrange to have at least one supporter second your proposal, come to your defense, or admonish those in the body not paying attention. Feel free to ask the presiding officer to assist you, but appeal to the GM only as a last resort.

Immerse yourself in the game. Regard it as a way to escape imaginatively from your usual self—and your customary perspective as a college student in the twenty-first century. At first, this may cause discomfort because you may be advocating ideas that are incompatible with your own beliefs. You may also need to take actions that you would find reprehensible in real life. Remember that a Reacting game is only a game and that you and the other players are merely playing roles. When others offer criticisms, they are not criticizing you as a person. Similarly, you must never criticize another *person* in the game. But you will likely be obliged to criticize their *persona*. (For example, never say, "Sally's argument is ridiculous." But feel free to say, "Governor Winthrop's argument is ridiculous," though you would do well to explain exactly why!) When spoken to by a fellow player—whether in class or out of class—always assume that person is speaking to you in role.

Help create this world by avoiding the colloquialisms and familiarities of today's college life. The presiding officer, for example, should never open a session with the salutation "Hi,

A NOTE ON COSTUMES

When entering into a Reacting to the Past game many students want to dress the part of their characters. Unfortunately, hurtful stereotypes concerning Mexicans are based on the historical dress from the time period of the Mexican Revolution. Because of this, we request that you not dress the part of any of the characters in this game.

guys." Similarly, remember that it is inappropriate to trade on out-of-class relation-ships when asking for support within the game. ("Hey, you can't vote against me. We're both on the tennis team!")

Reacting to the Past seeks to approximate of the complexity of the past. Because some people in history were not who they seemed to be, so, too, some roles in Reacting may include elements of conspiracy or deceit. (For example, Brutus did not announce to the Roman Senate his plans to assassinate Caesar.) If you are assigned such a role, you must make it clear to everyone that you are merely playing a role. If, however, you find yourself in a situation where you find your role and actions to be stressful or uncomfortable, tell the GM.

Game Requirements

Your instructor will explain the specific requirements for your class. In general, a Reacting game will require you to perform several distinct but interrelated activities:

- **Reading:** This standard academic work is carried on more purposefully in a Reacting course, since what you read is put to immediate use.

- **Research and Writing:** The exact writing requirements depend on your instructor, but in most cases you will be writing to persuade others. Most of your writing will take the form of policy statements, but you might also write autobiographies, clandestine messages, newspaper articles, or after-game reflections. In most cases, papers are posted on the class website for examination by others. Basic rules: Do not use big fonts or large margins. Do not simply repeat your position as outlined in your role sheet; you must base your arguments on historical facts, from ideas drawn from assigned texts, and from independent research. (Your instructor will outline the requirements for footnoting and attribution.) Be sure to consider the weaknesses in your argument and address them; if you do not, your opponents will.

- **Public Speaking and Debate:** Most players are expected to deliver at least one formal speech from the podium (the length of the game and the size of the class will affect the number of speeches). Reading papers aloud is seldom effective. Some instructors may insist that students instead speak freely from notes. After a speech, a lively and even raucous debate will likely ensue. Often the debates will culminate in a vote.

- **Strategizing:** Communication among students is a pervasive feature of Reacting games. You should find yourself writing emails, texting, and attending meetings on a fairly regular basis. If you do not, you are being outmaneuvered by your opponents.

Skill Development

An Associated Press article on education and employment made the following observations:

> The world's top employers are pickier than ever. And they want to see more than high marks and the right degree. They want graduates with so-called soft skills—those who can work well in teams, write and speak with clarity, adapt quickly to changes in technology and business conditions, and interact with colleagues from different countries and cultures. . . . And companies are going to ever-greater lengths to identify the students who have the right mix of skills, by observing them in role-playing exercises to see how they handle pressure and get along with others . . . and [by] organizing contests that reveal how students solve problems and handle deadline pressure.[3]

Reacting to the Past, probably better than most elements of the curriculum, provides the opportunity for developing these "soft skills." This is because you will be practicing persuasive writing, public speaking, critical thinking, problem solving, and collaboration. You will also need to adapt to changing circumstances and work under pressure.

Learning Objectives:

The goal of this game is to demonstrate the political and social turmoil that swirled beneath the veneer of the Porfiriato (the name given to the era of leadership of former president Porfirio Díaz) and the guise of "Order and Progress" just after Mexico's centennial celebration in 1910.

Students will

1. Apply political ideologies of the time and examine how they intersect with decisions regarding conflicts and the perpetuation of the violence of the Mexican Revolution. Some of the ideologies include Comtian positivism, Social Darwinism, agrarianism, anarchism, Social Catholicism, feminism, liberalism, and communism.

2. Demonstrate knowledge of state formation, the rural and urban divide, some early-twentieth-century political ideologies, and of U.S.–Mexican relations at the start of the twentieth century.

3. Grapple with answers to the following questions: How is success and progress demonstrated to your neighbors, your peers, your electorate, and foreign nations? By what means does one nation claim to be superior to another and by what means does one class of people claim superiority over

another? To what degree are these claims accurate and according to whom? How might the people in the implied inferior position have a different meaning of success? What happens when these ideas collide and cannot find seamless resolution?

4. Understand, evaluate, analyze, and locate primary and secondary sources and employ them for the use of both public speaking and effective and properly cited writing. The writing will involve citations in a recognized style.

5. Demonstrate knowledge of the major players and events leading up to and continuing through the Mexican Revolution via formal assessments (e.g., exams or papers).

 PART 2: HISTORICAL BACKGROUND

CHRONOLOGY

1810	Start of Mexican independence movement.
1821	Treaty of Córdoba signed, awarding Mexico independence.
1846	United States invade Mexico.
1848	In the Treaty of Guadalupe Hidalgo, Mexico cedes half its territory to the United States.
1854	In the Gadsden Purchase, the remainder of what constitutes the modern-day borders of Arizona and New Mexico is sold to the United States.
1855	Benito Juárez and allies overthrow Antonio Lopéz de Santa Anna.
1857	Benito Juárez and allies reform the government, in part to stem U.S. expansionist ideas. Ley Juárez, Ley Lerdo, and Ley Iglesias are three of the most significant laws passed.
1858–61	War of Reform.
1863	France invades Mexico and establishes the reign of Emperor Maximillian.
1867	France withdraws troops; Benito Juárez executes Maximillian and captures Mexico City.
1877	Porfirio Díaz overthrows President Sebastián Lerdo de Tejada and becomes president.
1906	Cananea Consolidated Copper Company miners strike.
1907	Río Blanco Textile Mill workers strike.
1907–1910	Food crisis due to major crop failures.
1908	James Creelman interviews Porfirio Díaz, who states he will not run in the 1910 election.
1910	Porfirio Díaz holds centennial celebration of Mexican Independence.
	• Porfirio Díaz emphasizes Mexico's indigenous roots, but would not allow individuals who were culturally Native American to attend the festival.

- Porfirio Díaz decides to run for president again, despite the Creelman interview.
- Francisco Madero loses the presidential bid in a landslide vote for Porfirio Díaz (quite possibly through ballot tampering). The Revolution starts shortly after.

1911   Massacre of Chinese in Torreón by Maderista forces (those loyal to Madero).

- Porfirio Díaz goes into exile.
- New elections held; Francisco Madero assumes the presidency.
- Emiliano Zapata issues the Plan de Ayala and rebels against one-time ally Francisco Madero.

1912   (Jan.–Mar.) Pascual Orozco issues the Plan de Santa Rosa and rebels against Madero.

- General Victoriano Huerta is recalled from retirement by Madero and sent with Pancho Villa to confront Orozco.

MEXICO: PRECONTACT TO THE EARLY NINETEENTH CENTURY

The ramifications of a decision made by an individual, let alone a country, can have an impact hundreds of years later. This is clearly evident with the colonization of the Americas. As such, to better understand why some groups, such as the Zapatistas, were as impatient as they were in 1912 we need to step back to the sixteenth century. The complex issues swirling around at the outset of the Mexican Revolution did not come from nowhere. While the following historical background is forcibly oversimplified (it isn't possible to do justice to the richness of all that led to the Revolution in a few brief pages), having a sense of the deep historical complexities that led to current conflicts will help you to better understand the context surrounding the issues at play in the game, how things have changed (or not) over time to get here, how the past impacts the present, as well as how all this impacts your character's positions and their relationship to others.

Mesoamerica before 1492

Before the arrival of Spaniards on the shores of present-day Mexico, the population of Mesoamerica resided largely in central and southern Mexico. These peoples were mostly organized in ethnic-states (known as *altepetl* in Nahuatl, *cah* in Maya, and *ñuu* in Mixtec). The majority of the people in the region were sedentary. Broken into various ethnic and language groups, most communities in the populated centers paid tribute to one or another larger ethnic-state, which was in turn ruled by an elite group of people. Aside from the politics involved in each of these areas, trade, religion, and warfare played a significant role in Mesoamerican life. Land control came in a variety of types. To oversimplify, the two most basic types were communal (controlled by the local authorities, but worked by the members of the communities) and individual (owned, individually, by men and women). When Hernando Cortés and his fellow conquistadors arrived on the shores of Veracruz in 1519, it was the Mexica of Tenochtitlan (commonly known today as the Aztecs) who held the predominant power in the region. The ethnic-states within their orbit of control gave them tribute. This tribute was delivered in the form of goods from each region; the goods came as raw materials (such as turquoise or feathers), food, or finished goods (such as clothing).

Following Mexica Defeat: Hapsburg Rule (1521–1700)

Under the leadership of Hernando Cortés, the Spaniards established their capital city on the ruins of the Mexica ethnic-state Tenochtitlan. They named the capital Mexico City and called the new viceroyalty New Spain. While the Mexica were defeated, the authority and power of the Spaniards was far from absolute since they remained a minority among an indigenous population numbering in the tens of millions. The Spaniards managed their military and political accomplishments through close alliances with the indigenous enemies of the Mexica, especially the Tlaxcalans. Cortés and his fellow conquistadors knew they were outnumbered and needed the assistance and cooperation of their indigenous allies and the recently defeated. As such, they established a viceregal government in accordance with many of the precontact traditions. Landownership rules remained largely the same for indigenous communities (though Spaniards slowly started to purchase land in more urban environments), tribute was still collected (though the recipients were often Spaniards), and wars were still conducted by the ruling authorities (though the rulers had changed).

Many changes occurred as well. In 1524, efforts to convert the indigenous people to Catholicism started in earnest, but the number of priests available (initially under 100) for that effort in comparison to the number of potential converts (in the millions) created a question regarding the success of the proselytization efforts. Though scholars debate the extent to which indigenous conversion succeeded, there is little debate about the physical presence of churches in the indigenous communities. Native peoples were quickly put to work building large and imposing friaries, where many of the religious fathers resided, as well as indigenous chapels. Spaniards often ordered these built on top of precontact religious sites and occasionally directly on an indigenous pyramid.

This reaffirmed the indigenous peoples' connection to the religious centers within their own communities; that tie generally remained strong, regardless of the devotion the community displays on the outside. While the Catholic Church viewed the religious structures as their own property, the natives saw it as part of their communal property. This difference of opinion did not matter so long as the focus of that center was on supporting a community's spiritual needs.

The relative ease of transition from Mexica rule to Spanish was also facilitated by the existence of an appellate authority in Spain. By the 1530s, natives were training in the Roman alphabet, and as early as the 1540s they started recording information in an alphabetic Nahuatl. By the middle of the sixteenth century (at the latest) some natives were writing in Spanish and Latin as well. They quickly put these skills to use to sue Spaniards (or other natives) in the Spanish legal system or to petition the king and queen directly. The idea of having a higher authority to which they could appeal provided them a way to complain when they did not like the decisions being made by local authorities.

While natives, Spaniards, and Africans established a colonial society in central Mexico, they were also expanding the zone of contact between Europeans, Africans, and Native Americans as they went on military expeditions to the north, west, and south. These treks all started by the middle of the sixteenth century and were met with resistance and rebellions. However, in the long term, missions and settlements were established and maintained during the Hapsburg period in what would eventually become the borderland region between the United States and Mexico. These trips to the north also brought the discovery of silver lodes, the most important of which became Zacatecas. While the silver of Potosí in the viceroyalty of Peru was greater and more important during the sixteenth century and the early seventeenth century, Zacatecas eclipsed Peru's importance by the late seventeenth century and the eighteenth century.

Bourbon Rule (1700–1821)

The year 1700 witnessed the death of the final Spanish Hapsburg monarch, Charles II. Following his death, the War of Spanish Succession broke out between the two claimants to the throne, the Austrian Hapsburgs and the French Bourbons. The Bourbons eventually won the throne, but with the concession to England that the thrones of Spain and France could never be joined. The Bourbons won the throne, but they had taken over the Spanish Empire when Spain was in a state of financial decline. Their style of rule was also in stark contrast with that of the Hapsburgs. Whereas the Hapsburgs positioned themselves as father figures and ruled the empire through councils, the Bourbons followed the absolutist philosophy of their French patriarch, Louis XIV. Although the changes to rule began with Philip V, it was Charles III (r. 1759–88) who started the processes that came to be known as the Bourbon Reforms. The general idea behind the reforms was to make the empire more efficient in all things and thereby restock the royal coffers.

The reforms affected many sectors, but we will focus on their impact on mining, religion, landownership, and rule. To vastly oversimplify: the Bourbons instituted a series of laws designed to increase the output of silver from the mining regions. The Bourbons believed that this could be best accomplished if more mining claims were controlled by a larger entity rather than small, individual mine holders. This was in essence true, as the Spanish monarchy held a monopoly on mercury, which was required for mining silver. Generally speaking, people with a larger stake in the mining industry purchased more mercury and had access to larger silver lodes. As mine ownership was consolidated, mining conditions changed as well, and fewer mine owners competed for mine workers. As a result, the relationship between workers and owners started to deteriorate.

The Bourbons also wished to further weaken the Catholic Church. The Hapsburgs had often used the Catholic Church as a balance against the power of the viceroy and the *audiencia* (the court) in the viceroyalties. When the Bourbons shifted the type of rule to absolutism, they saw less reason to balance the powers in the colony and instead focused on appointing loyal peninsular subjects (people born in Spain) to important posts in the colonies (more on the effect of this policy later in the game book). The Bourbons were not specifically against the Catholic Church, but they wanted people who were subject only to their rule to be in places of power. As such, they shifted the Church power in New Spain from the religious orders—such as the Franciscans, Dominicans, Augustinians, and Jesuits—to the secular priests (that is, those that did not belong to a religious order), who traditionally led mass and performed burial, marriage, and baptismal rights. The Hapsburgs had attempted to make this shift during their rule, and this was how things were organized in Europe. In the Americas, the religious orders had the closest ties to the indigenous peoples, and thus gained control over a large amount of land through gifts from the crown. These holdings grew with each passing generation as more people, both Spaniards and Natives, bequeathed land to the religious orders. Because the Church never died, its land never left its control.

Of the religious orders, the Jesuits were the biggest threat to the Bourbons. The Society of Jesus, as the Jesuit order is called, developed in the sixteenth century as a response to the Reformation. Their founder was Saint Ignatius of Loyola, and they were initially established in Spain. While they differed from the older orders (Franciscans, Dominicans, and Augustinians) in many ways, there was one vow in particular that made them a threat to European monarchs, including the Spanish kings. This was the fourth vow that all Jesuits took on entering the order, the vow of obedience to the pope. Initially the vow was considered innocuous, but, as the monarchs of Europe aimed to control more and more of the power within their domains, it was seen as dangerous. In the second half of the eighteenth century, monarchs across Europe began to rid the Jesuits from their empires. The Spanish Empire was no different, and in 1767, Charles III expelled the Jesuits from New Spain. Their exile left haciendas in northern New Spain open for purchase, giving the Spanish crown a much-needed influx of capital. Wealthier **peninsulars** and **criollos** (people of Spanish descent born in the Americas) purchased the most profitable of these haciendas, and the poorer haciendas were either reassigned to other religious orders or liquidated. When Spaniards purchased the land, no consideration was given to the indigenous people who lived on the missions. Their choice was to stay and work for the hacienda's new owners or to leave and find a new place to live.

peninsular/peninsulares People of Spanish descent born on the Iberian peninsula.

criollos People of direct Spanish descent, but born in the Americas.

Beyond the missions, the Bourbons also started transferring indigenous parishes from the control of the religious orders to the secular priests. This caused some divisiveness among the indigenous people and the religious orders that had been their spiritual advisers. The two sides wrestled for ownership over indigenous chapels, as the natives still saw the buildings as rightfully their property. Many of these cases went to courts, but all decisions regarding the actual ownership of the buildings were made on a case-by-case basis (in some instances the indigenous people retained control; in others the Church gained control). In the larger urban spaces this would eventually become less of an issue, but it still remains a point of contention in more rural areas of Mexico today.

Changes in Landownership. In Spain, as in other places in Europe, landownership had been based on ideas of vassalage. Simply stated, the king owned all of the land, and he awarded the use of that land to loyal subjects. Those subjects, in turn, could allow others to use the land as well, but the king could always take it away. The king, or his agents, often awarded land to loyal subjects for services rendered to the monarch (whether through military service, the payment of fees, or a number of other ways).

Native land tenure was generally based on two things: communal ownership and private. Generally speaking, the majority of indigenous people gained access to their land—and water—by being members of their community. It was the community who distributed the land. Early in the colonial enterprise the indigenous population was annihilated by disease, and during this period, communal land went unused, so Spaniards were able to claim much of it—either through purchase or as gifts from the crown—and would use this newly privatized land for commercial ventures such as farming or mining. As these colonial enterprises grew, so, too, did the need for more laborers. By the end of the eighteenth century, the indigenous population was starting to rebound, but they were finding that the land they required to sustain their communities was now controlled by wealthy landowners who were more interested in commercial agriculture than in subsistence. So the Spanish had a double incentive to retain control: beyond simply not wanting to give up what they had claimed, the hacienda and mine owners wanted cheap labor.

Move Toward Independence. With the arrival of the Bourbons came a definite preference for peninsulars over criollos in positions of colonial leadership. The general thought was that people born in Spain were smarter and more loyal to the crown than people born in the Americas. As such, the Bourbons started a process of instating peninsulars in positions that had previously been held by criollos. To add insult to injury, they also established new, well-paying positions that were also open only to peninsulars. This bias helped create a schism between some of the elite who had traditionally been allies, though in and of itself this policy was not enough to push New Spain toward a fight for independence. Changes in the militia, an avenue that had previously allowed for upward social movement for Afro-Mexicans and **pardos** alike, would play a significant role in independence movements.[4]

The term **pardos** refers to people of mixed European, Native American, and African ancestry.

However, the reign of Carlos IV (1788–1808) was weak and his son, Fernando the VII, desired the throne, which created only greater chaos. In 1808 Napoleon Bonaparte invaded Spain and forced the abdication of Carlos. Napoleon took the royal family to Paris and replaced them with his brother Joseph Bonaparte. People in Spain and the colonies revolted against the rule of Joseph and reaffirmed their ties to the Spanish crown. However, while the monarchy was in Paris the people had to rule themselves, and this sparked the independence movement. During this time, decisions regarding leadership, land, trade, and any other laws or rules generally reserved for the highest branches of government had to be sorted out at lower and more local levels. As such, land disputes were settled in regional power centers and often to the disadvantage of the indigenous people who lacked political power.

NINETEENTH-CENTURY MEXICO AND THE ASCENDANCE OF BENITO JUÁREZ

Mexico's push for independence started with the *Grito de Dolores* (the Cry of Dolores) on September 16, 1810, when Father Miguel Hidalgo rallied his parishioners and supporters to what ultimately proved a disastrous bid for independence from Spain. However, an eleven-year intermittent struggle followed, officially ending on August 24, 1821, when Spain and Mexico signed the Treaty of Córdoba awarding Mexico its independent status.

Mexico's political situation during this time was tumultuous at best. Though chaotic, this period witnessed significant changes in authority, land law, and official languages. In the early part of the independence period, an attempt was made to establish racial equality by defining citizenship in terms of who owned land. The idea was that everyone in Mexico could own property, and your race did not matter. However, by basing citizenship on *individual* landownership, the government inadvertently attacked indigenous customs and rights and stripped the possibility of citizenship from natives who worked only land held by the community. The changes further imposed state governments over indigenous municipal governments (which had technically been separate during the colonial period).

Beyond attacks on indigenous governments, the Mexican government declared Spanish as the official language of the country. Previously, under Spanish rule, individuals could use a choice of Spanish, Latin, or a number of indigenous languages when submitting paperwork to a court of law. Following independence, everyone in Mexico was to be "Mexican" and the criollos in charge decreed that Spanish was the language of the land. This decision ended official legal status for a number of languages and virtually ended their written tradition. It also made it much harder for rural citizens who did not know Spanish to seek redress in the courts.

Among the most significant laws redressing the earlier affront to communal indigenous communities was the 1828 *fundo legal*, which decreed that all lands "which have been unfairly taken" from indigenous communities be returned or that just compensation be paid. The goal was to define and divide communal lands. A significant problem with the law was the term *unfairly*. It is subjective, leading to multiple interpretations, and proved difficult to define legally. The law recognized legitimate landholders as those with the legal paperwork. Ancient communities did not have such paperwork. Again, this tended to favor large creole landholders over the communal, ancient traditions of the indigenous communities. In essence, private citizens were more able to claim "vacant" lands than were indigenous towns. Native towns were now subject to state governments.[5]

Politically this was a period of turmoil, with numerous changes in Mexican leadership. Antonio López de Santa Anna was the one constant authority figure for Mexico during its early independence era, but he claimed he did not wish to be president. The top military generals and political leaders in Mexico turned to him when they wished for a change in the direction of the government. He was the only person the multitude of political sides could agree on as a leader of Mexico. In 1836, during his presidency, Mexico replaced the Constitution of 1824 with the Seven Constitutional Laws, which strengthened the central government. As a result, many states rebelled against the government—the two most notable being Texas and Yucatán. While the Mexican government eventually regained control of Yucatan, the Caste War erupted and continued to vex the country until the early twentieth century. Texas's secession and eventual annexation to the United States led to the U.S.–Mexican War. This became a defining moment for Mexico and Santa Anna. The conclusion of the war saw the United States absorb half of Mexico. The end for Santa Anna came when he later sold part of the country to the Americans as well (the Gadsden Purchase).

The Rise of Benito Juárez

Aside from political uncertainty, nineteenth-century Mexico was shaped by the introduction of an array of intellectual ideas and modernization. This period witnessed the development of **liberalism**, **anarchism**, and **positivism** (see next page). Benito Juárez was of particular note because of his position in the midst of the intellectual swirl: his adoption and use of liberalism, his race (he was a Zapotec native of Oaxaca), his position as a "father" figure to future intellectuals who found themselves on opposite sides of debates during the Mexican Revolution, and his position as the president who led Mexico through the War of Reform and the French Intervention. In 1855, Benito Juárez and Ignacio Comonfort (president of Mexico, 1855–58) overthrew Mexico's dictator, Antonio López de Santa Anna. Juárez, Comonfort, and other liberals espoused the idea that Mexico needed to modernize so the United States would seek trade with Mexico rather than seek its land. This idea continued to be debated into the early twentieth century.

Their focus became rapid economic advancement for the country. In 1857, they passed a new constitution espousing some of these ideas. The three most important laws were the **Ley Lerdo**, which decreed that the Church had to sell any land not directly used for religious practice, the **Ley Juárez**, a moderate law that limited ecclesiastical and military privileges, especially their legal courts, and the **Ley Iglesias**, which regulated fees that could be charged to the peasants for church sacraments. The fees had traditionally been paid by hacienda owners, who then added the costs to the debt their workers owed them, making it harder for the workers to leave the hacienda for other work. Ultimately, the Ley Lerdo placed corporate or communal land into the hands of people willing to use it to generate wealth and ended up affecting lands communally held by indigenous towns as well. This, again, gave more property to the landed elite because they had the money and position to purchase the newly available land.

Ley Lerdo Part of the 1857 constitution, an important law directing the Catholic Church to sell any land not directly used for religious practice.

Ley Juárez Part of the 1857 constitution, an important moderate law that limited ecclesiastical and military privileges, especially their legal courts.

Ley Iglesias Part of the 1857 constitution, it sought to regulate the fees the Catholic Church could charge peasants for services related to the sacraments.

The passage of the liberal 1857 constitution turned moderates against the government, and Mexico descended into a civil war known as the War of Reform (1857–61). The Juárez government fled Mexico City. In 1861, the liberals (Juárez's coalition) retook Mexico City and ended the war. However, they also defaulted on foreign loans owed to Britain, France, and Spain. The question of whether Mexico should be a democracy or a monarchy was never fully put to rest following independence. The conservative opposition, still frustrated with Juárez, requested assistance from Napoleon III, who was eager to collect on French loans to Mexico. French troops entered Mexico in 1863 and established Maximillian, a Hapsburg prince and distant relative of the Spanish Hapsburgs, as the emperor of Mexico. French forces stayed in the country for four years. Maximillian was a liberal, but he was not Mexican. So, while he did not counter the reforms of the

IDEOLOGIES

LIBERALISM:

At the time of the Mexican Revolution, *liberal* refers to a political ideology that favors individual freedoms within a federalist government, a government with power divided between the federal and more local levels, and with limited Catholic Church and military power. Mexican liberalism is often most associated with an anticlerical stance that saw the Catholic Church as an obstacle to progress. Liberals supported small yeoman farming and looked to education as a means of modernization and assimilation.

ANARCHISM:

Anarchists advocate self-rule among individuals rather than government rule, claiming that laws are made by rich men in their own self-interests. They express a profound distrust in the possibility that any politician (Madero included), once in power, could adequately advocate for the poor. Mexican anarchists at the time of the Mexican Revolution believe that society is divided into two social classes—the exploiters and the exploited—and they support and advocate for the exploited.

POSITIVISM:

Positivism is a European philosophical ideology that rejects theological and metaphysical philosophies in favor of "positive" observable and experientially based facts, with an emphasis on science. Positivists stress intellect and reason as a means of coming to understand the physical world in contrast to the traditional religious emphasis on the spiritual. Within the context of Latin America, it was a means to personal and societal development. Positivists' ultimate goal was to become more like Great Britain.

See "Ideologies at the Time of the Revolution," later in this game book, for a fuller explanation of these ideas.

1857 constitution, the liberal government saw him as representing a foreign power, a loss of their sovereignty. In 1867, French forces withdrew from Mexico, leaving Maximillian behind. Juárez took advantage of the absence of military support to capture Maximillian and put the question of a monarchy to rest by executing him.

After taking control of the government in 1867, Juárez focused on modernizing the country and further weakened the Catholic Church by barring it from property ownership beyond houses of worship and by secularizing education and marriage. In 1871, he was elected again, much to the disgruntlement of opponents in his own party who believed the reelection was illegal under the constitution. In fact, Porfirio

Díaz, a supporter, ran against Juárez in 1870 under the slogan "Effective suffrage, no reelection" (a slogan that would later be turned against Díaz). When Juárez died in 1872, Sebastián Lerdo de Tejada, his vice president, became president. A new generation, represented by Porfirio Díaz, wanted power. An attempted coup failed.

PRESIDENT PORFIRIO DÍAZ AND THE PORFIRIATO (1876–1910)

In 1876, Sebastián Lerdo de Tejada ran for reelection. Porfirio Díaz, Lerdo's competition in the 1872 presidential race, rebelled on the grounds that reelection should not be allowed according to the constitution. Yet Lerdo won and was named president. Díaz retreated to the United States for six months, returned with military forces and U.S. financial support, and overthrew Lerdo. A few months later, in 1877, Díaz was elected president. He would rule until 1910, a period of Mexican history later referred to as the **Porfiriato**. He focused on bringing order to the country and an end to the violence. To accomplish this, he concentrated on modernizing the society and the economy. Ultimately Díaz was of the same strain of liberalism and positivism as Juárez and Lerdo; however, he understood the fear that regional elites possessed of a strong central government in Mexico City. Díaz assuaged regional leader's fears by playing them against each other. To further gain support, he styled himself as both a liberal and a patriot, but always made sure to emphasize his patriot credentials first. This gave him loyalty from his followers and respect from the opposition, allowing him to work with elites across the country toward a sense of stability and progress.

Porfiriato The time period between 1876 and 1910 when Porfirio Díaz ruled Mexico (directly or indirectly).

Establishing Order and Progress, 1876–1884

When Porfirio Díaz gained power in 1876, the presidency had changed hands seventy-five times in the preceding fifty-five years. While both Benito Juárez and Sebastián Lerdo de Tejada had provided some stability, they focused on asserting the central government's control, not on economic development. The turmoil and uncertainty of the period before Díaz caused Mexico to miss the industrial, scientific, and technological advances experienced in much of Europe and the United States. Along with the presidency, Díaz gained an empty treasury, a country in debt to many foreign powers, a bureaucracy whose paychecks were in arrears, a mining enterprise (once the crown jewel of the Spanish Empire) in shambles, and infrastructure—crucial to food supply, communications, transportation, and foreign trade—in such a wreck that the government even considered abandoning the most important port along the Gulf Coast, Veracruz.[6] In short, Díaz's coup, while successful, gave him the responsibility of sorting out a disaster.

Porfirio Díaz, like the two presidents before him, was a liberal who believed that Mexico needed **"order and progress"** to succeed. His hope was that reforms on all levels, including political, would change the image of Mexico internally and externally and that foreign and domestic investors would see Mexico as a safe place to invest. He embraced positivism and its ideas of order and progress. Order must come first, because with it you could then implement progress. Díaz's first term was focused on creating the order he saw as necessary for progress. He worked with the United States to secure the border between the two countries from banditry, he reduced smuggling, and he increased legal trade with the United States by establishing three Mexican consulates at the Texas border.[7] To show he was serious about shrinking the debt, he reduced his salary and those of his cabinet and fired many within the bloated bureaucracy. At the end of his term in office he stepped down, as the constitution required and as he said he would. Supporters urged him to change the law so he could stay in office longer to implement greater changes. He, however, wanted to show the world that Mexico had changed and that the improvements could be seen at the highest rungs of society.

Manuel González, Díaz's secretary of war, won the 1880 presidency in a landslide. Working from the order Díaz had helped establish, he focused on progress. His term witnessed modernization (and in fact he made Porfirio Díaz the head of the Department of Development for a time) but also increased debt and stories of corruption. The stories were damning and some were potentially fabricated. However, González changed land laws to allow governmental appropriation of "unused" land. The lands seized in this way could be sold to investors, thus furthering the development of the country. Unfortunately, many of the lands seized were taken from indigenous communities—again. When his term ended, he stepped down, and Díaz ran for office again, legally, and won. After this, Díaz would no longer honor the non-reelection position and would stay in office from 1884 to 1911.[8]

Díaz, the Científicos, and Modernization, 1884–1911

Diaz's time out of the presidency was productive. He made contacts in and out of Mexico that allowed him to hit the ground running when his new term started. The progress that followed was impressive; industrialization replaced human muscle and communications were simplified with the expansion of the telegraph (introduced in 1849) and the introduction of the telephone in 1882. Díaz also improved Mexico City's flooding and sanitation problems when he hired S. Pearson and Son, a British company, to build a thirty-mile canal and six-mile tunnel to drain the capital, though problems persisted.[9] Improvements continued in transportation, shipping, mining, sanitation, agriculture, finances, and oil drilling, among many other areas. Oil was growing in importance across the world at this time, exemplified in 1910 by Winston Churchill's decision to convert the Royal Navy to oil, and Mexico would not be left out.

Mexico During the Porfiriato

UNITED STATES OF AMERICA

Legend:
- Railroads at the time of the Porfiriato
- Railroads in 1884, prior to Díaz's rule
- State boundaries
- **OAXACA** State
- ⊛ Capital city
- ● City

Cananea

COAHUILA

Gulf of Mexico

Torreón

M E X I C O

San Luis de Potosí

YUCATÁN

Veracruz

Mexico City

Córdoba

PACIFIC OCEAN

MORELOS

OAXACA

CENTRAL AMERICA

400 miles

400 km

Díaz alone was not responsible for Mexico's "progress." His closest advisers were known as the *científicos*. These technocrats shaped and followed the positivist ideals of the regime by looking to ideas of Comte, John Stuart Mill, and Herbert Spencer. They generally loathed the poor and illiterate, especially those in the countryside, and believed they held Mexico back from its forward momentum. In 1894, Mexico had its first balanced budget in its short history when revenues exceeded expenditures. In addition, with the relative stability and peace at the time, this period saw the first sustained population boom since independence, nearly doubling from approximately 8,743,000 (in 1874) to 15,160,000 (in 1910).[10] Because of the efforts of Díaz and the científicos, Mexico's image abroad had improved and Mexico was active in the international community.

But progress came at a cost. The booms of modernization enjoyed in the urban environments of Mexico, especially Mexico City, were not felt in the countryside. While Díaz and the científicos maintained their power through political maneuvering and alliances (with local power brokers and hacienda owners), they were also willing to deploy military force or the *rurales* (the rural police force) to intimidate and openly force their policies—often at the expense of the rural poor, many of whom were indigenous—all in the name of preserving order.

Land Policy during the Porfiriato. In 1883, under Manuel González's presidency, a new land law was passed. The law aimed to encourage foreign investment and purchase of Mexican rural properties. Furthermore, it allowed foreign companies to survey public lands for subdivision and settlement. Once the companies submitted their reports, they received one-third of the land for free and could purchase the remainder at a low price. Oftentimes these were indigenous lands that had been held for generations (many since before the arrival of the Spaniards in 1519). However, the law required the indigenous towns to provide proof of ownership in the form of written documentation (something rarely available seeing as they had owned the land before the existence of such written documentation). If the people using the land did not have documents proving ownership, their land could be, and often was, seized as public property.

By 1894, eleven years after the issuance of the law, one-fifth of the land in Mexico was owned by land companies, many of them foreign. In 1894, the government altered the law to benefit the companies, making it even easier to get more land. By the early years of the twentieth century, 134 million acres, or 23 percent, of prime land was owned by just a few hundred wealthy families (many of whom were connected through a web of marriage alliances), and over half of all rural Mexicans lived on and worked for a *hacienda*. The wealthiest of all the landowners, also known as *hacendados*, was don Luis Terrazas of the northern state of Chihuahua. His hacienda system may have been the largest in all of the Americas.[11]

The rural villagers and the hacienda *peones* had a harder life than their ancestors just a century earlier under Spanish rule. The daily wage for agricultural workers remained at 35 centavos (100 centavos in a peso). Meanwhile the cost of basic foodstuffs, such as corn, had doubled, while others, like beans, increased sixfold. People who worked for a hacienda were poorer than an equivalent rural villager. Hacienda workers often received credit (rather than physical money) toward purchases at the *tienda de raya*. While they could charge things to the store, they were constantly in debt and forbidden from leaving the hacienda until their debt was paid off; debts were passed on to the next generation. Those who were illiterate suffered more than their friends, as they could more easily be taken advantage of in a society requiring physical records of transactions.[12]

Peón (pl. peones) A peasant; farmhand; laborer (often unskilled).

Tienda de raya A company store; like in the United States, workers were often paid with credit at the company store instead of cash and were permitted, even encouraged, to charge items, which indebted them to the hacendado and kept them working until they could pay off their ever-increasing debt, which would pass to their children.

Women's Roles during the Porfiriato. The Porfiriato was a period of marked growth for women entering into professional fields as well as factories. In 1887, the first woman earned her medical degree from the Medical School in Mexico City, and in 1903 a commercial school for women opened. These advances for women, especially in the urban middle class, created moral concerns as more women left the respectable spaces of the home to enter more public spaces. Respectability for women had for some time been tied to the home. Though by the early twentieth century this expectation wasn't as strong, some still worried that working women might be seen as lower class;[13] others associated female workers with prostitutes in terms of morality. Working women, in turn, often argued that these concerns were baseless, that they had a responsibility to support their family, and that with duty came honor, even if it meant working in a factory.[14] But even though women entered the workforce, they still legally needed the permission of their husbands or fathers to work outside the home, they could not vote, were paid less than men, and they were still expected to maintain their traditional roles within the family, particularly among urban middle and working classes.

Labor during the Porfiriato. Anarchist movements developed during the nineteenth century and helped form labor unions. With the increased industrial boom and a focus on cheap goods, laborers were forced to work long hours in unsafe conditions for poor pay. In cities, most workers labored seven days a week for eleven to twelve hours a day.[15] In rural areas, the pay was less and the abuse, as bad if not worse. Many companies operating in Mexico also employed American workers and paid them more for the same labor than their Mexican counterparts. The start of the major labor unrest came with the 1906 mine strike at U.S. investor Colonel William Greene's Cananea Consolidated Copper Company. The strike quickly turned violent, and Greene called friends in Arizona, asking them to send a volunteer force of Arizona Rangers across the border (by permission of the governor, though they were sent across as individuals) to patrol the streets of the town of Cananea. Deaths occurred on both sides of the engagement, and additional strikes rippled across the country.[16] The Cananea workers demanded the removal of a corrupt foreman, five pesos pay for an eight-hour workday, employment quotas requiring 75 percent of jobs to employ Mexicans, use of responsible and respectful people in the deployment of the mining cages that lowered and raised the workers from the underground mines, and promotion of Mexican workers based on their skill set just like that used with American workers. The strikes spread and intensified, the worst coming in 1907 at the French-owned Río Blanco textile mills. When the dispute started, the workers went to Porfirio Díaz and asked him to intervene. He agreed, but his decision supported the owners on the majority of accounts. On January 6, the workers decided to strike the next day. The violence started in the tienda de raya (company store), where women were denied credit for their food. The workers set the building on fire. The local political boss ordered in federal forces and the rurales. He had them shoot into the crowd, which included women and children. After the workers dispersed, they later returned to collect the bodies of the deceased and were fired on again by the forces. More than 100 people died.[17]

Religion during the Porfiriato. Porfirio Díaz was not openly hostile to the Catholic Church, despite being responsible for seizing much Church land. However, he saw the Church's separation from the state apparatus as essential to Mexico's modernization. He also realized the importance of the Church to the Mexican populace. As such, his second wife, Carmen Romero Rubio, worked with the Catholic Church, thus keeping it separate from the head of the state, but still close to the president. This separation was nowhere more evident than in the effort to proclaim the Virgin of Guadalupe as the patron saint of Mexico in 1895. Porfirio Díaz and the científicos remained outside the fund-raising effort for the event and left the organization and petitioning of the pope and other religious figures to doña Carmen and other female socialites (many of whom were married to científicos). These women brought the Catholic Church and the government of Mexico into a sort of truce.[18] Díaz did not return any Church lands (on the contrary, many Catholic properties, seized previously, were sold off during this period, some to Protestants), but he was not directly antagonistic either. During this period the Catholic Church turned to more social concerns, focusing on morality and avoiding outright political engagement. Specifically, Pope Leo XIII issued the **Papal Rerum Novarum** in 1891, a treatise on capital and labor. It sought both to find solutions to the hardships experienced by many in the working class while also working against the ideas of socialism and anarchism. Simply put, the Church tried to find a middle ground. As the Porfiriato started to decline, the Church continued to try to offer a moderating

The **Papal Rerum Novarum** was a decree issued by Pope Leo XIII in 1891 that sought to find a middle ground between the demands of capital and laborers.

voice. This did not keep the Church from speaking against conversion to Protestantism or Mormonism, both of which had missionaries entering into Mexico via the U.S. border.

The Fall of the Porfiriato

On February 17, 1908, Porfirio Díaz was interviewed by American journalist James Creelman. In the interview, the 77-year-old Díaz stated that he believed Mexico could sustain democracy and that he would not run for reelection in 1910. The Creelman interview prompted reformers (internal and external to Díaz's circle) to look for potential candidates. As the election grew closer, Díaz changed his mind and decided that he would run, but he would also allow Francisco Madero (the son of a wealthy landowner from Coahuila) to run against him. In a twist of irony, Madero ran under a campaign of "**Effective suffrage, no reelection.**" Díaz removed his competition by sending front runner Bernardo Reyes on a military mission to Spain to investigate the telegraph system and having Madero jailed in the run-up to the election, though he was eventually released. The election went ahead, and Díaz was proclaimed the winner in a landslide, so large that there was little doubt that there was electoral fraud.

Effective suffrage, no reelection (*Sufragio efectivo, no reelección*) was the campaign slogan of Francisco I. Madero, when running against Porfirio Díaz. It previously had been Díaz's slogan; by adopting it, Madero meant to point out electoral fraud and the abuses of the continued "reelection" of Díaz. Note that this slogan did not mean equal suffrage. Many agreed that it referred primarily to landowners, a category that tended to leave out women, indigenous peoples, and the poor.

In response to the election and his arrest, on November 20, 1910, Francisco Madero released the Plan of San Luis de Potosí calling for the overthrow of Díaz's government. However, the Revolution had started two days earlier in Puebla, on November 18, when Aquiles Serdán and his family were discovered to be in support of Madero. A gunfight broke out at their house, and most of the Serdán family was killed by the federal military. Two days later, the Revolution was in full force, and by the end of the year Pascual Orozco, Francisco (Pancho) Villa, and Emiliano Zapata had risen in support of Madero's plan. Based in Morelos (a state bordering on the south edge of Mexico City) Emiliano Zapata's forces, the Zapatistas, were able to apply a constant pressure on the Mexican military, which prevented the military from using their full strength against the northern revolutionaries led by Orozco and Villa. Revolutionary successes in battle eventually forced Porfirio Díaz to resign his position and go into exile on May 31, 1911. In an agreement with Madero, Francisco Leon de la Barra, a supporter of Díaz, became the interim president until elections could be held the following fall. Leon de la Barra focused on trying to violently stamp out revolutionaries who refused to give up their arms, such as the Zapatistas, who sought to implement the reforms promised by the Plan of San Luis de Potosí. Madero hoped that many would disarm because he and others within elite circles planned on reforming Mexico's political system. They believed that the legal process was the best way to address the land and labor problems that workers and the rural poor faced on a daily basis. To the workers and poor, such a process was slow and flawed.

COMMUNICATION AT THE TIME OF THE MEXICAN REVOLUTION

Sitting in a college classroom today we tend to take for granted our access to vast amounts of worldwide information at almost any moment through technology like smartphones. As we put ourselves into the shoes of our characters, we need to consider how information circulated at the time of the Mexican Revolution, when social class, language, and geographic location were barriers to communication. The elite who lived in Mexico City had more access to many forms of communication but still were out of touch with rural conditions.

Railway and telegraph lines constructed under the Díaz regime speeded the flow of information from urban centers to rural areas in new ways. The telephone entered Mexico in 1879, funded largely by foreign capital and companies. By the turn of the century, telephones were primarily used by the government.[19] In 1911, the country possessed approximately 16,000 telephones, with more than half in Mexico City for its population of over 300,000. Most of the phones were in the service of the military. Between 1910 and 1920, even with the number of telephones growing by about 2,000 per year, only 0.1 percent of the population, primarily businessmen, hacendados, politicians, and military, were using them.[20] A few of the more elite families might have had telephones in their homes, but more often local communication took the form of letters or messengers, and long-distance correspondence was carried by telegraph and mail that used the rail lines.

A **tertulia** is a discussion group formed of primarily elite men in urban centers who would gather in cafes or private homes to discuss literature, art, politics, etc.

Ideas also circulated through **tertulias**, discussion groups formed of primarily elite men in urban centers who would gather in cafes or private homes to discuss literature, art, politics, etc. Though these groups supported a variety of political stances, one of the more radical anti-Díaz groups was Ateneo de la Juventud (Athenaeum of Youth), a group of intellectuals that began meeting in 1906 for philosophical discussions about such ideas as anti-positivism, pro-humanism, anti-imperialism (especially U.S. imperialism), and a search for Mexican identity linked with **mestizaje**. They organized conferences, published the illustrated journal *Savia Moderna*, and organized art exhibitions. This group, whose participants included intellectuals such as José Vasconcelos and artists Dr. Atl, Diego Rivera, and Saturnino Herrán, became known as the "Generation of 1910" for their criticisms of the Porfirian regime during centenary festivities to commemorate Mexico's independence from Spain.[21]

Mestizaje refers to miscegenation—racial mixing between European and Indigenous backgrounds; related to the term *mestizo*, a person of mixed European and Indigenous descent.

In addition to these discussion circuits, the educated upper classes, especially those in urban areas, had access to more formal forms of communication, such as newspapers, books, pamphlets, illustrated journals, and magazines. A very small percentage, some of whom had been educated in the United States, read both Spanish and English publications from the United States and Mexico.

The Role of the Press

At the end of the nineteenth century, a mere 37.73 percent of the approximately 324,360 inhabitants of the Mexican capital were literate, including those who could read and write only poorly.[22] Outside the capital the literacy rate was even lower, and many people did not (and still do not) speak or read Spanish, speaking instead one of over seventy indigenous languages. The countrywide literacy rate of only 15 percent had important implications in publishing. As journalist Pete Hamill pointed out, "Good journalism, for most publishers, was bad business. In a country where 85 percent of the population was illiterate, newspapers naturally directed their energies towards those who could read and write . . . businessmen, large landowners, and the middle class that was emerging from the expanding bureaucracy."[23]

Much of the less literate population relied heavily on word of mouth and on less formal, more image-centered forms of communication. Print capitalism in Mexico City at the beginning of the twentieth century also included the publication of inexpensive illustrated magazines, broadsheets, and corridos in which images accompanied the text. Publishing houses such as that of Antonio Vanegas Arroyo in Mexico City, with the help of "graphic reporter" José Guadalupe Posada, specifically marketed to this population: people who did not necessarily identify with the more elitist newspaper culture.[24] (See, for example, "Gaceta Callejera," on p. 202.) His calaveras (skulls) contained images of skeletons in daily life and were often circulated around November 2 in celebration of the Day of the Dead. A calavera is also a kind of poem, written around that same time of year, that often satirizes people who are still living. He used "calavera prints as social reportage, as manifestos and as political and social satire."[25] Posada's work also frequently appeared in popular satiric penny press publications such as *El Diablito Rojo*, *La Guacamaya*; *El Diablito Bromista*. Robert Buffington attributes a growing working-class consciousness that intersected with perceptions of gender and masculinity to the penny press in Mexico City in the decade leading up to the Mexican Revolution.[26]

Beginning in 1900, advances in photographic reproduction made photojournalism a possibility over drawings and engraved images. Some journalists, such as Agustín Víctor Casasola (to whom most of the photos we have of the Mexican Revolution are accredited—sometimes dubiously[27]), began taking photos of the Revolution that would circulate in new ways and resulted in a decline in the use of sketch artists and engravers in newspapers: "[e]ditors and readers demanded what they considered to be the real thing. That meant photographs."[28]

A variety of newspapers circulated before and during the Revolution, some of which criticized the Porfiriato. *El Imparcial*, the most successful newspaper at the turn of the century, supported the Díaz regime.[29] Anti-Díaz newspapers such as *Anahuac*, *El Antirreeleccionista* (the official newspaper of the anti-reelection movement) and radical journals such as *El Demófilo* and *El Hijo de Ahuizote* circulated opposition views, with the latter considered "the most important illustrated periodical during the Porfiriato."[30] It may be somewhat surprising given the heavy hand of the Porfiriato, but "notwithstanding limits on the press, political cartoonists prospered during the Porfiriato, which tolerated some—but not all—adverse political commentary," offering alternatives to official versions of present and past events.[31]

PLM Partido Liberal Mexicano (Mexican Liberal Party), founded by Ricardo Flores Magón in 1906.

The Flores Magón brothers, Ricardo, Enrique, and Jesús, published their journal *Regeneración*, voice of the anarchist movement and the **PLM**, from exile in the United States. More positivist-leaning publications included *La Libertad*, *La Prensa*, *Siglo XIX*, and *México Financiero*. Women such as Dolores Jiménez y Muro found voice in feminist publications such as *Mujer Mexicana*. Probably the single most influential international reporting leading up to the Revolution occurred on February 17, 1908, when American journalist James Creelman published his interview of Porfirio Díaz in which the president announced he would not run again in 1910, prompting opposing groups to look in earnest for candidates.

In the early days of Madero's time as president, the press enjoyed unprecedented freedom from government control. This was a dramatic shift from the Porfiriato, when overt criticism of the regime meant risking imprisonment. Many of Madero's enemies used the openness of the press to directly attack him, yet he resisted censuring the press. The Revolution attracted an influx of foreign journalists, especially from the United States, who traveled to Mexico to write about the rebellion. One of the most important was John Reed who reported for *Metropolitan Magazine*, and *New York World* and helped shape the vision of the Revolution that circulated abroad.

Art and Architecture

More formal classic art forms, such as painting and sculpture, also grew in importance during the Porfiriato. Díaz specifically used art to promote his political agenda and worldview. He invested government funds for art projects that suited his, and his regime's, needs. He was particularly interested in projecting an image of Mexico as modern (to him this meant European and especially French) to the rest of the world to combat impressions of Mexico as backward and "barbaric." He understood that public art such as monuments, statues, sculptures, and buildings could help. The regime took advantage of international art exhibitions, such as the World's Fair, to promote this image, in part by glorifying the remote indigenous past while completely ignoring and even erasing the realities of the indigenous present such that "[l]iving indigenous people rarely appeared in official art during the Porfiriato."[32] Through emphasizing the Aztec Empire, art reinforced Mexico City (the previous Aztec capital, Tenochtitlan) as the center of power with Díaz at the helm.[33]

This same interest in projecting a modern (Europeanized) Mexico is reflected in the multiple architectural projects that redesigned the Paseo de la Reforma, a wide road running through the center of Mexico City, in the image of the Champs Elysees (a famous boulevard in Paris). The street was lined with statues—designed mostly by European artists and engineers—that paid tribute to select heroes from Mexico's past. Part of this vision included the monument to Independence, a column topped with a golden angel, completed in time for the celebrations of the 1910 centennial of independence from Spain. This monument to mark the anniversary of a separation from European rule nevertheless harkened back to Europe in its neoclassical design, "inspired by similar monuments in Paris and Berlin."[34]

Díaz also began several large architectural projects, including the Teatro Nacional (now known as Bellas Artes) and the Oficina Central de Correos (Central Post Office), both designed by the Italian architect Adamo Boari. Few of the building projects undertaken at this time included Mexican architects, and many of the buildings included imported materials, artistic styles, and artists. In his chapter on art and architecture in Mexico during the Porfiriato, art historian James Oles points out that "almost everything about these buildings was imported, except for the cheap labor."[35] The regime's reliance on foreign art forms and artists dovetailed with Díaz's interest in encouraging foreign investment—these buildings were to signal economic prosperity to the world, and especially to interested investors.

Such was the extent of Díaz's admiration for Europe that as part of the celebration to mark the centennial of independence from Spain in 1910, he organized an art exhibit with his minister of education (Justo Sierra) exclusively composed of Spanish artists. Some Mexican artists, especially those who were associated with a rising movement to promote national art that had been growing for several years (in particular among those associated with *Savia Moderna* and the *Ateneo de la Juventud*), were outraged by what they saw as a display of Porfirian-backed neo-colonialism. Dr. Atl (born Gerardo Murillo), who had actually received money from Porfirio Díaz to study art in Europe some years earlier, organized an alternative exhibition at the Academy of San Carlos dedicated to national art. Though it was not included in the official program of commemorative activities, the government did provide modest funding, though far less than for the official exhibit. The academy's Mexican artist exhibit featured Saturnino Herrán's triptych *Legend of the Volcanoes*, along with contributions from José Clemente Orozco, Diego Rivera, Jorge Enciso, and Roberto Montenegro, among others. Atl's organization for this exhibit demonstrated a growing interest in creating, funding, and promoting Mexican national art; a departure from previous academicism and teaching styles; and an interest in breaking with elitist artistic traditions. This movement toward a more "egalitarian spirit" was echoed in the way works of art were chosen to be included. Rather than showing a few select works of masters, "crowds of people from the street served as the jury, shouting opinions as objects were held up in their judgment."[36]

Some say that this exhibit planted the seeds of political action in the Academy of San Carlos's students, like David Alfaro Siqueiros, who, at the time our game begins, had been on strike demanding changes in the way art was taught. Their demands in many ways reflected the current political unrest. Those in power saw these strikes as dangerous. Students (and artists) were questioning authority and the centrality of power in Mexico City.

Corridos: The Music of the Revolution

Although corridos, a style of narrative song or ballad that tells stories of (usually male) heroes and/or key events (such as battles), had circulated in Mexico since the 1860s and 1870s, they are most associated with the Mexican Revolution and U.S.–Mexican border conflicts of the early 1900s.[37] Corridos tended to follow certain patterns, starting with the singer declaring he is singing a corrido, introducing the main character along with a date and location, and ending with a farewell or "despedida." (The lyrics to several corridos are included in Part 5 of the game book, as is a broadside example with an accompanying image by José Guadalupe Posada.)

These songs primarily circulated among the working classes at the time of the Mexican Revolution and generally took the perspective of the underdogs. Traveling with Villa's men, U.S. journalist John Reed witnessed the communal composition of a corrido in honor of Pancho Villa:

> One of them began to sing that extraordinary ballad, "The Morning Song to Francisco Villa." He sang one verse, and then the next man sang a verse, and so on around, each man composing a dramatic account of the deeds of the Great Captain. For half an hour I lay there, watching them, as they squatted between their knees, serapes draped loosely from their shoulders, the firelight red on their simple, dark faces. While one man sang the others stared upon the ground, wrapt [sic] in composition. . . . After a while I slipped away; I doubt if they even saw me go. They sang around the fire for more than three hours.[38]

Reed's account reflects a tradition of oral and communal composition. Some corridos were composed individually by those involved in the fighting or based on versions of events circulating in newspapers. Others were commissioned and some adapted new lyrics to previously existing music. Many were composed collectively and passed on by word of mouth, accounting for the many variations. Published versions of corridos accompanied by José Guadalupe Posada's illustrations found their way to public spaces such as plazas, parks, and markets around Mexico in cities and villages alike by way of traveling singers who would sell printed copies of the lyrics following their public performances. Posada's broadsides expanded a traditionally oral composition and transmission practice. Publishing lyrics on broadsheets tended to standardize the performed songs.

Reed's account also testifies to a social function of the corrido, by which composing and singing together provided not only entertainment for the troops but also a sense of community. The function of the corrido is still debated by scholars. Since the singers tended to find their subjects in current events (public figures, popular heroes, battles, scandals, etc.), some scholars see them as a kind of oral newspaper, transmitting news to illiterate masses. However, in some settings, especially in terms of local communities, news would have traveled by word of mouth before a corrido could be composed. In this context, the corridos had a more commemorative function and even depended on the listeners knowing the basics of the story.[39] Either way, these songs helped remind people of what was going on in their local communities as well as in other areas of the country. Beyond the stories they told, the ballads reflected larger concerns faced by poor Mexicans.[40]

The Advent of Film

Film arrived in Mexico in 1896 with representatives of the Lumière brothers introducing moving pictures to Porfirio Diáz, followed by public exhibitions a few weeks later. Soon after, Díaz became one of Latin America's first film stars, filmed by those same agents in quotidian family scenes and in Chapultapec Park on horseback. It didn't take long for cinemas of a variety of scales to appear in urban areas such as Mexico City, but film also traveled to the countryside by railroad where projectionists (who were sometimes also filmmakers) could set up make-shift cinemas in cafés, halls, or their own tents known as *carpas* such that by 1902, Mexico hosted approximately 300 cinemas.[41]

Film certainly shaped public perception of the Mexican Revolution both in Mexico and in the United States as filmmakers from both countries traveled with military troops. Their material was edited into newsreels, which tended to give the illusion of impartiality. U.S.-based Mutual Film Corporation was the most interested in recording the events in Mexico.[42] They had learned from those who had filmed previous wars (Greece-Turkey in 1897, Cuban independence in 1898, Boer War of South Africa in 1899) the importance of "reconstructing" news to attract an audience. That sometimes included reenacting scenes that were not captured live on film.

One of the most remembered Mexican filmmakers from the time, Salvador Toscano, began filming as early as 1898. The Toscano Archive, a family-managed Mexican archive, contains footage he shot and collected. He directed several films of Díaz, including *Don Porfirio Díaz paseando a caballo en el bosque de Chapultepec* (*Don Porfirio Díaz on Horseback in Chapultepec Park*) in 1899 and *Fiestas del centenario de la independencia* (*Celebrations of the Centenary of Independence*, 1910) before becoming more associated with anti-reelectionism as displayed in his film *La toma de ciudad Juárez y el viaje del héroe de la revolución Don Francisco I. Madero* (*The Taking of Ciudad Juárez and the Journey of Don Francisco I. Madero*, 1911). Under the Díaz regime filmmakers didn't show images that could cast a negative light on the government (like the strikes in Río Blanco or Cananea), perhaps, as film scholar Ángel Miquel suggests, due to their own class status and a desire not to make enemies with power. However, with the rise of Madero's call for revolution, some *cineastas* (filmmakers) began filming things that didn't necessarily coincide with the party line.[43] While Díaz allowed cineastas to use and circulate his image without personally financing or commissioning the films, Madero hired filmmakers to make propaganda films that were sometimes cloaked in the guise of news, thus marking the beginning of the "official film."[44]

Unfortunately, what we have today are only fragments of this footage. None of the films made at the time exist today in the form in which they would have been exhibited, in part because of a lack of archiving mentality and in part due to the unstable and flammable nature of filmstock, which made it dangerous to preserve.[45]

IDEOLOGIES AT THE TIME OF THE REVOLUTION

With the onset of the Industrial Revolution in the nineteenth century, the world struggled to come to grips with the rapid changes in labor, family life, religion, land use, and a number of other ideas—many of which were debated during the Mexican Revolution. In order to understand different perspectives that shaped attitudes and decisions at the time of the Revolution, and in order to better inhabit your characters, the predominant ideologies of the time are provided below. Use them to help inform your actions and arguments and to understand those of other Revolutionary figures as well.

Agrarismo (Agrarianism)

Agrarismo is a grassroots ideology focused on allowing individuals and indigenous communities to get their land, water, and foraging rights back from large haciendas. It also is focused on procuring political autonomy for indigenous towns and protection for their churches.[46] The best-known proponents of agrarianism are the Zapatistas; however, other groups from across the country, including communal farmers and independent farmers, are fighting for the ideas of agrarianism.[47]

While the term *agrarianism* is relatively recent, some of the basic questions of landownership it represents date back to at least to the 1700s. During the colonial period in Latin America, when indigenous populations were dwindling, Spaniards, the Crown, and the Church purchased, seized, and were given communal and individually held indigenous lands. As the native population started to rebound in the 1700s, some individuals, such as Bishop Manuel Abad y Queipo, objected to the continued occupation of indigenous lands.

Agrarianism, generally, refers to land reform formulated for people who have little to no land with the goal of increasing their access to landownership. Agrarianism does not include all land reform, which, in its broadest understanding, can refer to any reforms that seek to change landownership policies. For example, after independence, liberal land reforms of the middle and late 1800s, such as the Ley Lerdo (see "Liberalism" later in the game book), can hardly be considered Agrarianism. Designed to reallocate Church lands, this law continued to strip communal farmers of their land as well. The nineteenth-century reforms witnessed a drastic increase in private (and sometimes foreign-owned) estates. The large hacienda owners flourished under the policies of Porfirio Díaz's regime, and the selective and predatory land surveyors, to the detriment of small landholders and the communally held lands of the indigenous population.[48] At the beginning of the twentieth century, indigenous villages in southern Mexico still held approximately 40 percent of the arable land. By 1911, their holdings had been reduced to 5 percent, leaving the majority of the population in the south landless.[49] While this was land reform, it was not agrarianism. With the onset of the Mexican Revolution, the Zapatistas brought the world's attention to their brand of agrarianism, which focused on the return of communally held indigenous lands and water rights to indigenous towns and peasant farmers by a redistribution of hacienda-held lands. At its earliest moments, agrarianism aimed at improving life for the rural poor of Mexico at the expense of the wealthy hacienda owners. Populist in nature, its leaders tended to come from the peasant population it supported. By its very nature it developed in the countryside and generally ignored more urban environments. (See the "Plan de Ayala" and the "Agrarian Law" in Part 5 of the game book.)

Anarchism

Mexican anarchists at the time of the Mexican Revolution believe that society is divided into two social classes: the exploiters (those who own the businesses) and the exploited.[50] Anarchists support the exploited—the poor and working classes—and call for a "social revolution which is economic in nature and anti-authoritarian."[51] They see authority in its various forms (political, ecclesiastic, economic) as the enemy, the exploiters.[52]

Anarchists advocate self-rule among individuals rather than government rule, claiming that laws are made by rich men in their own self-interests. They express a profound distrust in the possibility that any politician (Madero included), once in power, could adequately advocate for the poor.[53] Rather than focusing attention on universal suffrage, claiming that the right to vote was merely an illusion of power, their struggle focuses on economic liberty, which they assert is essential for political liberty.[54] They see the key to economic freedom as intricately tied to land reform, advocating for communal land holding over the system of private property.

Anarchists suggest that private property is the root of poverty since it is what creates inequality of wealth and necessitates authority to protect it. As their 1911 "Manifesto" explains,

> Without the principle of private property there would be no reason for government, which is necessary solely for the purpose of keeping the disinherited within bounds in their quarrels or in the rebellions against those who hold the social wealth; neither would there be reason for the church, whose only object is to strangle the innate human rebellion against oppression and exploitation

through the preaching of patience, resignation, and humility, and through quieting the call of the most powerful and fertile of instincts through immoral, cruel, and unhealthy penances; and so that the poor will not aspire to enjoying the good things of the earth and thus constitute a danger to the privileges of the rich.[55]

A Brief History. Anarchism had its most significant effect on Mexican history during the nineteenth- and early-twentieth-century working-class movements. With the end of the colonial period, at the start of the nineteenth century, Catholicism turned inward to focus more on the individual than on the community and the rapid development of capitalism. Workers, artisans, and agriculturalists found themselves in need of mutually supporting aid societies. Anarchism came to provide a political defense of urban and rural working-class laborers at a point when power, land, and wealth were starting to rapidly centralize in the hands of the few.

In Mexico, the movement grew out of the centuries of communalism found in the native societies of Mexico combined with European mutual aid organizations, such as guilds and religious brotherhoods (known as confraternities). While anarchist-like mobilizations started in the late eighteenth century, it was the middle of the next century that really saw them spread. After the passage of the Ley Lerdo, which allowed for the privatization of lands owned by groups of people, held by institutions like the Catholic Church or indigenous communities, a boom in land privatization happened, and peasant land holdings dwindled from 25 percent of *all* Mexican arable lands to 2 percent. Percentage of control varied by geographical region. Middle- and large-size estates drastically increased in number. By 1878, there were approximately sixty-two active anarchist groups in Mexico. During the 1890s anarchist activity separated into worker groups and student groups. Workers, such as textile laborers, formed societies of resistance. They strove to improve their conditions in the workplace and had to avoid the attention of the rurales (rural police). If they avoided attention, they could survive, but a number were eventually violently repressed. Alternately, the movement started by the Flores Magón brothers, Ricardo, Enrique, and Jesús, did not shy from confrontation with law enforcement. This group became one of the most radical, with an emphasis on the communalism of the indigenous peoples. Of the three brothers who began the movement, Ricardo and Enrique joined the anarchists, and Jesús, the most moderate, aligned with Madero in support of democracy. Though Enrique and Ricardo fled to the United States, they helped successfully organize the anarchist movement in Mexico, and their writings, especially Ricardo's, formed much of the ideological basis of the anarchist movement during the Revolution.[56]

Demands. Anarchists believe that government is harmful and society should be organized around voluntary organizations that have no hierarchy. They want: an even distribution of property across Mexico, equal pay for workers regardless of race or sex, a secular society, child labor laws and a minimum wage, workers to have control of the companies of Mexico, not investors (foreign or local), equal access to public secular education; and they are willing to take whatever actions are necessary to achieve their goals.

For further insights into the ideology of the anarchist movement and the PLM (Partido Liberal Mexicano), see the core texts included in the game book that deal with anarchism, especially the "Manifesto" (1911, p. 106) and "Class Struggle" (1911, p. 101).

Feminism

To understand the demands and concerns of Mexican feminists leading up to the Revolution, we need to step back from our current concepts and attitudes regarding feminism. Keep in mind that gender roles (expectations of male and female behavior) are sociocultural and temporal in nature—they change across time and space. What was expected of "proper" women at the end of the nineteenth century in Mexico might surprise us today in the United States. Nor were (or are) expectations for gender the same across social classes or in different spaces (urban versus rural), even in the same basic geographic space and time period.

That said, feminism in Mexico in the late nineteenth and early twentieth centuries was largely centered in cities (namely Mexico City) and the Yucatán Peninsula among women of the middle classes. In 1912, socialist reformer and feminist Elvia Carrillo Puerto created the first Peasant Feminist League (*Liga Feminista Campesina*). Carillo Puerto worked with indigenous communities on the peninsula promoting hygiene, sobriety, secular education, equal rights, and in the 1920s, birth control.[57] In Mexico City, women's publications written by and for women began to appear in the 1880s, even before the term *feminism* entered circulation.[58] Early feminist demands centered on gaining access to education and vocational training. These feminists did not typically advocate for abandoning traditional roles in the home, but rather often argued that better education and training would make them better wives and mothers. Other principal concerns included improved wages and changes to the Civil Code of 1884 that would reduce legal inequality of (especially married) women. Though women participated in political organizations, including anti-Porfirian movements, liberal clubs, Magonist groups, and Maderista groups leading up to and during the Revolution, they generally saw themselves as helping the cause of the group, not as promoting women's rights.[59] Few women advocated women's active participation in the political sphere in their own right (e.g., through suffrage) at the outset of the Mexican Revolution. In 1916, however, the first Feminist Congress would take place in Mexico and included topics such as education, women's roles in the home, the role of the Catholic Church, revisions to the 1884 Civil Code, women's suffrage, and even a scandalous speech written by feminist Hermila Galindo Acosta de Topete that argued for women's rights, divorce, education reform, and sex education. Galindo's speech shocked many by claiming women were equal to men intellectually and sexually.[60]

Rights. During the time of the Porfiriato and the Mexican Revolution, women had neither the right to vote nor to hold public office—but few women anywhere in the world had the right to vote or hold office in 1912. By and large these issues were not foremost on Mexican feminist agendas, especially at the outset of the Revolution when our game begins.[61]

Though the primary concern of early feminists centered on education, there were movements to address the legal inequality of women. Genaro García, a liberal male who wrote his thesis on the inequality of matrimonial rights for men and women in 1891, argued that women were subordinated to men by the law—specifically the Civil Code of 1884 (adapted under Porfirio Díaz), which limited the rights of married women as compared to the 1850s and relegated women to a "kind of slavery."[62] Historian Anna Macías explains that "the Civil Code of 1884 accorded to adult single women almost the same rights accorded to all adult males, but a married woman really was treated as *imbecilitas sexus* ('an imbecile by reason of her sex')."[63]

Essentially, married women lost their ability to legally self-advocate. A married woman needed her husband's permission to enter into any legal contract or lawsuit. Though women retained ownership of their property when they entered into marriage, they lost to their husbands the legal ability to manage it and lost the right to file suit against husbands who mismanaged their property. This version of the Civil Code also stipulated adultery by a woman would always be cause for marital separation, whereas adultery by a man would justify separation only in certain circumstances.[64] The code also legally enforced a double sexual standard in that it allowed investigation of maternity, but not paternity. Where children were concerned, the husband had complete legal control and "if widowed, the wife's right to act as the guardian of her children was severely limited."[65]

Education. Some of the first feminist demands regarding access to secondary education for women grew from the liberal ideals of the equality of all citizens and the need for citizens to be educated.[66] In spite of liberal rhetoric to this effect, men and women were not equal (not to mention the inequalities along class or race lines).

Nevertheless, some of the early support for women's gains in education came from liberal men. In 1840, women had no access to secondary education. In general, liberal men at the time supported women's expanded education to the secondary level, at least in part because education would allow women to be better wives and mothers and thus strengthen the family unit in a time of social strife.[67]

Although the call for "equal education" existed, men and women still did not learn the same things.[68] For example, upper-class women generally received a superficial education in order to participate in polite conversation, play an instrument for guests, and maintain a domestic sphere suitable to her stature. Too much education was viewed as improper and as possibly tempting the weaker sex toward sin. When women did achieve access to secondary education with the opening of the first secular secondary school for women in Mexico City in 1869,[69] they were still discouraged, if not outright barred, from "masculine" pursuits such as medicine and law. In 1871, the Escuela de Artes y Oficios de Mujeres, a vocational school for women, was opened in Mexico City and offered fifteen courses in arts and crafts and eight in scientific subjects. As Macías asserts, "Apparently liberals were willing to countenance the idea of women studying the humanities, some science, and some vocational subjects deemed 'appropriate to their sex,' so that they might earn their living without competing economically with men."[70] In keeping with the image of women as self-sacrificing mother figures, women were encouraged to become elementary school teachers and even could become certified as secondary school teachers, though this access was limited to elementary-only under Díaz in 1889.[71]

Work. Education and entry into the workforce came as modernization, especially under Díaz, pushed women into the labor market in factories and offices.[72] However, "although careers for women existed, it was still often viewed as inappropriate for them to work outside the home unless absolutely necessary for survival, as in the case of those who were widowed or were granted the rare ecclesiastic separation (which did not permit remarriage) and therefore did not have a man to support them."[73] Nevertheless, women's role in Mexico's urban workforce grew and

> by the end of the Porfiriato thousands of middle-class women worked outside the home as schoolteachers, with another 1,785 women working for the government. Between 1888 and 1904 the first women were accepted, however reluctantly, in the schools of medicine, law, and commerce in Mexico City, and by 1910 a number of females began to work in commercial establishments without jeopardizing their reputation as respectable women.[74]

Men and Feminism. Some men spoke out against feminism, such as Porfirio Díaz's minister of public education, positivist writer Justo Sierra, who seemed to fear that feminism would entice women to want to act more like men. He specifically warned female teachers against entering the masculine sphere of politics.[75] In his 1904 book, *La mujer moderna,* Ignacio Gamboa expressed fear that feminism would lead to the end of the race given the anti-reproduction stance of feminists and that the women's movement promoted divorce (or not marrying at all) and lesbianism.[76] In general, however, liberal men supported women's access to education and some, like Genaro García, actively advocated for women's equality with men under the law.

Women in the Revolution. In addition to some of the intellectual contributions referenced previously, women participated actively in the Revolution in different ways, often in valuable support roles (cooking, finding supplies, smuggling, caring for soldiers, caring for children, medical support, etc.) but also as active female soldiers—some even dressing and living as men. Though some of these roles reinforced typical gendered expectations, the Revolution was a time that provided an elasticity of expectations for female roles,[77] allowing women to step out of the domestic sphere,[78] whether following husbands or fathers; or escaping homelessness or seeking employment as so many had during the Porfiriato.[79] Prior to the Mexican Revolution, women and children lived in the barracks and women played central roles "in the daily practices of the army. [The Porfirian soldadera] reflected a broader community of norms and expectations and embodied gendered relations of power." Even so, these women, who were neither military nor civilian, were seen as different from other women in Mexican society.[80]

Camp followers were relatively common in conflicts around the world through the mid-nineteenth century. After the advent of railways, which reduced the need for much of the support provided by these women, European armies, quickly followed by most armies worldwide, limited or eliminated female presence in the military.[81] But not so in Mexico. Though the exact number of soldaderas is difficult to estimate due to insufficient historical documentation, thousands of women actively participated in many capacities in armed conflict during the Mexican Revolution.[82]

Soldadera Literally, a female soldier. We use the term generally to refer to a woman who participated actively in the Mexican Revolution in a variety of roles, from a camp follower who played support roles (cooking, finding supplies, smuggling, caring for soldiers, caring for children, providing medical support, etc.) to an active female soldier who took up arms, served as a spy, and even commanded troops.

Unfortunately, **soldaderas** and camp followers are often remembered for their relationships with men rather than for their own merits. Some soldaderas did enter into sexual relationships with soldiers, some of which might have been considered prostitution, while others were more monogamous ad hoc relationships. Some women were already married (or sometimes married during the Revolution) and traveled with their husbands. In certain cases, women became the consort of another soldier if her husband abandoned her or died. These relationships ranged from coerced to consensual. Among the coerced, women were raped,[83] were manipulated by men who demanded or expected sex in exchange for protection or food, or felt they had no other choice. Among the consensual, women were motivated by love, pure practicality, and even economics, because these relationships offered a means for survival. It is important to emphasize that not all soldaderas or camp followers had relationships that included sex and that becoming a soldadera is *not* synonymous with becoming a prostitute. In fact, "relatively few became prostitutes, and indeed many became soldaderas precisely to avoid this fate."[84] Though unfortunately these women are often remembered for sexual promiscuity, soldaderas played many essential roles during the Revolution.[85]

Liberalism

To understand liberalism we must first divorce the terms *liberal* and *conservative* from current twenty-first-century U.S. political rhetoric. At its most oversimplified, liberal refers to a political ideology that favors individual freedoms within a federalist government, a government with power divided between the federal and more local levels, with limited Catholic Church and military power. Mexican liberalism is often most associated with an anticlerical stance that saw the Catholic Church as an obstacle to progress. Conservatives favored a strong central government (and some even supported the idea of a monarchy), where the interests of society as a whole took precedence over individual freedoms, and wanted the Church and the military to maintain power. Conservativism is often associated with a proclerical stance, specifically pro–Catholic Church. Note that liberalism changed over the years and did not champion the same causes in the same way at the time of the Revolution as it did earlier. It gradually split into two factions, one more elite than the other.

Liberalism as a political movement was especially influential in Mexico in the late 1800s. It emphasized individual freedom and fought to limit the power of "privileged groups such as merchant guilds, religious orders, and special military courts. Liberals typically called for the abolition of these organizations—often called corporations—in order to open opportunities" for what they hoped would be an emerging middle class that would improve Mexico's economic development.[86] In addition, liberal ideas regarding equality of all citizens and the need for citizens to be educated (even if mostly rhetorical in nature) helped feminists find, in liberal men, early support for women's gains in education.[87]

Liberalism is most often associated with Benito Juárez (president from 1858 to 1871), the Reform Laws, and the controversial constitution of 1857 (as discussed earlier in the game book).

Some of the most controversial changes in the constitution of 1857 from the constitution of 1824, composed only a few years after independence from Spain, involved the relationship between church and state. The most significant blow to the Catholic Church is arguably the removal of Article 4 of the 1824 constitution: "The religion of the Mexican nation is, and will always remain, Catholic, Apostolic, and Roman. The nation protects it by wise and just laws and prohibits the practice of any other faith."[88] It may come as no surprise that the Catholic Church reacted strongly against this constitutional change and those who swore to uphold it.[89] Reaction to these limitations on the Church (and other "corporations") resulted in the War of Reform.

Later, with the French occupation of Mexico, conservatives allied themselves with the French and with Emperor Maximilian of Hapsburg, who ruled Mexico from 1864 to 1867. Liberalism took on new significance by invoking patriotism and supporting Mexican president Benito Juárez against the French and a monarchical form of government. At the same time some of liberalism's basic tenets were abandoned, such as the liberal ideal of small government and limited executive power, as Juárez's government became more autocratic both in an effort to enact the radical changes in power structure called for in the constitution of 1857 (the enforcing of the separation of church and state required a strong central government) and in an effort to stabilize and unite a country after years of war—now divided not only between liberals and conservatives but also destabilized by infighting among the liberals themselves.[90]

After Juárez's death, in 1872 the new liberal president Sebastián Lerdo de Tejada (brother of Miguel Lerdo de Tejada of the Ley Lerdo) changed the constitution of 1857 to include liberal Reform Laws in the form of amendments that, among other religious restrictions, established marriage as a civil union, limited a religious institution's ability to purchase land, and most important, officially established the separation of church and state. Where the original constitution simply removed the stipulation of an official religion, the amendment went further to decree: "The State and the Church are independent of one another. Congress may not pass laws establishing or prohibiting any religion."[91]

Before becoming president, Porfirio Díaz supported the liberal cause, fought against the French invasion, and was perhaps most remembered for his part in the defeat of the French in the Battle of Puebla on May 5, 1862 (Cinco de Mayo).[92] As this bellicose period ended in 1867 with a liberal victory, Díaz shifted into politics and ran against Juárez. When Díaz took office in 1876, liberalism was in flux.

Liberalism had started to shift by the 1850s as positivism gained influence.[93] Under Díaz, liberalism became less anticlerical and antimilitary (he had reconciled with both organizations) and more about "the use of the national government to promote economic development," which included government contracts with foreign investors.[94]

During the Porfiriato, liberalism split into two groups: *puros* (pure) adhering to the Reform Laws and the constitution of 1857, and the *nuevos* (new), influenced by positivism, who favored order over freedom and were more sympathetic to the Díaz regime (though not uncritical of it). The puros were replaced at the intellectual and political center of Mexico by the nuevos during the 1890s.[95]

The 1900s saw reactions against this shift in the formation of the Partido Liberal Mexicano (PLM; Mexican Liberal Party), founded by Ricardo Flores Magón in 1906. This party combined anarchism and liberalism to redefine what was meant by *liberal*. Following traditional liberal doctrine, the PLM continued to emphasize limiting Church power but added demands for curtailing labor abuse in factories, ending "debt peonage," working off debts through labor, and fighting for land reform.[96] This party incarnated conservative fears that unchecked liberalism would lead to anarchy. Though not an anarchist, Madero espoused a middle ground in liberalist thought (although he leaned toward positivism), which permitted enough common ground with the PLM early on in Madero's run for the presidency that they came together against Díaz. One of the reasons the Magóns and Madero could join together temporarily was that the liberalism of the Porfiriato had swung so far away from its roots that Francisco Madero was able to champion a return to the "liberal" constitution of 1857 as part of his campaign against Díaz.[97]

Positivism

Positivism is a philosophical ideology that rejects theological and metaphysical philosophies in favor of positive observable and experientially based facts, with an emphasis on science. Positivists stress intellect and reason as a means of coming to understand the physical world in contrast to the traditional religious emphasis on the spiritual. And in fact, they believed that overcoming superstitious phases of society was necessary to achieving material and intellectual progress toward a European-style ideal.

Mexican positivism grew from tensions between liberal and conservative ideas. Like the liberals, Mexican positivists wanted to reduce the power of the Church, especially over education. They argued for a secular education based in the sciences, suggesting that science, not religion, would help modernize Mexico. Even as positivism and liberalism had some key points in common (e.g., a rejection of religious education in favor of science), they were not identical. Aguilar Rivera refers to positivism as a branch of conservatism within liberalism.[98]

At the time of the Revolution, positivist ideas in Mexico that stressed order maintained by a strong central government were a reaction to Juárez-era liberalism, especially as manifested in the constitution of 1857 and its emphasis on freedom. Positivist writers such as Justo Sierra suggested in *La Libertad*, a journal that espoused positivist and Social Darwinist ideals, that the emphasis on individual freedom was misplaced and that individual rights were secondary to the rights of society, which included peace and order.[99] Positivists feared that unchecked liberalism could lead to anarchy.[100] The break between the liberals and positivists occurred visibly with the 1892 elections, when the editors of *La Libertad* created a new political party, the Unión Liberal.

During the same time period, a positivist group of intellectuals known as the *ciéntificos* came together with a shared insistence that scientific progress would be key to Mexico's modernization, and they applied scientific methods to social and political issues.[101] According to Aguilar Rivera, "'scientific' positivism implied the conviction that scientific methods could be applied to find the solution for national problems. Politics was therefore seen as an experimental science, based on observable facts. Governors 'should no longer be guided by abstract theories and legal formulas that had only led to revolutions and disorder.'"[102]

Although they are often associated with the Porfiriato and remembered as advisers to Porfirio Díaz, the group of científicos had originally formed in opposition to Díaz. Díaz found the group to be convenient scapegoats and funneled public dissatisfaction toward them and away from him. Around 1903, however, this relationship shifted to one of mutual tolerance, if not outright support. According to Walter Breymann, "second only to their belief in science was [the ciéntificos'] desire to maintain uninterrupted peace for Mexico," such that they grew to "accept Díaz as the only alternative to anarchy." And as the ciéntificos began to lean more toward Europeanization and foreign investment as a means to modernize and stabilize Mexico, Díaz found them to be increasingly useful.[103]

Many ciéntificos and other positivists served in the Díaz administration as members of Congress and the cabinet or in high-ranking positions in banking, finance, and industry. However, not all ciéntificos or positivists supported Díaz, and though the Díaz administration, with its slogan of "Order and Progress," is often associated with positivism, it never officially defined itself as such, but rather as "liberal and Catholic, never positivist."[104]

Social Catholicism

Adherents to Social Catholicism want to challenge the notion of a secularized society without a place for religion, specifically Catholicism, in politics. The movement developed in response to nineteenth-century liberal reform ideas. By the start of the twentieth century a lot of movements had developed with the express aim of influencing public life through adherence to Catholic dogma and criticism of liberal society. Followers of Social Catholicism focused on the formation of a Christian state, the defense of workers and indigenous rights, land ownership, agrarian reform, literacy, the right to strike, alcoholism, fairer wages, and Church-related issues such as evangelization and indigenous idolatry. While these ideas lined up with anarchism and communism, the Catholic Church came out against the secularism of these ideologies. They agreed that something needed to be done about the social injustices, but believed that the Church should be at the heart of each of those movements.

Ultimately the focus of the movement was to apply Christian morals and principals directly to the daily interactions of adherents to the movement with other Mexicans. By applying Christian morals on a daily basis outside of the walls of the Church, followers hoped to reinvigorate the parish structure of Catholicism in Mexico. While priests and bishops were supporters of Social Catholicism, they were barred from direct political activity. As such, the Mexican people, and not the clergy, led Catholic political parties. The Catholic Church organized a series of conferences from 1903 through to 1911 that served to push the social problems of Mexico to the forefront of Catholic action.[105] In 1911, with the support of Archbishop José Mora y del Río, the National Catholic Party (PCN) formed. Though the hierarchy of the Catholic Church did not support Francisco Madero's movement, their party was the first to benefit from Porfirio Díaz's removal because Catholicism was allowed to return to politics.[106] Their movement has been viewed as an alternative to Madero's Revolution.[107]

Social Darwinism

Social Darwinism, as elaborated by Herbert Spencer, applied Charles Darwin's notions of survival of the fittest and natural selection to the social realm, arguing that the strongest people will naturally rise to the top. This theory tended to be used in the late nineteenth century and early twentieth century to justify power differentials by suggesting that class and racial divisions reflected this natural selection—the poor were poor because they were biologically not "fit" and government intervention or aid would interfere in a "natural" process.[108]

The leading Mexican intellectuals at the time of the Revolution would not have self-identified as a Social Darwinist. The Catholic Church vehemently rejected Darwin's work and therefore embracing anything related to Darwinian theory would mean going against the Church.[109] Yet ideas related to Social Darwinism had a profound influence on intellectuals and politicians alike.

Mexico's version of Social Darwinism diverged from the racist version circulating in Europe and the United States. European and American versions of Social Darwinism emphasized biological explanations for inferiority and superiority; Mexican versions emphasized cultural explanations as well as racial origins for these differences. Porfirian leadership (especially the científicos) used some form of Social Darwinism to justify elitist economic policies (policies that had negative effects on indigenous populations). And some Porfirian intellectuals, such as Francisco Bulnes and José Limantour, stressed the biological racial inferiority of the indigenous. Bulnes, for example, sought to promote a "whitening" of Mexico through European immigration. And many Porfirian intellectuals agreed that the indigenous population impeded Mexico's quest for modernization. However, especially considering that the ruling class was not solely "white" but rather was made up of mestizos (those of mixed European and indigenous descent), many intellectuals focused on *culture* over *race*. Justo Sierra, for example, spoke directly against Bulnes and his view of biology as destiny. Though he did suggest that Mexico's problems stemmed from the levels of poverty and illiteracy among the indigenous, instead of seeing this as part of natural selection due to being biologically unfit, Sierra (and later José Vasconcelos) argued that education of the indigenous peoples was the key. This solution did not entirely escape racist leanings, considering his emphasis on assimilating to "white" culture—needing to learn Spanish and white ways in order to be successful.[110]

Some intellectuals espoused the genetic superiority of mestizos over whites and indigenous peoples. Riva Palacio suggested that in fact, the combination of indigenous and European genetics would create a superior race, an argument that would later be developed by José Vasconcelos in his seminal *La raza cósmica* (The Cosmic Race).[111]

 PART 3: THE GAME

It is now March 9, 1912. Porfirio Díaz has been in exile since May 1911. Francisco I. Madero gained the presidency this past November. A month following his election, Emiliano Zapata rebelled in the south, followed quickly by General Pascual Orozco in the north. Forces led by Victoriano Huerta and Pancho Villa have been sent to confront Orozco. Madero, desirous of peace, has called a meeting to see if he can use the legislative process to reconcile his government with the Zapatistas and the supporters of Porfirio Díaz, and thereby stem the outbreak of violence.

MAJOR ISSUES FOR DEBATE

1. Effective Suffrage

Suffrage is the signature topic of Francisco Madero and his allies. While the Porfiriato had a number of things they wanted to change, there was no mechanism to create that change. *Effective* suffrage is not the same as *equal* suffrage. Most people in the early twentieth century (women included) did not see a need for women to vote. Some things to keep in mind while arguing this topic: Voting was public, which meant peer pressure could be applied. If someone lived on a hacienda or in a company town, they had to think carefully about voting against their boss's desire. The law at this point distinguished between married and unmarried men. Intimidation was very much an issue, Francisco Madero himself had been jailed by Porfirio Díaz before an election. Similarly, Francisco Madero's brother Gustavo (not in the game), had Francisco's main rival for the presidency, Bernardo Reyes, beaten bloody in the streets of Mexico City. In the countryside it was simply difficult to get to the polls.

2. Strong Federal Government vs. Strong State Governments

One of the central debates in early state formation for former European colonies was how strong the central, or federal, government would be versus that of the state governments. As an issue this was not isolated to Mexico or even Latin America; it was also a debate in the United States. A key question with this issue is whose laws were primary, the states', or the federal government's? You will not be able to answer all of these questions, but you should think about the following: What kind of government should Mexico have? What is the role of the federal government, and what role should state governments play? How should power be shared between the federal and state governments? Who should contract foreign debt?

Who should possess a military? Who should determine taxes, citizenship, etc.? As with suffrage, which determines who can vote, the decision on this debate influences enforcement of that law. Some characters possess a lot of power in their home states, so they would oppose a strong federal government as it would weaken their own power. This debate is largely determined by the perspectives of the characters and what will benefit their goals.

3. Land Reform

Land reform is probably the most iconic debate in the game. Indigenous communities had a history of communal landownership that existed before the arrival of the Spaniards in 1519. Indigenous groups, such as the Zapatistas, want communal ownership back. This is different in northern Mexico, where the indigenous populations are smaller and many people have been relocated to Henequen plantations on the Yucatan Peninsula. In the north, revolutionaries are looking for ways for small land holders to gain access to smaller tracks of individually owned land. To do any sort of reform, land will need to be taken from those who currently hold it (wealthy Mexicans and foreigners) and then redistributed. There are multiple sides to this issue, and allies will not always agree on which is best. Is it better to distribute land among the peasant classes and help build the economy from the bottom up or to promote centralization of landownership in an effort to use it more efficiently? What other options are there? What happens when there is an extremely unequal distribution of wealth? How does it affect stability? What happens when people's basic needs, such as access to food, shelter, and health, are not met?

4. Labor Reform

The late nineteenth and early twentieth centuries were important for labor reform around the globe. Anarchism was an early organizer of the labor movement, and this was no different in Mexico. A multitude of questions arose. Foreigner laborers (especially from the United States) traveled to Mexico and received more money for their work than did Mexicans in an equivalent position. Should there be laws protecting Mexican workers? What about a minimum wage? Should there be guaranteed time off? How about a minimum workday or minimum workweek? Should there be laws governing child labor or women's labor or penal labor? What about forced labor for indigenous groups who rebel against the government?

5. Foreign Business Interests

During the Porfiriato, Díaz actively sought foreign investment as a way to move Mexico forward and make it less appealing to the United States territorially, the theory being that if investment in Mexico was good, then the United

States would not want to take more of its territory than it already had in the mid-nineteenth century. Foreigners were responsible for a lot of developments, but those developments (such as train, radio, and film) benefited the urban elite and not those in rural areas. What role should the government play in supporting foreign investment? What are the pros and cons of inviting foreign investors into the country? How much influence, if any, should those investors have on determining policy in the country? Should one country's investments be favored over those of another? Is there a way to minimize foreign investors' impact on the Mexican economy?

6. Education Reform

Imbedded in the questions tied to education are the cultural values of a society and its hope for the future. In many ways the battle over education was as much about what it means to be Mexican as it was the traditional objectives of education, such as literacy and mathematics. Some of the questions under consideration are the following: Should women be educated? Should priests and nuns be allowed to continue as teachers? Should indigenous languages be taught or suppressed? Should a certain amount of education be required of all Mexicans? Can the Catholic Church be involved in education at all? How does Mexico pay for an increase in schools? How does Mexico train teachers to meet increased demands? Should Mexican education be Western or something else? What is the role of government in education?

7. Religious Reform

Catholicism had been the official religion of Mexico, but that changed at the end of the nineteenth century. The Catholic Church still has a lot of followers and a lot of influence in many areas of Mexican life. What role, if any, should the Church be allowed to play in politics? Should other religions be treated similarly? In what ways should the Catholic Church be connected to education, land reform (it lost a lot of land with the 1857 constitution), or women's rights? Should more limitations be placed on the clergy? Should they take an oath to the constitution? Should they be forced to (or at least allowed) to revoke their vows? Should the Church become more Mexican? If so, what does that look like?

8. Women's Rights

The rights of women were just starting to come to the forefront during this period. Questions related to all of the preceding topics also relate to them. This very categorization of the rights of women is fundamental, but there are issues to think about: Should women be considered "other" or should all laws passed apply equally to them and men? Can they own their own businesses, or work outside of the home, without being subject to the dictates of their father, husband, or brother?

Can they initiate a divorce? Can they obtain an equivalent education? Can they pursue higher degrees? Can they sign contracts and contract debt? How might marital status impact women's rights? To what degree should the rights of single women, married women, widowed women be the same?

9. Freedom of the Press

While this topic does not have a day dedicated to it specifically, the ideas around it are constantly present and players should be thinking about ways to expand or decrease the impact of the journalists. The press was just starting to form its identity during this time. Questions from the moment are not all that different from those still being asked today: Should slander and libel be permitted? Are journalists allowed to attack the government? Should the government control journalists? What penalties can be applied to journalists? How might a free press or other means of communication (such as art and film) be used and/or abused in relationship to all of the topics being discussed in the game?

BASIC OUTLINE OF THE GAME

The recommended time segments in this outline are for 50-minute and 75-minute class periods. Check with your instructor (the Gamemaster) if you're unsure which recommendations to use.

Flow of Each Game Session

1. The first 5–10 minutes of class are for paying for food, plotting, and/or for the secretary of war to arrest friends or enemies. NOTE: No assassinations can happen at the start of a Game Session.

2. The central 30–45 minutes of the class are for debating the topics at hand. Each day, this period starts with a brief presentation of the Official Timeline Mural (see p. 70) by the presidential secretary. Following the presentation, characters will give speeches at the podium or they may question someone who gave a speech at the podium. During this period, the secretary of war may arrest people.

3. The final 15–20 minutes of class are for *voting* on a new policy or an amendment to the constitution and for setting the second agenda item for the next session (see "Major Issues for Debate," for a list of topics). Something must be voted on at the end of each Game Session. Referendums that pass will be assumed to be amendments to the 1857 constitution, unless otherwise stipulated in the official wording of the document. Topics can be revisited at a later date only if the GM allows.

   a. The class must decide on a second debate topic for the next class session. The sitting president has final say on what it will be and needs to choose one item from the Major Issues for Debate list. The topic chosen will be important for potential votes on constitutional changes and thus faction victories.

   b. This is also the time when assassinations or coups can happen. *If* the sitting president is removed during this time the character(s) responsible for his removal *must* immediately issue the agenda for the next Game Session from the debate list. If they choose "presidential election" they *must* also choose one other topic for debate.

People must accept the president's decision, even if his agenda does not align with their preferences. The Podium Rule, allows them to attempt to take the discussion in another direction, but only items on the official agenda may be voted

> **NOTE**
>
> *During the final introductory session, the second agenda item for the first Game Session is set by Francisco Madero.*

on during that session. Thus lobbying the president to make sure that your issues are on the agenda is a good idea.

Schedule of Classes

The schedule and topics are subject to change at the discretion of Gamemaster and characters active in the game.

SETUP SESSION 1

INTRODUCTION TO THE PEDAGOGY AND RECEIPT OF ROLE SHEETS

Before starting discussion on the history of the Mexican Revolution, your instructor will hand out the role sheet for your assigned character and any government position handouts (such as the presidential secretary role sheet). The Gamemaster will briefly explain the pedagogy. Read your role sheet before the first lecture/discussion so you have a point of reference for this information. As you read (and reread) the historical background, you will gain a better understanding of how your character feels about the history of Mexico.

SETUP SESSION 2

LECTURE/DISCUSSION ON THE FIRST HALF OF NINETEENTH-CENTURY MEXICO

Ensure you have read your role sheet and "Part 2, Historical Background," of the game book by this point. This session provides the opportunity to better understand the causes that led to the Mexican Revolution. The final 20–30 minutes of class should be dedicated to faction time. The three main factions will gather in different spaces to learn who is playing which character and to start planning their strategy. Your instructor will start meeting individually with the Indeterminates. If you have an Indeterminate role, feel free to mill around the room and listen to conversations the factions are having. Your instructor may also meet with students who are occupying government positions.

WARNING! *When your faction meets, do not share any of your secrets.*

LECTURE/DISCUSSION OF THE PORFIRIATO

Depending on your instructor's preferences, you may have a second introductory session, which will largely follow the format of Setup Session 2. The final 20–30 minutes of class is dedicated to faction meetings. If you are an Indeterminate, you may listen in on the faction conversations. The instructor will continue to meet with individual characters and answer questions that may arise from the faction meetings.

• GAME BEGINS •

THE YEAR IS 1912

President Francisco Madero is in charge of the day and can control the amount of time people are allowed to have at the podium. The first topic of debate is effective suffrage. The second topic was announced in the final setup session.

Game Flow

1. Collect Money: The secretary of hacienda should set up to collect money for food, being sure to record who pays on his sheet. The price for the first day is ten pesos. While this is occurring, factions should be meeting and planning. When the collection is finished, the secretary of hacienda should let the Gamemaster know if anyone is in danger of starving. NOTE: The GM may ask the presidential secretary to help collect money.

2. Debates: After money has been collected President Madero will welcome everyone and give his speech. Other speeches will follow. While specific characters must speak on the topic at hand, others can approach the podium as well. A debate on suffrage and what law, if any, should be adopted to amend voting policy must be discussed. If that debate ends before the allotted 30–45 minutes, the debate will turn to the second topic (the one the president chose the session before).

3. Vote: After the debate, the final 15–20 minutes of this class are dedicated to voting on suffrage. A vote on the second topic can happen only after the first topic has been voted on. Players cannot delay a vote on suffrage past this session. Just before the vote the GM will

ask players if they are using Power of the Press or using money to buy votes. (Assassinations and military action cannot happen yet.) The presidential secretary will ask the characters to raise their hand and fingers, indicating the number of votes they are casting for or against (e.g., if Félix Díaz bought a

NOTE

Players can use the Power of the Press only if they activated it. See p. 76 in the game book.

vote, he would hold up two fingers indicating the weight of his vote). The presidential secretary and others should be vigilant to make sure people barred from voting—based on law—are not voting. The GM and the presidential secretary will tally the votes. Based on that tally, the issue will pass or not. The remaining time of the class is dedicated to plotting for the next Game Session.

4. After the Vote: President Madero will announce the second topic for Game Session 2.

GAME SESSION 2

THE YEAR IS 1913

President Francisco Madero is in charge of the day and controls the podium. The class must discuss strong federal government vs. strong state governments (even if it was the second topic in Session 1). Food prices may have increased (the GM will make this announcement).

Game Flow

1. Collect Money: The secretary of hacienda collects money, recording who pays on his sheet. When the collection is finished the secretary of hacienda should let the Gamemaster know if anyone is in danger of starving. (See Game Session 1 for more details.)

2. Timeline Mural: The presidential secretary sets up the first panel of the Timeline Mural. Once this is set up he may help the secretary of hacienda. After the money has been collected, the presidential secretary will explain why he chose the three images he did for timeline. One image will be from something that occurred in the game during Game Session 1, another will cover something that historically occurred in the Revolution in 1912, and the third will cover something that happened in world history in 1912 that potentially had an influence on the Revolution.

3. Debates: President Madero will start the debates for the day. Players will debate on the strength of federal government versus state governments. If that debate ends before the

allotted 30–45 minutes, the debate will turn to the second topic (the one the president chose the day before). (See Game Session 1 for more details.)

4. Vote: After the debate, players will vote on a strong federal government versus strong state governments. A vote on the second topic can happen only after the first topic has been voted on. The presidential secretary and others should be vigilant to make sure people barred from voting—based on law—are not voting. The GM and the presidential secretary will tally the votes. Based on that tally, the issue will pass or not. (See Game Session 1 for more details.)

5. After the Vote: The remaining time of the class is dedicated to plotting for the next Game Session; however, assassinations and military action may now happen. For an assassination to occur the required information must have been turned in to the GM twenty-four hours before the class started. For the military action to happen it must be activated. If anyone's character dies, the player will receive a new role from the GM at the end of class. If there is a new president, that character must choose a second topic for next Game Session. The player should also receive the president's role sheet from the old president.

GAME SESSION 3

THE YEAR IS 1914

The president is in charge of the day and controls the podium. The class must discuss land reform (even if it was the second topic in Session 2). Heated debate should be happening, especially on land reform. Note that new characters will arrive in the game and some of the starting characters will disappear.

Game Flow

1. Collect Money: Food prices may have increased; the GM will make this announcement. (See Game Session 1 for more details.)

2. Timeline Mural: The presidential secretary sets up the Timeline Mural and will explain why he chose the three images. One image will be from something that occurred in the game during Game Session 2, another will cover something that historically occurred in the Revolution in 1913, and the third will cover something that happened in world history in 1913 that potentially had an influence on the Revolution.

3. Debates: The president will start the debates for the day. Players will debate on land reform. If that debate ends before the allotted 30–45 minutes, the debate will turn to the

second topic (the one the president chose the day before). (See Game Session 1 for more details.)

4. Vote: After the debate, players will vote on land reform. A vote on the second topic can happen only after the first topic has been voted on. The GM and the presidential secretary will tally the votes, and based on that tally, the issue will pass or not. (See Game Session 1 for more details.)

5. After the Vote: The remaining time of the class is dedicated to plotting for the next Game Session; however, assassinations and military action may now happen. The president must choose a second topic for the next Game Session. (See Game Session 2 for more details.)

GAME SESSION 4

THE YEAR IS 1915

The president is in charge of the day and controls the podium. The class must discuss labor reform (even it was the second topic of Game Session 3). If Francisco Madero is still president, there will be an election at end of class for a new president. Note that this will make the end of class tighter for this Game Session.

Game Flow

1. Collect Money: Food prices may have increased; the GM will make this announcement. (See Game Session 1 for more details.)

2. Timeline Mural: The presidential secretary sets up the Timeline Mural and will explain why he chose the three images. One image will be from something that occurred in the game during Game Session 3, another will cover something that historically occurred in the Revolution in 1914, and the third will cover something that happened in world history in 1914 that potentially had an influence on the Revolution.

3. Debates: The president will start the debates for the day. Players will debate on labor reform. If that debate ends before the allotted 30–45 minutes, the debate will turn to the second topic (the one the president chose the day before). (See Game Session 1 for more details.)

4. Vote: After the debate, players will vote on labor reform. A vote on the second topic can happen only after the first topic has been voted on. The GM and the presidential secretary will tally the votes, and based on that tally, the issue will pass or not. (See Game Session 1 for more details.)

5. Presidential Election: If Francisco Madero is still president, there will be a vote for a new president. Francisco Madero will step down and leave the game. The new president will choose the second topic for the next game session and will receive the president's role sheet. The player of Francisco Madero will receive a new character.

6. After the Vote: The remaining time of the class is dedicated to plotting for the next Game Session; however, assassinations and military action may now happen. (See Game Session 2 for more details.)

THE YEAR IS 1916

The president is in charge of the day and controls the podium. The class must discuss foreign business interests (even if it was the second topic in Game Session 4).

Game Flow

1. Collect Money: Food prices may have increased; the GM will make this announcement. (See Game Session 1 for more details.)

2. Timeline Mural: The presidential secretary sets up the Timeline Mural and will explain why he chose the three images. One image will be from something that occurred in the game during Game Session 4, another will cover something that historically occurred in the Revolution in 1915, and the third will cover something that happened in world history in 1915 that potentially had an influence on the Revolution.

3. Debates: The president will start the debates for the day. Players will debate on foreign business interests. If that debate ends before the allotted 30–45 minutes, the debate will turn to the second topic (the one the president chose the day before). (See Game Session 1 for more details.)

4. Vote: After the debate, players will vote on foreign business interests. A vote on the second topic can happen only after the first topic has been voted on. The GM and the presidential secretary will tally the votes, and based on that tally, the issue will pass or not. (See Game Session 1 for more details.)

5. After the Vote: The remaining time of the class is dedicated to plotting for the next game session; however, assassinations and military action may now happen. The president must choose a second topic for the next game session. (See Game Session 2 for more details.)

THE YEAR IS 1917

The president is in charge of the day and controls the podium. The class must discuss education reform (even if it was the second topic in Game Session 5).

Game Flow

1. Collect Money: Food prices may have increased; the GM will make this announcement. (See Game Session 1 for more details.)

2. Timeline Mural: The presidential secretary sets up the Timeline Mural and will explain why he chose the three images. One image will be from something that occurred in the game during Game Session 5, another will cover something that historically occurred in the Revolution in 1916, and the third will cover something that happened in world history in 1916 that potentially had an influence on the Revolution.

3. Debates: The president will start the debates for the day. Players will debate on education reform. If that debate ends before the allotted 30–45 minutes, the debate will turn to the second topic (the one the president chose the day before). (See Game Session 1 for more details.)

4. Vote: After the debate, players will vote on education reform. A vote on the second topic can happen only after the first topic has been voted on. The GM and the presidential secretary will tally the votes, and based on that tally, the issue will pass or not. (See Game Session 1 for more details.)

5. After the Vote: The remaining time of the class is dedicated to plotting for the next Game Session; however, assassinations and military action may now happen. The president must choose a second topic for the next Game Session. (See Game Session 2 for more details.)

THE YEAR IS 1918

The president is in charge of the day and controls the podium. The class must discuss religious reform (even if it was the second topic in Game Session 6).

Game Flow

1. Collect Money: Food prices may have increased; the GM will make this announcement. (See Game Session 1 for more details.)

2. Timeline Mural: The presidential secretary sets up the Timeline Mural and will explain why he chose the three images. One image will be from something that occurred in the game during Game Session 6, another will cover something that historically occurred in the Revolution in 1917, and the third will cover something that happened in world history in 1917 that potentially had an influence on the Revolution.

3. Debates: The president will start the debates for the day. Players will debate on religious reform. If that debate ends before the allotted 30–45 minutes, the debate will turn to the second topic (the one the president chose the day before). (See Game Session 1 for more details.)

4. Vote: After the debate, players will vote on religious reform. A vote on the second topic can happen only after the first topic has been voted on. The GM and the presidential secretary will tally the votes, and based on that tally, the issue will pass or not. (See Game Session 1 for more details.)

5. After the Vote: The remaining time of the class is dedicated to plotting for the next Game Session; however, assassinations and military action may now happen. The president must choose a second topic for the next Game Session. (See Game Session 2 for more details.)

GAME SESSION 8

THE YEAR IS 1919

The president is in charge of the day and controls the podium. The class must discuss women's rights (even if it was the second topic in Game Session 7). If someone has been president for four consecutive years, there will be an election at the end of class for a new president. Note that this will make the end of class tighter for this Game Session.

Game Flow

1. Collect Money: Food prices may have increased; the GM will make this announcement. (See Game Session 1 for more details.)

2. Timeline Mural: The presidential secretary sets up the Timeline Mural and will explain why he chose the three images. One image will be from something that occurred in the

game during Game Session 7, another will cover something that historically occurred in the Revolution in 1918, and the third will cover something that happened in world history in 1918 that potentially had an influence on the Revolution.

3. Debates: The president will start the debates for the day. Players will debate on women's rights. If that debate ends before the allotted 30/45 minutes, the debate will turn to the second topic (the one the president chose the day before). (See Game Session 1 for more details.)

4. Vote: After the debate, players will vote on women's rights. A vote on the second topic can happen only after the first topic has been voted on. The GM and the presidential secretary will tally the votes, and based on that tally, the issue will pass or not. (See Game Session 1 for more details.)

5. Presidential Election: If the current president has served for four consecutive years, there will be a vote for a new president. If not, the sitting president should announce who he would support as his successor when his term ends.

6. End game.

FINAL SESSION

DEBRIEF

Game Flow

1. The presidential secretary will post the final panel of the Timeline Mural and will explain why he chose the three images. One image will be from something that occurred in the game during Game Session 8, another will cover something that historically occurred in the Revolution in 1919, and the third will cover something that happened in world history in 1919 that potentially had an influence on the Revolution.

2. Other actions may occur at the GM's discretion.

3. The GM will distribute post-Revolution biographies of the characters, so you can learn what happened to your character in later years.

4. As a class, you will discuss actions you took during the game and reveal your secrets.

5. Your instructor will compare the history of the Mexican Revolution to what happened in the game and will set the historical record straight.

Movement of Time

Each session of the game represents a single year in the course of the Revolution. What occurs during any of these Game Sessions is largely up to you, the players, though certain actions will trigger certain outcomes. Do not delay your actions if you suspect someone will stop being president in the next Game Session (remember, each session is a year in terms of the game). Generally speaking, knowing what year you are in is important for understanding world events that may impact Mexico (such as a U.S. presidential election).

Assignments

Each character has at least two different assignments, which are outlined on the role sheet. For example, one might be a speech your character will give in session (albeit ad hoc, without reading it); the other might be a more creative assignment such as a media piece (a newspaper article, homemade movie clip, piece of art, song, etc.), or piece of propaganda related to your character's goals. If you have any questions, ask the Gamemaster.

All media pieces should be submitted to the student characters who have access to publication venues. These students will act as publishers and editors and have the right to reject any piece not fitting their revolutionary agenda. Should a student be unable to find a character to publish her piece, she should approach an outside journalist (the GM will play this role). Other students will be able to use published information during the Game Session debates. This assignment must be informed by primary source documents from the period.

Over the course of the game, some students will play multiple roles. If this happens, consider how many assignments you have submitted before starting any assignments for your new character, as you will likely have written at least one already (if your character died before you submitted the assignment, you should still turn it in for credit). If you have completed one assignment, then you need to complete only one of the assignments listed in the role sheet for your new character (talk to the GM about which one). If you haven't done an assignment yet, then you will need to do all of the assignments. If you have done all of the assignments from a previous character, then you don't need to do any from your new character; *however, you still need to be able to discuss your new character's point of view and present it to the class.*

COUNTERFACTUALS

1. Gatherings involving the characters in this game *never* occurred in history. The closest such event was the 1914 gathering in Aguascalientes, from which the idea for this game is based.

2. For the purposes of the game, some characters appear on the scene later or earlier than they did historically in the Mexican Revolution. These inconsistencies are noted on the individual role sheets.

3. To make sure a variety of ideas from the Revolution are represented, some characters, such as Francisco Bulnes and Enrique Clay Creel, are in Mexico for the game, even though in truth they spent the Revolution in exile.

4. The presidential secretary position in this game did not exist. Abraham González, who starts the game in this position, was governor of Chihuahua and secretary of the interior. The position was created to help aid the flow of the game.

5. Historically, Victoriano Huerta was not secretary of war until later in the Revolution.

6. Some of the core texts, such as "The Social Question in Mexico," which was not presented until January 1913, are included in the game because they are important to debates that occur later in the game. No matter the year of the Game Session, each of the texts in the game book can be used to support your ideas, even if that particular text had not yet been published.

RULES AND PROCEDURES

Objectives

Your objective is first to learn in detail about your historical character. Like all people you will have a personality, a point of view, and a set of talents that make you unique. You will be acting this character during the game and must make decisions as the character would. You have topics of interest specifically assigned to your character (see your role sheet) and will share information on that topic with the class. Second, you must become conversant with the range of problems of the times and with the potential solutions. Each character's goal in the game is to achieve what he or she believes is best for the country of Mexico. The main mechanism for making this happen is through informed debate (by reading the sources included in the game book or found through careful research) followed by a vote. But, as happened in the actual Mexican Revolution, the individual actions of characters in the game (through bribery, military violence, the press, or assassination) can often derail careful plans. You must be ready and willing to stand and speak extemporaneously on all of the major issues for debate, as you never know when someone will encourage you to change your vote. If a topic is not listed on your role sheet, then you should ask in-depth questions of the presenters about why the topic is important. Call them on their sources and ask them to verify their arguments with evidence. Expect to be required to do the same. You will speak when assigned in the role of your character but also whenever you have some ideas to contribute. Speaking is required. Audacity is part of the game. Do not hold back. Take action.

Victory Conditions

While winning does not affect your grade, it does give you the opportunity to do a happy dance or whatever other kind of celebratory cheer you might do when you win a game. In the course of this game there are at least four different ways to win: two individual wins and two collective or faction wins.

Character Wins (Detailed in Your Role Sheet)

1. Big Win: Each character has a set of victory objectives. These are the goals that each character would like to achieve by the end of the Revolution. Just as in real life, it is next to impossible to get everything you would like, but this does not mean you should not try. To achieve the Big Win you must get *all* of your victory objectives. As you will quickly notice, getting all of what you want will prove difficult, so you may decide that compromise allows you to accomplish what is more important to you. Because of this you might be willing to bend on certain things when your fellow citizens ask for help.

> **TIP**
>
> Taking responsibility for the Timeline Mural can help with your character's legacy. Likewise, writing articles for the newspaper is a legacy achievement.

2. Legacy Win: You have to accomplish fewer goals to secure a Legacy Win, which involves how, and if, your character will be remembered by future generations.

Faction Wins

1. Governmental Control: If you are even loosely associated with the side that is in control of the Mexican government at the end of the game, you are considered to be on the winning side. To accomplish this goal, you must still be acting out the major goals of your character.

> **TIP**
>
> The way to a Memory win is to publish articles, write Mexican ballads (*corridos*), create silent films, take part in the creation of the Timeline Mural, or present your own creative works.

2. Memory: This win option is perhaps the most nebulous and difficult to predict over the course of the game. Winning the Memory means that ten, fifteen, twenty years or more in the future people will look back on the Mexican Revolution and will be talking about what you wanted the Revolution to mean.

Attendance

The Mexican Revolution was an incredibly violent period of history, especially for revolutionaries. To simulate the deadliness of the period—due to revolutionary violence, disease, general accidents (such as being thrown from a spooked horse), or Arizona Ranger involvement along the border—characters who are absent from a Game Session will have a 50 percent chance of dying due to a random malady as decided by the GM. Students who have a character die in this way will be assigned a new character as soon after the missed session as possible. They are expected to learn their new character immediately and be ready to play their new character at the start of the next Game Session.

Female vs. Male

There are both male and female characters in this game. Male and female students may be called on to play a member of the opposite sex. Because of this, it is necessary to distinguish who is playing a female character and who is playing a male character. Female characters in the game will need to wear a red bandana (or some other identifying article as determined by the GM) on their person. A portion of the bandana must be visible at all times. All students are expected to act professionally about the random gender assignments.

Timeline

Several of the murals painted following the Revolution by Diego Rivera, José Clemente Orozco, and David Siqueiros can be viewed as historical timelines. *Del porfirismo a la Revolución*, by David Siqueiros, is a famous mural painted decades after the Revolution that depicts its most famous events. The mural is easily found online. In one section, Siqueiros highlights the Cananea Mine strike of 1906 as a pivotal moment in the decline of the Porfiriato. Other segments dramatize different events during this crucial period in Mexican history.

Over the course of the game, students will generate a similar mural, which will serve as a timeline. Students will create a panel for each Game Session. Whoever is the presidential secretary at the end of a given Game Session gets to choose what images are included in the timeline or he may delegate this responsibility to someone else. Each panel, however, must include at least three images. The first must reflect what happened in the previous Game Session. The second is the "mirror image" of the first, showing what actually happened in Mexico for the chosen event. The final image reflects something that occurred elsewhere in the world that had a direct bearing on Mexico at the time. These images may be created by one or more students or may be copies of actual images of the period. They should be arranged in a collage format.

The Declining Balance and the Starvation Clock

As the Mexican Revolution progressed, money was harder to obtain and food became scarce and more expensive. At the start of each Game Session, characters must provide the *secretaría de hacienda y crédito público* (secretary of finance and public credit), known as the secretary of hacienda in the game, with the going cost of food. Initially this is set at ten pesos, but it will change over the course of the game. The secretary of hacienda is essentially providing your character with food in return for the money. If you fail to provide the secretary of hacienda with money on time, he or she may charge interest for your late payment. Deciding to do so is up to that character. There are ways around purchasing your food from the secretary of hacienda, but this is up to you (individually or collectively) to figure out. If you think of an idea, run it by the GM, and the GM will let you know if you need to keep paying.

Failure to pay the secretaría de hacienda at the start of a Game Session will start the "starvation clock." *If your character fails to provide the requisite money by the end of that Game Session, you will starve to death.* If your character dies, you will receive a new role.

Powers

Powers are assets of influence that you can activate by doing research. They are either general powers or special powers. General powers are available to everyone. They may be supplemented with special powers as indicated on your role sheets. The instructions that follow describe the powers and what you need to do to be able to use each one.

General Powers

1. Power of the Podium. Though the people in power did not listen to everyone during this period in Mexican history, in the game we want to hear all viewpoints. Therefore, everyone gets a chance to speak when they approach the podium, regardless of political alignment. The "podium" will be a physical location in the room, decided at the beginning of the game. The length of time you have to speak at the podium could vary, depending on who is in power, though no one will have less than a minute. If need be the Gamemaster will enforce this rule. *To Activate:* Approach the podium.

2. Power to Vote. Many things in the game require votes by the characters, such as electing a president or passing an amendment to the constitution. Something will be voted on during each Game Session. These votes move factions closer or farther from their goals. Mexico, at the time, was striving to be a functioning democracy (or at least some people in Mexico were hoping it would be). The idea of suffrage and casting a vote was supremely important. Women, foreigners, and men under the legal voting age (eighteen if married, twenty-one if a bachelor) did not have suffrage. However, in the course of creating a new constitution, students may widen suffrage to include any disenfranchised group. Votes will be cast publically. Journalists have the Power of the Press, which allows them one vote each time they publish a newspaper. In other words, three published newspapers means three extra votes. To cast a vote you *must* be in class (absentee voting is not allowed) and cannot be in jail. *To Activate*: Be present in class and be a character who has the right to vote.

3. Power of Money. All characters in the game are given an initial amount of money that reflects their financial status at the time of the Mexican Revolution. This money is needed to pay for food at each Game Session. The cost of food will vary during the game. If you ever find yourself in need of more money, you must try to obtain it from other characters, by asking for help, pillaging, or through other means or talents associated with your character. If you wish to earn more money, you must ask those with money to give you a job. However, they are under no obligation to hire you. *To Activate*: Have money.

What Your Money Can Buy

1. Food: See "Declining Balance and the Starvation Clock" (p. 71).

2. Bribery: Should you wish to bribe another character, you can do so without the presence of the Gamemaster. Offer money to other characters to encourage them to vote or act the way you would like them to. But beware; an exchange of money does not bind anyone to the stated agreement.

3. Hire an assassin. See "Power to Assassinate (below)."

4. Stamp Tax: It is possible for the president to levy a Stamp Tax on different goods. Should this happen, characters directly affected by the tax will need to pay. The president will provide more information on the Stamp Tax, should he decide to collect.

4. Power to Assassinate. The Mexican Revolution was an incredibly deadly time in Mexican history. During this period, Mexicans worked to sort out their differences first by negotiation, then by sidelining someone politically through arrest or exile, and ultimately by killing them. Díaz, like others, realized that Mexico was precariously balanced, so when journalists irritated him, he had them imprisoned—often. Only rarely did he seek to have them killed. Francisco Madero's revolt unhinged this. Díaz's search for stability drove him to try more negotiations. If this failed to reconcile a difference, then violence was a real option. Due to historical and ideological conflicts, you may find it beneficial to have a character "assassinated," or removed from the game. But remember that assassination attempts are not always successful, nor were they during the Mexican Revolution. Violence always carries a risk. *To Activate*: If you wish to assassinate a character you must first draw up a plan in writing and submit it to the GM at least twenty-four hours before the assassination can take place. The plan is a small research paper.

1. Part one of your plan *must* include an explanation of what ideological conflict you have with the intended target. It *must* be 100 to 300 words in length, *must* reference specific unacceptable actions on the part of the target, and *must* justify the attempt by using primary sources from the game book or elsewhere. You *must* cite your sources. The assassination attempt cannot be purely for vengeance. You must have reasons supported by your character's ideological beliefs.

> **NOTE**
>
> Assassinations *cannot* happen until the end of the second session of game play.

2. Part two of your plan needs to include the name of the character to be assassinated and the signatures of all individuals supporting your attempt.

Assassinations can happen *only* at the end of a Game Session or between sessions. If between sessions, it *must* happen at least twenty-four hours before the start of the next Game Session.

Be aware that all choices carry possible consequences. When you submit your signed contract for assassination to the Gamemaster you are handing it to a character in the game, not the professor of the class. Word of the plan might leak if a bribe is offered to the character who received the plan. You can attempt an assassination on a particular individual only every other Game Session. However, you may attempt to assassinate multiple people.

Figuring out the results: The Gamemaster will roll three six-sided dice outside of class and consult a chart. Depending on the roll of the dice and the strength of your plan, the GM will determine whether your assassination attempt succeeds or fails. There are multiple ways to increase your chances of success.

ADVICE FOR STRENGTHENING AN ASSASSINATION ATTEMPT:

1. **Scoping the Scene**. Research the where, when, and why of the scene and add details to your plan. For example, if your character is trying to assassinate a Zapatista known to have raided haciendas, you might find the name of an actual early-twentieth-century hacienda in the state where the revolutionary was known to operate. The more research you have, including sources beyond the

game book, the better your chances. Consider it scoping out the scene. You need to cite where you find this information.

2. **Build Allies**. Both in your faction and out of your faction. The more people who sign your plan, the higher its chances of success. On the other hand, the more people who know, the greater the possibility of opposition characters finding out who is behind the attempt. Presenting a rousing speech in front of the class, even though it may also warn the enemies that you are coming, may convince others of your view and encourage them to sign your plan.

RESULTS OF SUCCESSFUL ASSASSINATIONS:

If your character is assassinated, you will receive a new role. Note that your new character may very well be on the opposite side of the Revolution from your original character. Of course, when you return as a new character, you have all of the historical information and secrets you learned when acting as your previous character. *Note that you cannot assist with any attacks or plots you knew about in your previous life without first consulting with the GM.* You can act on previous knowledge only if another character choses to share that same information with you in your new role. This is on the honor system.

ASSIGNMENTS AFTER THE DEATH OF YOUR CHARACTER:

In the game you are responsible for the assignments associated with your character. If you have completed a written an assignment but have not yet turned it in when your character dies, you must still submit the assignment for a grade. You will not, however, be able to give a speech on the assignment, because that character is dead. You will be expected to give a speech as your new character, but you do not have to turn in a second written assignment. If you have not written anything for your first character before his or her death, then you must complete both the written and oral work associated with your new character. When you shift characters, the number of assignments to complete during the game remains the same (your workload neither increases nor decreases). If you are uncertain of what to do, talk to the GM.

NOTE

The president and the secretary of war are the only characters who may not be arrested or removed from the chambers.

5. **Power to Arrest.** The secretary of war (a character in the game) has the *exclusive* ability to arrest anyone in the game, except the president. *To Activate*: The secretary of war announces the arrest to the GM.

The student playing the arrested character moves to the back of the classroom (the jail cell). This detainee is unable to speak for the next 10–15 minutes of the Game Session (length of silence depends on the length of the Game Session) and is unable to vote. While incarcerated, the character may not communicate with other revolutionaries or vote. After the time is up the detainee may return to the debate chambers, but must refrain from outbursts for the rest of that Game Session (the GM will enforce this). The secretary of war may arrest as many characters as he likes over the course of a session. He may not, however, arrest a character more than one time during a single session.

Character-Specific Powers

In the Mexican Revolution there are three special powers that individual characters in the game may have at their disposal: the Power of Military Action, the Power of the Press, and the Power of Currency Reserves. Every character has at least one of these special powers, and some have more. Your character's powers are detailed on your role sheet. Activation often requires the submission of a small paper or a speech. These are not graded, but their submission will be considered a part of your participation; however, check with your GM for specific requirements. When you turn in your larger written assignments for a grade you will also activate your power for that Game Session.

If your character has multiple powers you may use all of them the same day, but each requires its own unique activation.

1. Power of Military Action. Characters in charge of military forces (official forces, such as those of a government, or guerilla forces, such as revolutionary fighters) may activate one, and only one, of the following actions in any one Game Session. Only those with the Power of Military Action can participate in a confrontation.

Overthrow/Defend the Mexican Government. If you wish to overthrow or defend the Mexican government, note that you are initiating a military conflict, battle, or raid undertaken to change the current leadership of the country. *To Activate*: To attempt an overthrow of the government, you must give a short speech declaring your intent to revolt. The speech must use your character's ideology and cite written sources to justify your actions. Success is more likely when a group of like-thinking people take simultaneous military action. Only those inciting the action, however, must make a speech. Supporters must have the Power of Military Action and must indicate they are using their power.

Results of a military action are determined as follows:

- To determine the winner of the conflict, the Game-master will count all of the military actions taking place on each side of the conflict. The side with the most participants wins. If there is a tie, then victory goes to the defenders. Because the secretary of war has better trained forces, his support counts as three participants when tallying number of characters involved.

- The leader of the winning side becomes the new president.

> **TIP**
>
> There is a lot of money floating around in this game. If you want to see who has it, watch the size of the bills that change hands with the secretary of hacienda at the start of any Game Session.

- If you lose, you have expended your Power of Military Action and cannot use another one that Game Session.

2. Power of the Press (PoP). Characters with the Power of the Press have influence over the general public through their publications. This influence is demonstrated through their ability to cast multiple votes when characters are voting on ratification of laws. Most male Mexican citizens in the game have one base vote. Foreigners, women, and youth have zero votes, unless they purchase votes with cash. Journalists, however, can earn multiple votes. NOTE: This is the only action that may be used multiple times in a Game Session. Each use requires its own activation.

Public Influence. A journalist may activate Public Influence up to four times in one Game Session. This action represents the journalist's readership.

To Activate: Write a 250-word article using sources (you must cite them) from the game book related to the topic you are voting on. Show the article(s) to the GM at the beginning of the Game Session. The GM will determine the number of votes allowed in that Game Session. Generally, you'll receive one extra vote per activation for any voting that occurs in that Game Session.

3. Power of Currency Reserves. People with lots of money often have more power in society than those with none. This was definitely the case in Mexico before, during, and after the Revolution. Currency reserves, meaning money in the bank, are there to demonstrate the economic imbalance in the country.

Characters with the Power of Currency Reserves have financial reserves in the bank that they may access up to four times over the course of the game. For example, a character who has this power and a starting peso value of 200 may withdraw an additional 200 pesos from the bank with each activation of the Power of Currency Reserves he or she takes during the course of the game. *You may activate this power only once per Game Session but four times over the entire game.*

To Activate: To activate the Power of Currency Reserves, you must write a 250-word letter to your investors or supporters stating why you need the money and how you will use it to support your goals. The GM will evaluate and approve your letter, sanction the withdrawal from your account, and give you the cash. If approved, you will gain an amount of cash equal to your starting peso value.

ALTERNATIVE MEANS OF ACTIVATING POWERS

The following list offers additional ways to activate general or special powers. Any of the following may be used to replace the standard activation option. *You must clear it with the GM before using any of these methods.*

- Getting a friend from outside the class to visit and play a role. (*GM needs a minimum of twenty-four-hour notice.*)

- Drawing up a plan for a new faction and sharing it publicly.

- Writing a corrido in the traditional style.

- Performing a corrido.

- Generating a period piece of art or an analysis of one.

- Creating a silent film.

- A creative endeavor of your own choosing that reflects the time period.

Destabilize Mexico. Characters with Currency Reserves may choose to pull their money and investments out of Mexico. Each character who takes this action increases the financial insecurity of the country, which is reflected by a 10-peso increase in the cost of food per participant in the action, to be paid at the start of each Game Session. Several characters could do this simultaneously, causing the price of food to jump substantially from one session to another. For example, the base price of food is 10 pesos, so if two characters decide to remove their funds from Mexico, the base price of food jumps to 30 pesos per Game Session (a 10-peso increase as the result of each investor's withdrawal). If, as an investor, you decide at any point to stop defunding Mexico, you can do so by alerting the GM of your decision. However, while you are defunding Mexico you cannot use your funds for anything other than for food. You cannot use your money to buy votes or to pile up cash.

To Activate: To destabilize Mexico, you must give a speech stating and supporting your ideological reasons for withdrawing your investments from the country.

 PART 4: ROLES AND FACTIONS

Maderistas

Led by Francisco Madero, the Maderistas are a cross-section of Mexicans from peasants to the wealthy. They reflect the diversity of opinions that comes with such a wide group. Their leadership and much of their membership comes from northern Mexico. The principal aim, of the leadership at least, is to pass suffrage reform. Many in the group were part of the anti-reelectionist movement and their reforms reflect a desire to shift the status quo, but predominantly by reforming the constitution. This group also has people who stand on both the left and the right of the political spectrum. They have joined with Madero in an effort to create stability in the country.

Francisco Madero He encouraged the people of Mexico to stand up to Porfirio Díaz and even seems to have the interests of the lower classes at heart. He is a wealthy man (the son of a hacienda owner) who speaks of support for women, labor reform, land reform, freedom of the press, and many other reforms.

Abraham González Casavantes He is an intellectual from the state of Chihuahua and an ardent spokesman and supporter of Francisco Madero. He became the president of the anti-reelectionist group in Chihuahua and organized opportunities for Madero to meet with potential followers. While he prefers a peaceful approach, it is rumored he organized the Revolution on the ground level. He is currently sitting governor of the state of Chihuahua, and for the purposes of the game, he serves as the presidential secretary.

José Vasconcelos An intellectual from the state of Oaxaca, he has spent a lot of time in the United States. In fact, his time in the United States turned him against the culture of that country, especially the materialism. He has been one of Madero's strongest supporters since the beginning of the anti-reelectionist movement, spent time prior to the Revolution in Washington, D.C., representing Madero, and is a big proponent of education reform. He is also the main editor of the of the anti-reelectionist paper *El Antireeleccionista*.

Francisco "Pancho" Villa He is a northerner, supporter of Madero, and a known bandit. However, unlike Madero, he does not come from the upper class; rather, he is a man of the working class. Some believe he is a military genius.

Dolores Jiménez y Muro She is an intellectual, schoolteacher, anarchist, activist, and supporter of Madero. She grew up in San Luis Potosí and has been active for longer than some other revolutionaries have been alive. She is outspoken in her support of women's rights, workers' rights, and agrarian reform.

Antonio Díaz Soto y Gama He is a very outspoken lawyer and anarchist from San Luis Potosí. Since the beginning of the century, he has spent a lot of time in jail for his criticisms of the Díaz regime. He is an ally of Madero's and has recently toned his rhetoric down. He appears to be honestly interested in the plight of the indigenous people.

Victoriano Huerta He was an important general for Porfirio Díaz known for his ferocity. He is ruthless in the repression of rebellions and has earned the animosity of the Zapatistas because of it. In an attempt to reconcile the two sides of the Revolution, Francisco Madero made him secretary of war.

Manuel Peláez Gorróchtegui He is a wealthy landowner and *caudillo* (regional strongman) from the state of Veracruz. He has close ties to many foreign investors (especially the oil company El Águila and its owner, British businessman Weetman Pearson). Though he has not been actively involved in the anti-reelectionist movement, he came out in support of Madero's revolt against Porfirio Díaz.

Silvestre Terrazas A prolific journalist from Chihuahua, he is the distant cousin of wealthy landowner Luis Terrazas. His daily newspaper, *El Correo de Chihuahua*, is known for its Catholic and moralistic content. However, in the last few years he has used the paper to target corruption and seek reform of the political status quo. He is especially known for his articles on workers' movements and against the corruption of recent governorships in Chihuahua.

Ernesto Madero Farías He is Francisco Madero's uncle and the current secretary of hacienda. He was a successful banker under the Porfirian regime and followed José Limantour (Díaz's secretary of hacienda). Porfirio Díaz asked Ernesto to negotiate the terms of his surrender on his behalf. Ernesto also served in his current position under the interim presidency of Francisco León de la Barra. He is known to support foreign investment for the good of the Mexican economy.

Felipe Ángeles A talented military leader, he openly criticized his superior officers, for which Porfirio Díaz exiled him to France for insubordination. He was one of the few high-ranking military officers who was absent during the entirety of the rebellion against Díaz. Francisco Madero recently recalled him from France.

Zapatistas

Followers of Emiliano Zapata, the Zapatistas represent the interests of southern hacienda workers and the indigenous people. Based out of the state of Morelos, their proximity to Mexico City makes them a constant threat. While interested in many reforms, their main focus is land reform. Although some of their membership includes urban intellectuals, the majority of the faction are indigenous, particularly Nahua. They seek redress for grievances inflicted on their community by past laws that stripped the possibility of communal landownership. In 1910, they allied themselves with Francisco Madero. However, since the defeat of Díaz they have become dissatisfied with Madero's delays regarding land reform and refuse to return hacienda land that they received. Despite efforts to come to an agreement, talks between the two groups broke down; within a month of Madero gaining the presidency, the Zapatistas went into open rebellion against him.

Emiliano Zapata An indigenous leader from the state of Morelos. After Madero issued the Plan of San Luis de Potosí, Zapata sided with him in the rebellion. While he was never able to physically join up with the northern forces, the position of his forces just south of Mexico City brought significant pressure on the Porfirio Díaz regime. Quickly frustrated with Madero's leadership since the fall of Díaz, Zapata issued the Plan de Ayala in November 1911 and has been in revolt against Madero since that time.

Otilio Montaño An indigenous leader from the south, he is the second in command of the Zapatistas and is potentially the brains of the outfit. He worked as a traveling schoolteacher of sorts and is the good friend of Emiliano Zapata.

Manuel Palafox He is an urban intellectual. He initially went to the Zapatistas to negotiate on behalf of the hacienda owners of Morelos. Rather than winning Zapata over to the hacienda owners, he joined Zapata and has been an ardent supporter ever since.

Ángel Robles An amazing Zapatista fighter, he has the best interests of the agrarian people in mind. At times, he is a bit hotheaded and likely to challenge someone when he is insulted or has his honor called into account.

Félicistas

Brought together by Félix Díaz, the Félicistas represent the interests of the supporters of Porfirio Díaz. They would like to maintain the status quo in Mexico. They have strong relations with foreign investors and hold the majority of the wealth in the country. They believe that for Mexico to succeed it must be done through economics and modernization. While some of the members of the group disagreed with Porfirio Díaz's decisions, they supported the stability and investment (or "order and progress") that he brought to the country. Many of them fear Francisco Madero has tampered with a precariously balanced government and worry that Mexico will fall to chaos.

Félix Díaz He is the nephew of Porfirio Díaz and a general in the military. While he became governor of Oaxaca at the end of his uncle's reign, Porfirio preferred to give Félix lesser posts, such as the head of police forces in Mexico City. Both Félix and his wife are wealthy landowners in their own right. That combined with his family ties makes Félix one of the most important leaders in the opposition to Francisco Madero.

Francisco Bulnes An older statesman, he sided with Sebastian Lerdo de Tejada against Porfirio Díaz when Díaz first gained power. A professor, writer, and politician, he eventually served in Porfirio Díaz's administration. A científico, positivist, and Social Darwinist, he criticizes the power of the Catholic Church. Bulnes believes in authoritarian rule in Mexico and sees Madero's triumph as proof that Díaz lost his strength as a leader.

Luis Terrazas The wealthiest landowner in the state of Chihuahua and the entirety of Mexico, he was a key supporter of Benito Juárez during the War of Reform against Prince Maximillian. While he was against Porfirio Díaz for a period, he eventually joined with him at the start of the twentieth century. His son-in-law is Enrique Creel. He is also distantly related to the journalist Silvestre Terrazas.

Enrique Clay Creel Cuilty He is the son of Abraham Lincoln's U.S. consul to Chihuahua and son-in-law to Luis Terrazas. He is a dual citizen of Mexico and the United States and has served as the governor of Chihuahua, acted as translator for the historic meeting between Presidents Howard Taft and Porfirio Díaz, and was, until recently, Mexico's ambassador to the United States. An incredibly successful banker and businessman, he was the second most important person in financial matters during the Díaz regime. Many foreign investors use him as a middleman to get things accomplished in Mexico. He is also a científico and has been publically called out for possible corruption by Silvestre Terrazas.

Emilio Rabasa An ardent supporter of Porfirio Díaz and the peace and progress the regime brought to Mexico, he advocates reform from within the political apparatus. He has served in various governmental positions, including as governor of Chiapas (despite his father being a foreigner) and as a senator. He is committed to reforms, provided they happen within the apparatus of the government. He believes that order is essential for progress.

Juana Catarina Romero She is a wealthy, unwed, businesswoman from Tehuantepec, Oaxaca, and a major power broker in the city who was instrumental in getting the railroad built. She was a good friend and ally of Porfirio Díaz. She is a strong supporter of the Catholic Church and of education reform. With her own money she opened two primary schools in Tehuantepec and hired priests and nuns to teach there.

Indeterminates

While the Indeterminates have interests that align with members of the Maderista, Zapatista, and Félicista factions they, for various reasons, have not joined any of those factions. Gaining their support for crucial votes could very well sway many different issues.

Archbishop José Mora y del Río Proactive in social and moral reforms, the archbishop has established the stance of the Catholic Church as a middle ground between the sides. He believes that mutual respect of all parties and by all parties is required to bring peace.

Pascual Orozco He was the first leader Madero promoted to general. He, like Villa, is of a lower social class than Madero. His main followers are anarchists and Protestants. He and his family are also known to be of the Protestant faith. This past February, he revolted against Madero and has allied himself with the Zapatistas, though he is not officially a part of their faction.

José Guadalupe Posada He is an artist and printer in Mexico City who creates the woodcuts for corridos and cheap magazines.

David Alfaro Siqueiros At the start of the game, he is 15 years old. He is a student living in Mexico City and attending the prestigious art school Academia de San Carlos, also known by its more recent title, the National School of Fine Arts (ENBA, Escuela Nacional de Bellas Artes). He has been active in the student strikes at the school.

Father Alfredo Méndez Medina He is a Jesuit priest who has just returned from Europe with ideas for labor organizing based on Social Catholicism. He seems to be causing a stir both in the Church and among lay labor organizers.

Amelio Jímenez At the start of the game, he is 16 years old. He is a Zapotec mestizo from Tehuantepec whose Spanish father owned a hacienda; however, he has been supporting the indigenous hacienda workers and fought against Díaz in Oaxaca.

Wong Foon Chuck He is a Chinese businessman and naturalized Mexican citizen from the state of Chihuahua. He has business interests in banking, rail, restaurants, real estate, and many other areas. In the 1890s the United States deported him to Mexico, despite cries from liberal sources like the *Washington Post*. He is a competitor with the Maderos and has had some run-ins with them as well. When Maderista forces took the town of Torreón from Porfirian forces, they massacred

303 people of Chinese descent. A number of them worked for Wong, and he knew most, if not all, of them. Currently China is asking Mexico to pay reparations for the massacre.

Dr. Atl (Gerardo Murillo) He is an artist and writer from Guadalajara who recently returned from Europe. His questioning of classical teaching techniques and support of indigenous art have created some trouble at the Academia de San Carlos, the prestigious state art school also known as the National School of Fine Arts (ENBA, Escuela Nacional de Bellas Artes).

Chepa Moreno She is a Yaqui Indian looking for work in Mexico City.

Foreigners

The following individuals are visiting Mexico and have an array of interests in Mexico. Do not take their lack of electoral rights for granted. Many of them have deep pockets—enough to buy votes and lots of influence in important political circles.

Henry Lane Wilson. As the ambassador of the United States, he was friendly with Porfirio Díaz and believes Mexico needs to continue to modernize. He has been adamant in his support of U.S. governmental interests and U.S. landholders in Mexico.

Weetman Dickinson Pearson (Baron Cowdray) A British entrepreneur, he represents many of the interests of Great Britain (a country second only to the United States in foreign investment). He was very close to Porfirio Díaz and his allies. His investments in oil, rail, and real estate are quite significant, especially in the areas of Veracruz and the Isthmus of Tehuantepec. He has spent time and energy working to weaken U.S. business interests in Mexico, especially in regard to railways and oil. He and Edward Doheny have a known rivalry, and both have spent considerable capital working to smear each other in various newspapers.

Edward Doheny He is a U.S. entrepreneur with oil and other interests in Tampico and Veracruz. After U.S. Standard Oil's dissolution in May 1911, Doheny became the number one U.S. oil investor in Mexico.

Paul von Hintze As the German minister of foreign affairs to Mexico, he wants Mexico to continue to modernize, but is hoping they do it with a preference for Germany.

Félix Sommerfeld A German businessman and confidant of Francisco Madero, he has worked as an assayer for mines and as a part-time reporter for the Associated Press along the U.S.–Mexican border.

Late Arrivals

Late arrivals are all important actors within the Mexican Revolution. Their roles in events will become more apparent as other characters leave the game.

Venustiano Carranza He is a wealthy hacienda owner from and governor of Coahuila who supports liberal reforms. He was not overly active in the early phase of the Revolution, although he had previously rebelled against Díaz. Though not a military leader, he served as secretary of war for a while. He is a vocal supporter of women's rights.

Álvaro Obregón A self-made man from the state of Sonora, he is a member of the middle class and has just started becoming more active in the Revolution.

Plutarco Elías Calles He is from the state of Sonora, is middle class, and has held some minor political offices. He is an outspoken critic of the Catholic Church.

Anacleto González Flores He is a Mexican of lower-income status from Jalisco.

Hermila Galindo Acosta de Topete A teacher from northern Mexico, she currently resides in Mexico City and is active in local politics there. She is very outspoken for women's rights and has written speeches and articles in favor of laws allowing divorce, women's suffrage, and the intellectual (and sexual) equality of men and women. Many consider her a bit scandalous.

Genovevo de la O He is an indigenous general who has been fighting in northern Morelos separate from the leadership of the Zapatistas. Though he has remained independent of the Zapatistas so far, his causes are similar to theirs.

John Reed A journalist from the United States, he supports the Revolution and appears to be completely enamored of Pancho Villa.

Juan Pérez Jolote A Chamulan native from Chiapas and a common foot soldier in the federal army. He speaks Tzotzil, one of many indigenous languages spoken in Mexico, and primarily in Chiapas.

 PART 5: CORE TEXTS

The sources that follow are required reading for the game. Your role sheets will emphasize those with which you should be especially familiar. Beyond the information in the game book, you are encouraged to look for period information on the Mexican Revolution in newspaper archives. The *New York Times* was especially prolific, but it was not the only U.S. paper covering the Mexican Revolution. You are also encouraged to seek out additional primary source materials in print or electronic format. Generally speaking, you are allowed to reference intellectual ideas from anything before 1920, even if the day you use it on happens before the publication of that source. For example, the Plan Felicista (which Félix Díaz wrote in 1913), may be used on the first day (1912); however, you cannot refer to events such as betrayals, assassinations, battles, etc. Rather, you can refer only to intellectual ideas (such as mentioning his support of foreign investment, modernization, or positivist ideas).

From "Political Constitution of the Mexican Republic," 1857

This constitution takes the place of the constitution of 1824 (composed only a few years after independence from Spain). Some of the most controversial changes involved the relationship between church and state. Some of the articles included here demonstrate new limits on Church power, though the most significant blow to the Church is arguably the removal of Article 4 of the 1824 constitution: "The religion of the Mexican nation is and will always be Apostolic Roman Catholic. The nation protects it through wise and just laws, and prohibits the practice of any other [religion]." It may come as no surprise that the Church reacted strongly against this constitution and those who swore to uphold it.

Created by the reform government of Benito Juárez, the constitution of 1857 was the document by which Porfirio Díaz's opponents criticized his regime. It is also the document under which Francisco Madero and the anti-reelectionists promised to govern. The sections reprinted here highlight key debates in the game as well as topics discussed, but not directly debated, such as citizenship.

SOURCE: *Manuel Dublan and Jose Maria Lozano, eds. and trans.*, Constitution of 1857: With Additions and Reforms Since 1901, *pp. 385–399.*

TITLE I

Section I: The rights of man

Article 2: In the Republic, all are born free. Slaves who set foot on national territory, recover, by this act alone, their freedom, and have the right to protection under the law.

3: Education is free. The law will determine which professions require a degree to be practiced and the requirements to earn said degree.

4: Every man is free to embrace the profession, industry, or work of his choice, being useful and honest, and to take advantage of its products [...]

5: No one can be obligated to perform personal service without just compensation and without full consent. The law cannot authorize any contract with the purpose of the loss or irrevocable sacrifice of human freedom, be it caused by work, education, or religious vows. Neither can the law authorize agreements in which man agrees to his exile.

7: The freedom to write and publish writing on any subject is inviolable. No law nor authority can establish censorship, nor demand bond from authors or printers, nor restrict the freedom of the press, that has no limits beyond respect of private life, morals, and public peace. Offenses of the press will be tried by a jury that describes the act, and by another that applies the law and designates the punishment.

27: People's property cannot be occupied without their consent, except for reasons of public utility and upon compensation. The law will determine the authority charged with expropriation and the requirements with which said authority must comply.

No civil or ecclesiastic corporation, independent of its character, denomination, or purpose, will have legal capacity to acquire property or administer real estate, with the sole exception of buildings immediately and directly intended for service or the purpose of the institution.

Section II: about Mexicans

30: They are Mexicans:

1: All those who are born within or outside of Mexican territory, to Mexican parents.

2: Foreigners who become naturalized according to the laws of the federation.

Foreigners who acquire real estate in the Republic or have Mexican children, provided that they do not demonstrate the intention to conserve their nationality.

31: It is the obligation of every Mexican:

1. To defend the independence, territory, honor, rights, and interests of his country.

2. To contribute to public expenses, to the federation as well as the state and municipality in which he resides, in a proportional and equitable manner as provided by law.

32: Mexicans will be preferred over foreigners, in equal circumstances, for all employment, posts or commissions named by authorities, in which citizenship is not indispensable. Laws will be issued to improve the condition of working Mexicans, rewarding those who distinguish themselves in any science or art, stimulating employment and founding grammar schools and art and trade schools.

Section IV: about Mexican citizens

34: Citizens of the Republic are all those who, having the status of Mexican nationality, also comply with the following:

1. Have reached eighteen years of age if married, or twenty-one if unmarried.
2. Have an honest means of living.

35: The prerogatives of a citizen are:

1. Voting in popular elections.
2. The ability to be voted into all publicly elected posts, and named to any other employment or commission, having the qualities that the law establishes.
3. Form partnerships in order to address political affairs of the country
4. Take up arms in the military or in the National Guard for the defense of the Republic and its institutions.
5. Exercise the right of petition in all types of business.

36: Obligations of a citizen of the Republic are:

1. To enroll in the register of his municipality, stating the property he has, or the industry, profession, or employment from which he subsists.
2. Enlist in the National Guard.
3. Vote in popular elections, in the corresponding district.

[...]

TITLE II

Section I: regarding national sovereignty and the form of the government

Section II: regarding integral parts of the federation and national territory

TITLE III: REGARDING THE DIVISION OF POWERS

Section I: about legislative power

Section II: about executive power

2) The exercise of supreme Executive power of the Union is entrusted to one individual who will be called "President of the United States of Mexico."

3) The election of the president will be indirect in the first degree and by secret ballot, under the terms of electoral law.*

---

* See "Ley Orgánica Electoral 1857," the "Ley electoral 1901," and the "Ley Electoral of 1911," updated by Francisco Madero.

6. Requirements to be president: be a Mexican citizen by birth, in possession of his rights, 35 years old at the time of the election, not belong to the ecclesiastic state, and reside in the country at the time that the election takes place.

7. The president will take office the first of December and will remain in charge for four years.

*REFORMED by Porfirio Díaz 5 May 1878 to read:

"The president will take office the first of December and will remain for four years, not being able to be reelected in the period immediately following, nor occupy the presidency for any reason, until four years after having ceased exercising presidential functions."

For the purposes of the game, it is a four-year term with no reelection.

*REFORMED by Porfirio Díaz in 1904 to 6 years; also added office of Vice President

*REFORMED by Francisco Madero 7 November 1911: presidential term of 6 years with no reelection of president or vice president.

Section III: about judicial power

TITLE IV: REGARDING THE RESPONSIBILITY OF PUBLIC OFFICIALS

TITLE V: REGARDING THE STATES OF THE FEDERATION

TITLE VI: GENERAL PREVENTIONS

123. Exercising the intervention designated by law in matters of religious worship and external discipline corresponds exclusively to federal powers.

TITLE VII: REGARDING THE REFORM OF THE CONSTITUTION

TITLE VIII: REGARDING THE INVIOLABILITY OF THE CONSTITUTION

128: This Constitution will not lose its force or vigor, even when its observance is interrupted by a rebellion. [...]

[REFORMS of NOTE for the game (though there were others):]

1. As noted above, both Porfirio Díaz and Francisco Madero made changes to executive power (among other changes not noted here).

2. In 1873, Sebastian Lerdo de Tejada (brother of Miguel Lerdo de Tejada) changed the Constitution of 1857 through the "adoption of the following Reform laws as Amendments to the Constitution on the twenty-fifth of September, 1873: *Article 1:* The State and the Church are independent of one another. Congress may not pass laws establishing or prohibiting any religion.

'Art. 2: Marriage is a civil contract. This and the other acts relating to the civil state of persons belong to the exclusive jurisdiction of the functionaries and authorities of the civil order, within limits provided by laws, and they shall have the force and validity which the same attribute to them.

'Art. 3: No religious institution may acquire real estate or capital fixed upon it, with the single exception established in Article 27 of this Constitution.

'Art. 4: The simple promise to speak the truth and to comply with the obligations which have been incurred, shall be substituted for the religious oath, with its effects and penalties."

And to Article 5 of the original Constitution were added the words:

'The law, consequently, may not recognize monastic orders, nor may it permit their establishment, whatever may be the denomination or object with which they claim to be formed.' "

RICARDO FLORES MAGÓN

"Manifesto to the Nation: The Plan of the Partido Liberal Mexicano," 1906

Leader of the anarchist movement in Mexico, Ricardo Flores Magón fled Mexico for the United States in 1904, fearing for his life. He spent much of his time in the United States publishing in secrecy or in jail. His writings in 1906 and the following years helped spur early revolts against the dictatorship of Porfirio Díaz. This manifesto calls on workers, mentioning their poor pay, to rise against Díaz and foreign investors. As with so many in Mexico from this time (including Díaz), Magón links himself and his followers to former president Benito Juárez.

SOURCE: *Chaz Bufe and Mitchell Cowen Verter,* Dreams of Freedom: A Ricardo Flores Magon Reader *(Chico, California: 2005), pp. 125–129.*

JULY 1, 1906

Mexicans:

*Y*ou have here the program, the banner of the Partido Liberal, under which all of you should unite who have not renounced being free men, all of you who are smothering in this ignominious atmosphere which has enveloped you for thirty years, all of you who are ashamed of the enslavement of the country (which is your own slavery), all of you who hold against your tyrants the rebellion-blessed rebellion—of those restless under the yoke, because that feeling of rebellion is the signal that dignity and patriotism have not died in the heart that shelters them.

Think, Mexicans, of what it would mean for the country if the program of the Partido Liberal Mexicano, today raised like a shining banner, were put into effect—a program calling you to a holy struggle for liberty and justice, to guide your steps along the way of redemption, to show you the luminous goal that you can reach only if you decide to unite your forces in order to stop being slaves. The program, of course, is not perfect—no human work is—but it is benevolent, and under the present circumstances in our country it is our salvation. It is the incarnation of many noble aspirations, the remedy for many evils, the correction for many injustices, the end of many infamies. It's a radical transformation: the end of a world of oppression, of corruption, of crimes that will give way to a freer, more honorable, more just world.

Everything will change in the future.

Public offices won't be for sycophants and schemers, but for those who, by their merits, make themselves worthy of the public trust; public functionaries won't be these depraved, vicious sultans who are today protected by the dictatorship and authorized to dispose of the homes, lives, and honor of the citizens; on the contrary, they will be men elected by the public to watch over the public's interests, and who, if they don't do so, will have to answer before the same people who had favored them; this disgusting venality that today characterizes the tribunals of justice will disappear, because there will be no dictatorship bestowing judicial robes upon its lackeys, but rather the people will designate with their votes those who administer justice, and because the responsibility of functionaries will not be a myth in the democratic future; the Mexican worker will stop being what he is today—an outcast in his own land; instead he'll be master of his own rights, dignified, free to defend himself from this vile exploitation which today is imposed upon him by force; he will not have to work more than eight hours per day; he will not receive less than one peso per day; he will have time to rest, to have a good time, to educate himself, and to enjoy various comforts which he could never afford with his present salary of 50, or even 25 centavos per day[†]; there won't be a dictatorship to counsel the capitalists who rob the worker and to protect the foreign forces who answer with a rain of bullets the peaceful petitions of Mexican workers; in contrast we'll have a government that, elected by the people will serve the people and which will watch over its compatriots, without attack from foreign interests, but also without permitting the excesses and abuses so common at present; the vast holdings that the big landowners hold empty and uncultivated will cease being silent and desolate testimony to the sterile power of a man and, collected by the state, will be distributed among those who want to work them; they will be converted into fertile and happy fields which give sustenance to many noble families; there will be lands for all who want to cultivate them, and the wealth they produce will not be for the enjoyment of a boss who puts in not

---

[†] There are 100 centavos to a peso.

the least effort in producing it, but it will be for the active worker who after opening a furrow and throwing in the seed with a hand trembling with hope, will bring in the harvest that is his through his sweat and effort; with the throwing from power of the insatiable vampires who today exploit him, and who because of their greed crush him with debts and government loans; taxes will be reduced considerably; now, the fortunes of the government take their leave of the public treasury—when this doesn't happen, there will be a giant savings, and the taxes will have to come down, lowering absolutely, of course, personal taxes and taxes upon moral capital, which today are truly intolerable; there will be no obligatory military service, this pretext under which the current honchos yank men from their homes because they dislike their prideful attitudes or because they're obstacles to the desires of the corrupt little tyrants to their abusing helpless women; education will be widespread, which is the basis of the betterment of all peoples; the clergy, this unrepentant traitor, this subject of Rome, this irreconcilable enemy of native liberties, in place of finding tyrants to serve and from whom to receive protection, will find instead inflexible laws which will put a limit on their excesses and which will confine them to the religious sphere; the expression of ideas will find no unjustifiable restrictions which impede the free judgment of civic men; the inviolability of private life will disappear, which so often has been a shield for corruption and evil, and public peace will stop being a pretext under which governments persecute their enemies; all liberties will be restored to the people and not only will the citizens have won their political rights, but also a great economic improvement; not only will there be a triumph over tyranny, but also a triumph over misery. Liberty, prosperity: here is the synthesis of the program.

Think, fellow citizens, of what it would mean to the country if these redemptory ideas were realized; look at our presently oppressed nation—oppressed, miserable held in contempt, a prisoner of foreigners whose insolence grows larger with the cowardice of our tyrants; look at how the despots have trampled on the national dignity, inviting foreign forces to invade our territory; imagine to what disasters and to what ignominy these traitors whom we tolerate in power, who counsel that the Mexican worker be robbed and mistreated, who have claimed to recognize the debt contracted by the pirate Maximilian to support his usurpation, who have continually given proofs of the contempt they hold for the nationality of which we compatriots of [Benito] Juárez and Lerdo de Tejada are proud; imagine to what disasters and what ignominy these traitors can conduct us. Contemplate, Mexicans, that abyss the dictatorship is opening under your feet, and compare this black chasm with the shining summit shown to you by the Partido Liberal so that you'll dispose yourselves to climb it.

Here, slavery, misery, shame; there, liberty, well-being, honor; here, the country in chains, exhausted by so much exploitation, subjected to whatever the foreign powers want to do to it, its dignity trampled upon by its own and by foreigners; there, the country free of yokes, it will prosper, with the prosperity of all its children, great and respected because of the lofty independence of its people; here, despotism with all its horrors; there, freedom in all its glory. Choose!

It is impossible to present to you in simple, benumbing words the picture of the sovereign, luminous nation of tomorrow—redeemed, dignified, full of majesty and grandeur. But don't let this stop you from appreciating this magnificent picture, since you yourselves will bring it forth with your enthusiasm if you are patriots, if you love this soil which your fathers sanctified, irrigating it with their blood, if you haven't denied your race which has known crushing despotisms and monarchs, if you haven't resigned yourselves to death as slaves beneath the triumphal chariot of dominating caesarism. It's useless for us to attempt to lift from your eyes the veil of the future, to show you that which will come into being through you yourselves: you will see what we could show to you. Console yourselves for the sorrow of our current servitude by evoking the picture of the free country of the future; you, the good Mexicans, you who hate the yoke, will illuminate the blackness of current oppression with the radiant vision of tomorrow and the expectation that from one moment to the next your visions of liberty will become real.

From you springs the hope of the country's redemption, from you, the good sons, the ones immune to the cowardice and corruption that the tyrants sow, from you, the loyal, the unbreakable, those who feel yourselves full of faith in the triumph of justice; respond to the call of the country: the Partido Liberal has reserved a place for you beneath its banners, which are raised in defiance of despotism; all of us who fight for liberty have a place open in our ranks; come to our side, contribute to strengthening our party, and so push for the realization of that which we all desire. Let us unite; let us add together our efforts; let us unify our purposes and the program will become a fact.

Utopia! A dream! shout those who, hiding their terror through abject rationalizations, intend to stop the popular reclamations so as not to lose a lucrative post or a less-than-clean business. It's the old refrain of all of those who resist the great advances of the peoples; it's the eternal defense of infamy. They call "utopian" what is redemptory in order that it be attacked or destroyed; all those who have attacked our wise constitution have wanted to excuse themselves by saying that it's unrealizable; today the lackeys of Porfirio Díaz repeat this thing necessary to hiding the crimes of the tyranny, and these miserable persons do not remember that this constitution, which they call so utopian, so inadequate for our people, so impossible to put into practice, was perfectly realizable under noble rulers like Juárez and Lerdo de Tejada. For evildoers, good must be unrealizable; for the cunning, honor must be unrealizable. The mouthpieces of despotism judge that the program of the Partido Liberal is impractical and even absurd; but you, Mexicans who aren't blinded by convenience nor by fear; you, noble men who desire the good of the country, will come to the simple realization of how much rudimentary justice this program contains.

Mexicans:

Upon the proclamation of its program by the Partido Liberal, with the inflexible purpose of putting it into practice, you are invited to take part in this great and redemptory work which must be done in order to have forever a free, respectable, happy country.

The decision is irrevocable. The Partido Liberal will fight without rest to fulfill the solemn promise that it makes today to the people, and there will be no obstacle that it will not overcome, nor any sacrifice that it will not accept to achieve its end. Today we call you to follow its banners, to fill its ranks, to augment its strength, and to make less difficult and less painful the victory. If you listen to the call and come to the post that befits your duty as Mexicans, you'll have a lot to thank the party for, since you'll be working for your own redemption; if you see with indifference the holy struggle to which we invite you, if you refuse to aid those who fight for right and justice, if through egotism or timidity you make yourselves accomplices of those who oppress us, the country owes you nothing other than contempt, and your rebellious conscience will never stop shaming you with the memory of your failure. Those who refuse to support the cause of liberty deserve to be slaves.

Mexicans:

Between that which despotism offers you and that which the program of the Partido Liberal offers you, choose! If you want shackles, misery, humiliation before foreigners, the grey life of the debased outcast, support the dictatorship which gives you all of this; if you prefer liberty, economic improvement, the raising up of the Mexican citizenry, the noble life of the man who is master of himself, come to the Partido Liberal that fraternizes with the noble and the virile, and join your efforts with those of all of us who fight for justice, to hurry the arrival of the radiant day on which tyranny will fall forever and the awaited democracy will surge forth with all the splendor of a star which never ceases shining brilliantly on the clear horizon of our country.

Reform, Liberty, and Justice.

RICARDO FLORES MAGÓN

1906 PLM Program

The 1906 PLM Program was generated by Ricardo Flores Magón through the suggestions of his readers and correspondents.[112] *While not all of the items in the list were adopted during the course of the Revolution many of the grievances did receive consideration, while others were eventually acted upon.*

SOURCE: *Chaz Bufe and Mitchell Cowen Verter, eds. and trans.,* Dreams of Freedom: A Ricardo Flores Magón Reader *(Oakland, CA: AK Press, 2005), pp. 131–134.*

CONSTITUTIONAL REFORMS

1. Reduction of the presidential term to four years.

* * *

4. Elimination of obligatory military service and the establishment of a national guard. Those who lend their services to the permanent army will do so freely and voluntarily. * * *

5. To reform and put into effect constitutional articles 6 and 7, eliminating the restrictions that private life and public peace impose upon freedom of speech and freedom of the press. * * *

6. Abolition of the death penalty, except for treason.

* * *

9. Elimination of military tribunals in time of peace.

THE IMPROVEMENT AND ENCOURAGEMENT OF EDUCATION

10. An increase in the number of primary schools on such a scale that they will more than take the place of those that will be closed because they belong to the clergy.

11. The obligation to provide overall secular teaching in all the schools of the republic, be they those of the government or private, declaring it to be the responsibility of their administrators if they don't comply with this principle.

12. Declaring instruction to be obligatory until 14 years of age, with the responsibility being the government's to provide protection, in whatever form possible, so that poor children, because of their misery do not lose the benefits of education.

* * *

RESTRICTIONS ON THE ABUSES OF THE CATHOLIC CLERGY

17. The churches will be considered as commercial establishments, remaining therefore obligated to keep books and to pay proportionate taxes.

18. Nationalization, in accord with the laws, of the real estate that the clergy owns in the power of third parties.

* * *

20. Elimination of the schools directed by the clergy.

CAPITAL AND LABOR

21. To establish a maximum of eight hours of work and a minimum wage in the following proportion: one peso overall in the country in areas where the average wage is less than that cited, and more than one peso in those regions in which

the cost of living is high and in which this wage [one peso] isn't enough to save the worker from misery.

* * *

24. Absolute prohibition of the employment of children under 14 years of age.

25. To obligate owners of mines, factories, workshops, etc. to maintain their properties in good hygienic conditions and to make hazardous places as safe as possible for those working in them.

* * *

27. To obligate bosses to pay indemnities for work accidents.

28. To declare null and void the present debts owed by agricultural workers to their bosses.

* * *

31. To prohibit the bosses, under severe penalties, from paying for work in any other manner than in cash * * * and to eliminate company stores.

* * *

33. To make Sunday an obligatory day of rest.

LANDS

34. The owners of lands are obligated to work productively all that they possess; whatever part of the lands that they leave unproductive will be recovered by the state, which will employ them in conformity with the following articles:

35. Mexicans living in foreign lands who ask for it will be repatriated at government expense and will be given lands to cultivate.

36. The state will give lands to whomever asks for them, with no other conditions than that they dedicate themselves to agricultural production and that they don't sell the lands.

37. So that these benefits are not taken advantage of solely by those few who have the necessary means to work the lands, but also by the poor who lack these means, the state will create or foment the creation of an agricultural bank that will give poor agricultural workers loans at low interest, repayable over time.

TAXES

* * *

40. To increase the taxes on speculation, luxury goods, and vices, and to lighten the taxes on articles of basic necessity. * * *

* * *

47. Measures to eliminate or restrict speculation, pauperism, and lack of articles of basic necessity.

48. Protection of the indigenous race.

* * *

50. Upon the triumph of the Liberal Party, the goods of those functionaries who were enriched under the present dictatorship will be confiscated, with the proceeds applied to the redistribution of the lands, especially restitution to the Yaqui, Maya, and other tribes, communities, or individuals whose lands were confiscated. * * *

51. The first national congress after the fall of the dictatorship will annul all of the changes to our constitution made by the government of Porfirio Díaz; it will reform our Magna Carta in the manner necessary to put into effect this program. * * *

SPECIAL CLAUSE

52. It will remain the responsibility of the Organizing Junta of the Partido Liberal Mexicano to address as quickly as possible the foreign governments, making it manifest to them, in the name of the party, that the Mexican people do not want any additional debts placed upon the country and that, therefore, it will not recognize any new debt that under any form or pretext the dictatorship has thrown upon the nation. * * *

RICARDO FLORES MAGÓN

"To Women," 1906

In this call to women, Magón acknowledges the important role women play in society. In the letter he speaks to the traditional roles they were expected to hold but also to the injustices society placed on them due to their sex. He discusses unequal pay and uses a historical approach to demonstrate that though society has progressed in the West, women continue to hold a lesser status. Finally, Magón discusses the continuing debasement of women as more young men are carted off. For the good of the country he calls on women to convince the men in their lives to pick up guns and fight. Ironically, though he refers to women as an army, he does not encourage them to pick up arms.

SOURCE: *Chaz Bufe and Mitchell Cowen Verter, eds. and trans.,* Dreams of Freedom: A Ricardo Flores Magón Reader *(Oakland, CA: AK Press, 2005), pp. 233–236.*

Regeneración, September 24, 1910.

Women comrades, the cataclysm is afoot, her eyes furious, her red hair blowing in the breeze, her nervous hands ready to knock upon all the doors in the country. Wait for her calmly. Although she carries death in her bosom, she is the announcement of life; she is the herald of hope. She will destroy and create at the same time; she will tear down and construct. Her fists are the formidable fists of the people in rebellion. She does not bring roses or kisses; she carries an axe and a torch.

Interrupting the millennial feast of the complacent, sedition raises its head and Balthasar's phrase changes with the times into a shaking fist, suspended above the head of the so-called managing class.

The cataclysm is afoot. Its torch will light the blaze that will consume privilege and injustice. Women comrades, do not fear this cataclysm. You constitute half of the human species, and whatever affects it affects you as an integral part of humanity. If men are slaves, you will be, too. Shackles do not recognize gender; the infamy that shames man disgraces you as well. You cannot separate yourselves from the degradation of oppression. The same claw that strangles men's necks strangles yours as well.

It is therefore necessary to be in solidarity in the great contest for freedom and happiness. Are you mothers? Are you wives? Are you sisters? Are you daughters? Your duty is to aid man: be with him when he vacillates—inspire him; fly to his side when he suffers to soothe his pain; and laugh and sing with him when triumph smiles. What if you do not understand politics? It is not a question of politics: it is a question of life and death. The chains of men are your own. Ay! Yours are perhaps heavier and blacker and more degrading. Are you a worker? Just because you are a woman, you are paid less than a man, and you are made to work more; you have to suffer the insolence of the foreman and the boss. If you are pretty as well, the bosses will assault your virtue, they will surround you, they will embrace you until you surrender your heart to them, and if you give up, they will steal it from you with the same cowardice that they steal the products of your labor from you.

Under the empire of social injustice where humanity rots, a woman's existence oscillates within the restricted field of her destiny, whose frontiers are lost in the blackness of fatigue or hunger and the shadows of matrimony or prostitution.

It is necessary to study, it is essential to see, it is indispensable to scrutinize page by page this somber book called life, this bitter briar patch that tears the flesh of the human heart, in order to realize exactly how woman participates in this universal suffering.

The misfortune of woman is so ancient that its origin is lost in the shadow of legend. In the infancy of humanity, the birth of a girl was considered to be a misfortune by the tribe. The woman worked the earth, fetched firewood from the forest and water from the stream, tended the herd, milked the cows and the goats, built the cottage, made fabric into clothing, cooked the food, and cared for the sick and the children. The dirtiest jobs were performed by the woman. If an ox died of fatigue, the woman took its place hauling the plough. When a war flared up between two enemy tribes, the woman's owner changed, but she continued, under the lash of her new master, to perform the tasks of a beast of burden.

Later, under the influence of Greek civilization, woman ascended a few steps in the regard of men. She was no longer the primitive clan's beast of burden, nor did she live a cloistered life as in Oriental societies. At that time, if she belonged to a free family, her role was that of producer of citizens for her country, or of slaves, if she had the rank of a helot.

Christianity arrived after this, worsening the situation of woman with its contempt for the flesh. The Great Fathers of the Church focused their hatred against feminine graces. Saint Augustine, Saint Thomas, and other saints before whose images poor women kneel, called woman the daughter of the devil, a vessel of impurity, and condemned her to suffer the tortures of hell.

The condition of woman in this century varies according to her social class, but, despite the softening of customs, despite the progress of philosophy, woman continues to be subordinate to man by tradition and by law. Eternally treated as a minor, the law places her under the tutelage of her husband. She cannot vote or be elected, and she would have to be extremely fortunate to enter into civil contracts.

Throughout the ages, woman has been considered to be an inferior being to man, not just by the law, but also by custom, and this erroneous and unjust conception is responsible for the hardship she has suffered ever since humanity barely lifted itself above primitive fauna through its use of fire and the flint axe.

Humiliated, scorned, tied by strong bonds of tradition to the pillory of an irrational inferiority, familiarized by a priest with the affairs of heaven, but totally ignorant of the problems of Earth, woman finds herself suddenly swept up by the whirlwind of industrial activity that needs workers, cheap workers above all, that takes advantage of the fact that she is not educated like men and are for the industrial struggle, that she is not organized with those of her class to fight with her brother workers against the rapacity of capital.

To this we owe the fact that women, who work more than men but earn less, are abused and abased and held in contempt today like they were yesterday—that these are the bitter fruits she harvests for a life of sacrifice. A woman's salary is so paltry that frequently she must prostitute herself to be able to support her family when she cannot find a man who will marry her in the matrimonial market, which is another kind of prostitution sanctioned by the law and authorized by a public functionary. And marriage is nothing other than prostitution when a woman weds without love, but solely with the intent of finding a man to support her, that it, as she does in the majority of marriages, she sells her body for food, just like a fallen woman.

And what can be said about the immense army of women who do not find a spouse? The growing shortage of primary goods, the disturbing decrease in wages for human labor resulting from the perfection of machinery, together will [sic] all of the more and more pressing demands of the modern world creates, are incapacitating man economically from taking upon himself the burden of maintaining a family. Obligatory military service, which seizes a great number of strong young males from the bosom of society, further diminishes the masculine supply in the matrimonial marketplace. The emigration of workers, provoked by various economic and political reasons, reduces the number of men capable of entering into matrimony even further. Alcoholism, gambling, and other vices and illnesses reduce even more the quantity of marriage candidates. All this results in an extreme reduction in the number of men suitable for marriage and, as a consequence, the number of single women is alarming. As single women's financial situation is very stressful, prostitution increasingly expands its ranks and the human race degenerates further through the debasement of the flesh and the spirit.

Women comrades: this is the dreadful scene that modern societies offer. In this scene, you see that men and women suffer equally from the tyranny of a political and social environment that is in complete disaccord with the development of civilization and the advances of philosophy. In your moments of worry, stop raising your beautiful eyes to heaven: that is where are those [*sic*] who have contributed most to making you eternal slaves. The remedy is here on Earth, and it is rebellion.

Make your husbands, your brothers, your fathers, your sons, and your male friends take up the rifle. Whoever refuses to raise a firearm against his oppressors, spit in his face.

The cataclysm is afoot. Jimenez and Acayucan, Palomas, Viesca, Las Vacas, and Valladollid are the first gusts of this formidable storm. It's a tragic paradox: freedom, which is life, can only be conquered by meting out death.

RICARDO FLORES MAGÓN

"Class Struggle," 1911

Here, Magón works in binaries. He discusses the capitalists and the workers. While he is focused on labor relations, he also discusses politics and leadership. As he was living in the United States at the time he wrote this, he especially calls out the failures of U.S. democracy.

SOURCE: *Chaz Bufe and Mitchell Cowen Verter, eds. and trans,* Dreams of Freedom: A Ricardo Flores Magón Reader *(Oakland, CA: AK Press, 2005), pp. 187–190.*

*R*egeneración, March 4, 1911

Humanity is divided into two classes: the capitalist class and the working class. The capitalist class possesses the lands, the machinery, the factories, the workshops, the tools of labor, the mines, the houses, the railways, the ships, and other means of transportation, and as the keeper of all of these, it can count on the government in any of its forms: absolute monarchy, constitutional monarchy, and republic, be it in centralized or federated form. The working class possesses no more than its arms, its brains, and the essential energy invested in performing any kind of labor—while it can remain on its feet.

The capitalist class, under whatever form of government, can live idly, because it is in a materially advantageous situation in respect to those who have nothing, that it, the workers; and the capitalist class enjoys by the same measure a great deal of independence and a great deal of liberty, since not only can it satisfy its needs without being beholden to anyone, but in addition it is supported by the governmental apparatus upon which it depends, with its laws, judges, police, soldiers, and prisons. In short, the capitalist class has all the means necessary to guarantee its free enjoyment of its riches.

The poor class, in virtue of finding material wealth monopolized by the rich, is forced to depend on the rich. If the poor man wants to work the earth, he has to rent himself for a price ("wages") which represents a small part of what he produces with his arms. If the workers want to work in a factory, in a mine, on a ship, on a railway, in construction building a house, or any other kind of work, he equally has to rent his arms in order to receive a wage which represents, always, a small part of what he produces. It has been calculated that the bosses pay only a tenth the value of what is produced by the worker's labor, and in Mexico it's even worse, because as is well known wages in our country amount to little more than alms. Nine-tenths of what a worker produces passes into the pockets of the boss as profit, despite his having worked nowhere near as hard as the worker. This profit, naturally, is protected by the law which, as I've said many times, is a product, as are all laws, of the capitalist class; this class, of course, has to make laws that benefit itself, laws that protect the exploitation of workers by their bosses. These laws prevail in all parts of the world, in all of the so-called civilized countries, from those ruled by absolute monarchs to those governed by constitutional presidents, as in the United States and Switzerland, both renowned as "free" countries, as "model" republics.

The worker, then, is a slave everywhere. A slave in Russia, a slave in the United States, a slave in Mexico, a slave in Turkey, a slave in France—a slave literally everywhere. The famous political liberties which Maderismo [the movement to put Francisco Madero in power] wants to conquer, such as the rights to vote, to meet publicly, to think freely, and many others, are in truth nothing but swindles which divert the proletariat from its sacred mission: economic liberty. Without economic liberty, it's not possible to enjoy political liberty.

There are countries, such as Russia, for example, where there are no political liberties and, nonetheless, the worker is no more unfortunate than he is in the United States, the country which trumpets its "freedom." In the streets of Saint Petersburg, Moscow, or Odessa you'll see the same rags, the same pallid faces as in the streets of New York or Chicago. This is to say that in Russia, that barbarous and oppressive country, there exists the same problem, the same social question as exists in the United States, the country that boasts of being free and civilized.

In Canada, despite there being no law guaranteeing everyone the right to vote, that is, in that land where there is nothing called "universal suffrage," where only those with property can vote, the worker lives with more ease than in the United States where universal suffrage exists, that it, where every man of a certain age can elect his rulers.

This proves that it is not the vote, not the right to think freely, not the right to meet freely, nor any of the other political rights conferred by law which gives the worker food to survive. The right to vote is a joke. Here, in the United States, we have proof of this. The people of this nation have always had the right to vote and, nonetheless, the miserable ghettos of New York, Chicago, St. Louis, Philadelphia, and of all of the other great American cities are eloquent witnesses to the inefficiency of the vote in bringing about the happiness of the people. In these ghettos, hundreds of thousands of persons rot, both physically and morally, in squalid tenements, and in the entire nation, every morning four million human beings leave these palaces of filth and hunger to search for work so that they can return to these palaces with a crumb of bread for their wives and children; but as they often don't find work, they return with empty hands, their stomachs pinched, and they go out again the next day on their perilous, wandering journey in search of bosses to whom to rent their arms. And when election time rolls around, these hungry wretches clamor to fill out ballots to elevate another ruler who will continue to weigh down upon their necks.

If we have this example before us, why would we attempt to gain the illusory power of the right to vote? Wouldn't it be better to dedicate ourselves to the conquest of the lands, the lands which are the fount of all riches and which, in the hands of the people, would assure to all the means of life, and by the same measure economic liberty—and as a consequence of this true liberty?

Material well-being is what the people need to be free. That the people take possession of the earth and of the instruments of production is what the Partido Liberal wants. When the people themselves are the lords of the earth, everything else will fall into their hands through the force of this circumstance. Is this crazy? That's what the cowards, the ignorant, and all those who have an interest in the continuation of the present system of exploitation of the working class say. All of those who desire to occupy great or small public offices, all of those who want to live at the expense of others, desire that Madero will triumph. But those conscious workers who possess no more capital than their callused hands—callused by the hard work to which they've been subjected by the bourgeoisie—those workers who have understood what *Regeneración* has taught, these will not follow Madero; they can't follow those who make politics their means of living. Rather, they are disposed to continue the class struggle, the struggle against capitalism, until it crumbles to dust.

There are two social classes: that which exploits and that which is exploited. That which exploits has as its interest that Madero rises to power, so that it can continue to exploit. The exploited class, for its part, has as its interest that the lands be shared by all, that there be no bosses—and that there be no more misery.

Comrades, follow the banner of the Partido Liberal which carries this motto: Land and Liberty.

RICARDO FLORES MAGÓN

"The Mexican People Are Suited to Communism," 1911

Written after the defeat of Porfirio Díaz but before Francisco Madero's inauguration, this article discusses Mexico's suitability for communism. Magón, of indigenous descent himself, discusses a utopic view of indigenous communal living, claiming that it was a form of communism itself.

SOURCE: *Chaz Bufe and Mitchell Cowen Verter, eds. and trans.,* Dreams of Freedom: A Ricardo Flores Magón Reader *(Oakland, CA: AK Press, 2005), pp. 176–177.*

Regeneración, September 2, 1911

The inhabitants of the state of Morelos, like those of Puebla, Michoacán, Durango, Jalisco, Yucatán and other states, in which vast areas have been invaded by proletarians who have immediately dedicated themselves to cultivating the lands, have shown the entire world, with their acts, that one doesn't need a society of savants to solve the problem of hunger.

To arrive at this result they took possession of the earth and the instruments of production in Mexico. They didn't need "leaders," nor "friends of the working class," nor "paternal decrees," nor "wise laws"—they didn't need any of this. Their actions did it all and continue doing it all. Mexico is marching toward communism more quickly than the most extreme revolutionaries had hoped for, and the government and the bourgeoisie now find themselves not knowing what to do in the presence of acts they believed were very far from being carried out.

It wasn't even three months ago that Juan Sarabia, in a long, sickening open letter directed to me, which was published in the bourgeois press in Mexico, told me that the working class didn't understand what we are advocating and that the people were satisfied with the fruits of Madero's revolt: the electoral ballot. But facts have shown that we members of the PLM are not under illusions, and that we fight convinced that our actions and propaganda respond to the necessities and to the manner of thinking of Mexico's poor.

The Mexican people hate, by instinct, authority and the bourgeoisie. Everyone who has lived in Mexico can assure us that there is no one more cordially hated than the policeman, that the word "government" fills the simple people with uneasiness, that the soldier, admired and applauded in all other places, is seen with antipathy and contempt, and that anyone who doesn't make his living with his hands is hated.

This in itself is enough for a social revolution which is economic in nature and anti-authoritarian, but there is more. Four million Indians live in Mexico who, until twenty or twenty-five years ago, lived in communities possessing the lands, the waters, and the forests in common. Mutual aid was the rule in these communities, in which authority was felt only when the tax collector appeared periodically or when "recruiters" showed up in search of men to force into the army. In these communities there were no judges, mayors, jailers, in fact no bothersome people at all of this type. Everyone had the right to the land, to the water to irrigate it, to the forests for firewood, and to the wood from the forests for the construction of small houses. The plows passed from hand to hand, as did yokes of oxen. Each family worked as much land as they thought was sufficient to produce what was necessary, and the work of weeding and harvesting was done in common by the entire community—today, Pedro's harvest, tomorrow Juan's, and so on. Everyone in the community put their hands to the work when a house was to be raised.

These simple customs lasted until authority grew strong enough to pacify the country, until it was strong enough to guarantee the bourgeoisie the success of its businesses. The generals of the political revolts received large grants of land; the *hacendados* [plantation owners] increased the size of their fiefdoms; the most vile politicians received vast tracts of "barren" lands; and foreign adventurers obtained concessions of lands, forests, rivers, of, in sum, everything, leaving our Indian brothers without a clot of dirt, without the right to take from the forests even the smallest branch of a tree; they were left in the most abject misery, dispossessed of everything that had been theirs.

As regards the mestizo population [of mixed Indian and Spanish heritage], which is the majority of the people of Mexico—with the exception of those who inhabited the great cities and large towns—they held the forests, lands, and bodies of water in common, just as the indigenous peoples did. Mutual aid was also the rule; they built their houses together; money was almost unnecessary, because they bartered what they made or grew. But with the coming of peace authority grew, and the political and financial bandits shamelessly stole the lands, forests, and bodies of water; they stole everything. Not even twenty years ago one could see in opposition newspapers that the North American X, the German Y, and the Spaniard Z had enveloped an entire population within the limits of "his" property, with the aid of the Mexican authorities.

We see, then, that the Mexican people are suited for communism, because they've practiced it, at least in part, for many centuries; and this explains why, even when the majority are illiterate, they comprehend that rather than take part in electoral farces that elect thugs, it's better to take possession of the lands—and this taking is what scandalizes the thieving bourgeoisie.

All that's left to be done is that the workers take possession of the factory, the workshop, the mine, the foundry, the railroad, the ship, in a word, everything—that they recognize no bosses of any type. And this will be the culmination of the present movement.

Forward comrades!

RICARDO FLORES MAGÓN, LIBRADO RIVERA, ANESLMO L. FIGUEROA, ENRIQUE FLORES MAGÓN

"Manifesto," 1911

This manifesto calls for an end to private property, authority, and the Church. He refers to them as a "dark trinity" where authority and the Church are in place for the sole purpose of protecting private property. He calls on women and men to stand up and contest anyone (be it Madero and his followers or someone else) who supports the ideas of the dark trinity.

SOURCE: *Chaz Bufe and Mitchell Cowen Verter, eds. and trans.,* Dreams of Freedom: A Ricardo Flores Magón Reader *(Oakland, CA: AK Press, 2005), pp. 138–144.*

MANIFESTO

September 23, 1911

Mexicans:

The Organizing Junta of the Partido Liberal Mexicano views with sympathy your efforts to put into practice the lofty ideals of political, economic, and social emancipation, whose reign upon the earth will finally put an end to the long battle of man against man, which has its origin in the inequality of wealth born of the principle of private property.

Abolishing this principle means the annihilation of all political, economic, social, religious, and moral institutions that comprise the ambient within which free initiative and the free association of human beings are smothered—human beings who see themselves obligated, in order to avoid perishing, to undertake a bloody competition from which exit triumphantly not the good, not the self-denying, not the most gifted physically, morally, or intellectually, but rather the most cunning, the most egotistical, the least scrupulous, the hardest of heart, and those who place their personal well-being above any consideration of human solidarity.

Without the principle of private property there would be no reason for government, which is necessary solely for the purpose of keeping the disinherited within bounds in their quarrels or in the rebellions against those who hold the social wealth; neither would there be reason for the church, whose only object is to strangle the innate human rebellion against oppression and exploitation through the preaching of patience, resignation, and humility, and through quieting the call of the most powerful and fertile of instincts through immoral, cruel, and unhealthy penances; and so that the poor will not aspire to enjoying the good things of the earth and thus constitute a danger to the privileges of the rich, the church promises to the humble, to the most resigned, to the most patient, a heaven extending to infinity, beyond the stars one can see. ✱　✱　✱

Capital, Authority, Clergy: this is the dark trinity which makes of this beautiful earth a paradise for those who have managed to clutch in their claws, through cunning, violence, and crime, the product of the sweat, blood, tears, and sacrifice of thousands of generations of workers and these same three things create a hell for those with whose arms and minds work the earth, operate the machinery, build the houses, and transport the products. In this manner humanity is divided into two classes with diametrically opposite interests: the capitalist class and the working class; the class which possesses the lands, the machinery of production, and the means of transporting wealth, and the class which has nothing other than its arms and minds to provide sustenance.

Between these two social classes there cannot exist any ties of friendship or fraternity, because the possessing class is always disposed to perpetuate the economic, political, and social system that guarantees it the tranquil enjoyment of its plunders, while the working class makes efforts to destroy this iniquitous system in order to install one in which the lands, the houses, the machinery of production, and the means of transport are for everyone's use.

Mexicans: The Partido Liberal Mexicano recognizes that every human being, by the simple fact of coming to life, has the right to enjoy each and every one of the advantages that modern civilization offers, because these advantages are the product of the effort and sacrifice of the working class in all ages.

The Partido Liberal Mexicano recognizes that work is necessary to subsistence, and therefore all, with the exception of the old, the physically impaired, and children, must dedicate themselves to producing something useful in order to provide necessities.

The Partido Liberal Mexicano recognizes that the so-called right of individual property is an iniquitous right, because it subjects the larger number of human beings to work and to suffer to satisfy and keep in idleness a small number of capitalists.

The Partido Liberal Mexicano recognizes that Authority and the Clergy are the support for the iniquity of Capital, and therefore the Organizing Junta of the Partido Liberal Mexicano has declared solemn war upon Authority, Capital, and the Clergy.

Against Capital, Authority, and Clergy the Partido Liberal Mexicano has raised the red banner on the fields of action in Mexico, where our brothers battle like lions, contesting victory from the followers of the bourgeoisie, be they followers of Madero, Reyes, Vazquez, or be they "científicos" or any others whose only purpose is to elevate some man to the head of state or to conduct some shadowy business without consideration of the entire Mexican population; and they all recognize as sacred, every one of them, the right of individual property.

In these moments of confusion, so propitious for attacking oppression and exploitation; in these moments in which Authority, broken, reeling, vacillating, harassed on all sides by the forces of unleashed passions, by the tempest of appetites revived by the hope of a coming feast; in these moments of sinking feelings, of anxiousness, or terror for all the privilege, the compact masses of the disinherited invade the lands, burn the property titles, place their creative hands upon the fertile earth, and shake their fists at everything that was respectable yesterday: Authority, Capital, and Clergy; they open the furrow, spread the seed, and wait, emotionally, for the first fruits of free labor.

These are, Mexicans, the first practical results of the propaganda and the actions of the soldiers of the proletariat, of the noble holders of our egalitarian principles, of our brothers who defy all impositions and all exploitation with the cry of death to those above and life and hope for those below: Long live Land and Liberty!

The storm grows fiercer day by day: partisans of Madero, Vazquez, Reyes, De la Barra, and the "científicos" call to you, Mexicans, to fly to defend their faded flags, to protect the privileges of the capitalist class. Don't listen to the sweet songs from these sirens who want to take advantage of your sacrifices in order to establish a government, that is, a new dog to protect the interests of the rich. On your feet everyone!—but in order to bring about the expropriation of the goods kept for themselves by the rich!

Expropriation must be carried out through blood and fire during the course of this great movement, as is being done by our brothers, the inhabitants of Morelos, Southern Puebla, Michoacán, Guerrero, Veracruz, northern Tamaulipas, Durango, Sonora, Sinaloa, Jalisco, Chihuahua, Oaxaca, Yucatán, Quintana Roo and regions of other states, as even the Mexican bourgeois press has to confess, in which the proletarians have taken possession of the lands without waiting for some paternal government to decree that they're worthy of happiness, conscious that they cannot expect anything good from governments and that "the emancipation of the workers must be the task of the workers themselves."

These first acts of expropriation have been crowned by the smile of success; but it's not necessary to limit oneself to taking possession of the lands and agricultural implements; it's necessary that the workers themselves determinedly take possession of all the industries, ensuring in this manner that the lands, mines, factories, workshops, foundries, cars, railways, ships, warehouses of all kinds, and the houses remain in the power of each and every one of the inhabitants of Mexico, without sexual discrimination.

The inhabitants of each region in which such an act of supreme justice is carried out have nothing else to do but to come to an accord that all the things found in the stores, warehouses, granaries, etc. be taken to a place easily accessible to all, where men and women of good will take a careful inventory of everything that's been gathered in order to calculate how long these things will last, taking into account the needs and the number of inhabitants who need to make use of these things, from the moment of expropriation until the first harvest is taken from the fields and the other industries produce the first articles.

With the inventory taken, the workers in the different industries will come to a fraternal understanding among themselves on the management of production. In this manner, during the course of this movement, no one will lack anything, and the only ones who die of hunger will be those who don't want to work, with the exceptions of the old, the handicapped, and the children who will have the right to the use of everything.

All that is produced will be sent to central community warehouses from which everyone will have the right to take everything that they need, according to their needs, with no other requirement than that they show proof that they work in one or another industry.

The aspiration of the human being is to have the maximum amount of enjoyment with the minimal amount of effort, and the best way to ensure this result is to work the land and the other industries in common. If the land is divided and each family has a plot, besides the grave danger of falling again into the capitalist system—because there will be no lack of cunning men or of those in the habit of saving who will manage to amass more than others and eventually will be able to exploit their brothers—there is also the fact that if a family works a plot of land, it will have to work more or less like it does today under the system of private property in order to obtain the same mean result. While if the land is held and worked in common, the workers will labor less and produce more. Of course there will be no lack of land for everyone to have their own house, as well as a good plot to put to use however they want. The same can be said of working the factories, workshops, etc., as of working the land. But each person, according to his temperament, desires, and abilities will have to choose the type of work he wants to do, and with this enough will be produced to cover his necessities, and to ensure that he won't be a burden on the community.

Working in the manner indicated, that is, following immediately after the expropriation of production, free of bosses and based upon the needs of the inhabitants of every region, no one will lack anything despite the armed movement, until, with the end of this movement and with the end of the last member of the bourgeoisie and the last representative of authority, with the law sustaining privilege broken into pieces and with everything in the hands of those who work, all of us will stretch our arms in a fraternal embrace and celebrate with cries of jubilation the installation of a system which guarantees every human being bread and liberty.

Mexicans: This is what the Partido Liberal Mexicano fights for. This is what the pleiades of heroes shed their blood for. This is what is fought for under the renowned cry, "Land and Liberty!"

The liberals haven't put down their arms despite the treaties between the traitor Madero and the tyrant Díaz, and despite, also, the urgings of the bourgeoisie who have tried to fill the liberals' pockets with gold. This is because the liberals are men who are convinced that political liberty will not be taken advantage of by the poor, but rather by the seekers after offices, and our object is not to obtain offices or honors, but rather to snatch everything from the hands of the bourgeoisie so that everything will be in the hands of the workers.

The activity of the various political bands in these moments is in dispute of supremacy, that is, following the triumph, who will do exactly the same thing as Porfirio Díaz, because no man, no matter how well intentioned he might be, can do anything in favor of the poor once in power. But his political activity has produced the chaos of which the disinherited can take advantage, that is, taking advantage of the special circumstance in which the county finds itself in order to put into practice on the march, without wasting time, the sublime ideals of the Partido Liberal Mexicano, without waiting for peace to carry out expropriation. Because if we wait, by then the provisions in the stores, granaries, warehouses, and other places will have been exhausted, and at the same time, because of the state of war in which the country finds itself, production will have been suspended and hunger will result; but if we carry out expropriation and organize work in a free manner during the revolutionary movement, no one will lack what he needs during the movement or thereafter.

Mexicans: if you want to be free, do not fight for any cause other than that of the Partido Liberal Mexicano. Everyone offers you political liberty after the triumph: the liberals invite you to take the lands, the machinery, the means of transport, and the houses immediately, without waiting for anyone to give you all this, without waiting for some law to decree these things, because the laws are not made by the poor, but rather by the frock-coated bosses who guard well against making laws to the disadvantage of their own caste.

It's the duty of all the poor to work and to struggle to break the chains that enslave us. To leave the solution of our problems to the educated and rich classes is to voluntarily put ourselves in the grasp of their claws. We are the plebeians; the ragged; the hungry; those who don't have a clod of dirt on which to lay heads; those who live tormented by the uncertainty of having bread for our women and children; those who, when we become old, are fired ignominiously because we can no longer work. We must look to our own powerful efforts, our thousand sacrifices to destroy to its foundation the edifice of the old society which has been until now a caring mother for the rich and a wicked and evil stepmother to those who work and are good.

All of the evils that afflict the human being originate in the present system, which obliges the majority of humanity to work and to sacrifice itself so that a privileged minority has all of its needs, and even its caprices, filled, while living in idleness and vice. And it wouldn't be so bad if all the poor were assured of work; but production in not arranged to satisfy the needs of the workers, but rather to provide profits to the bourgeoisie, who take pains not to produce more than they can afford; and from this results the periodic work stoppages in industry or restrictions on the number of workers, which also comes from the improvements in machinery which supplant the arms of the proletariat.

To put an end to all this it's necessary that the workers have in their hands the lands and the machinery of production, and that it be themselves who organize the production of the wealth while paying attention to their own needs.

Robbery, prostitution, murder, arson, and swindles are all products of the system which places men and women in conditions under which, if they don't want to die of hunger, they are obligated to seize what they can or to prostitute themselves, since in the majority of cases, even if they have a great desire to work they can't find it, or the pay is so low that their wages don't cover even the most urgent necessities of the individual and the family; and the hours of labor under the capitalist system and the conditions under which it is carried out destroy the health of the worker in little time, if they don't kill him outright in an industrial accident which has no other origin than the contempt with which the capitalist class views those who sacrifice themselves for the benefit of the capitalists.

The poor man, angered by the injustice of which he's the object; choleric before the insulting luxury which those who do nothing flash before him; beaten in the streets by the police for the crime of being poor; obligated to rent his body to work at jobs he dislikes; badly paid; despised by all those who know more than he does or by those who believe themselves superior because of their money; contemplating a sad old age and the death of an animal dispatched from the stable for being unfit to serve; nervous about the possibility of being without work from one day to the next; obliged to see as enemies the members of his class, because he doesn't know if they will be the ones who rent themselves to the capitalists for less than he does—it's natural that under these circumstances antisocial instincts develop in the human being, instincts which are unleashed in crime, prostitution, and betrayal: the fruits of the old, hateful system which we want to eradicate down to its deepest roots in order to create a new system of love, equality, justice, fraternity, and liberty.

Let everyone arise as a single man! In the reach of all are tranquility, well-being, liberty, the satisfaction of all healthy appetites—but not if we allow ourselves to be guided by rulers. Let everyone be the master of himself. Let everything be arranged by mutual consent between free individuals. Death to slavery! Death to hunger! Long live Land and Liberty!

Mexicans: With our hands placed on our hearts and our consciences tranquil, we're making a formal and solemn call for you—everyone, men and women—to adopt the lofty ideals of the Partido Liberal Mexicano. While there are poor and rich, rulers and ruled, there will be no peace, nor is peace to be desired, because such peace would be founded in the political, economic, and social inequality of millions of human beings who suffer hunger, outrages, prison, and death, while a tiny minority enjoys all types of pleasures and freedom for doing nothing.

To the struggle! Expropriate with the ideal of benefiting all, and not just a few, so that this war will not be a war of bandits, but of men and women who desire that all be brothers and, as such, enjoy all the good things provided by nature and by the arms and minds of the men who create them, with the only condition being that everyone dedicates himself to truly useful work.

Liberty and well-being are within the reach of our hands. The cost is the same in effort and sacrifice to elevate a ruler, that is, a tyrant, as it is to expropriate the wealth held by the rich. Choose, then: either a new ruler, that is, a new yoke, or redemptive expropriation and the abolition of all religious, political, indeed all types of impositions.

Land and Liberty!

Written in the city of Los Angeles, state of California, United States of America, on the 23rd day of the month September 1911.

—Ricardo Flores Magón, Librado Rivera, Aneslmo L. Figueroa, Enrique Flores Magón

RUDYARD KIPLING

"The White Man's Burden"

Written in 1899 following the Spanish-American War and the U.S. takeover of the Philippines, Kipling's poem highlights the racist ideas of Western imperialism at the time and the notion of Western Social Darwinism. William Taft, the first U.S. governor-general of the Philippines (and later U.S. president at the start of the Mexican Revolution) referred to Filipinos as "Little Brown Brothers." Despite the poem's timing in relationship to U.S. actions, Kipling was Britain's imperial poet. This poem represents ideas firmly rooted in European societies.

SOURCE: *Franz Rehbein, Joshua Cole, ed.,* Das Leben eines Landarbeiters *(Jena: Eugen Diederichs Verlag, 1911), pp. 238–240.*

Take up the White Man's burden—
Send forth the best ye breed—
Go bind your sons to exile
To serve your captives' need;
To wait in heavy harness,
On fluttered folk and wild—
Your new-caught, sullen peoples,
Half-devil and half-child.

Take up the White Man's burden—
In patience to abide,
To veil the threat of terror
And check the show of pride;
By open speech and simple,
An hundred times made plain
To seek another's profit,
And work another's gain.

Take up the White Man's burden—
The savage wars of peace—
Fill full the mouth of Famine
And bid the sickness cease;
And when your goal is nearest
The end for others sought,
Watch sloth and heathen Folly
Bring all your hopes to nought.

Take up the White Man's burden—
No tawdry rule of kings,
But toil of serf and sweeper—
The tale of common things.
The ports ye shall not enter,
The roads ye shall not tread,
Go mark them with your living,
And mark them with your dead.

Take up the White Man's burden—
And reap his old reward:
The blame of those ye better,
The hate of those ye guard—
The cry of hosts ye humour
(Ah, slowly!) toward the light:—
"Why brought he us from bondage,
Our loved Egyptian night?"

Take up the White Man's burden—
Ye dare not stoop to less—
Nor call too loud on Freedom
To cloke your weariness;
By all ye cry or whisper,
By all ye leave or do,
The silent, sullen peoples
Shall weigh your gods and you.

Take up the White Man's burden—
Have done with childish days—
The lightly proffered laurel,
The easy, ungrudged praise.
Comes now, to search your manhood
Through all the thankless years
Cold, edged with dear-bought wisdom,
The judgment of your peers!

FRANCISCO MADERO

The Presidential Succession of 1910

Written in 1908 following Porfirio Díaz's interview with James Creelman, wherein Díaz announced he would not run for election in the 1910 presidential race; in the book, Madero discusses what he believes needs to happen in Mexico in order for it to move forward after the retirement of Díaz. The excerpts reprinted here discuss topics central to the Mexican Revolution and the debates in the game.

SOURCE: *Francisco I. Madero,* The Presidential Succession of 1910, *Thomas B. Davis, trans. (New York: Peter Lang, 1990), pp. 148–163, 207–213, 219–221.*

PUBLIC INSTRUCTION

Indubitably, public instruction is the base of all progress, of all advancement, the only thing which will elevate the intellectual and moral level of the Mexican people in order to give it the force necessary for successfully leaving behind the torments which menace it. To dedicate the country to achieve it was the great necessity of the Fatherland. General Diaz himself has understood this, but despite his efforts, he has failed in his work because with the system of administration which he has implanted, he has to make use of inept persons because his range of vision, no matter how penetrating it may be, cannot embrace a wide radius.

According to the census of 1900, it appears that only 16% of Mexicans know how to read and write. So that one may have an idea of the pitiful significance of this figure, we cite the latest statistics of Japan where 98% of the school age males attended institutions of instruction within that growing empire, and 93% of the women do so. This is the most eloquent proof of the failure of the administration of General Diaz in an area of vital importance for the country. Even the Federal District itself, which is where the action of the executive is most, felt, the average of those who know how to read and write is 38%.

We will not begin to comment upon the type of teaching which is given in official schools and which have been so roughly attacked by Dr. Vazquez Gomez, and we shall limit ourselves to affirming a fact: The youth which has been educated in the official institutes has graduated from its school perfectly trained for the battle for a livelihood. All possess full knowledge which places them in a situation for making a fortune soon enough because they possess the principle factor—the adaptability to fit into all situations, to act in all roles. With the same imperturbable serenity, we see them call for the fulfillment of the law; that they are the first to violate it, as we now find them declaiming against the government while they are the first in supporting it.

In contrast, that gilded youth is possessed of the most discouraging skepticism and the great words *Fatherland* and *Liberty*, which move so deeply the hearts of all men, leave them indifferent, cold, imperturbable. He who has faith, he who loves his country and is resolved to sacrifice for it, passes before their eyes as a crazy person or, somewhat less, they treat him kindly as somewhat disoriented.

Nevertheless, the sap of the Fatherland is so vigorous that in youth enthusiasm for all that is grand and all that is beautiful is manifested in all its splendor. What happens is that the official schools, and even more the middle class schools, keep on undermining those noble and optimistic sentiments and plant in their hearts discouraging skepticism, cold incredulity, love of the positive, of what they can touch. When they come to the age of maturity, that is the only thing which they consider real and they classify the words such as Fatherland, Freedom, and Abnegation as metaphysical, which they are accustomed to disdain.

FOREIGN RELATIONS

*O*ur policy of Foreign Relations has always consisted in an exaggerated condescension toward the neighboring Republic of the North, as between individuals, each concession constitutes a precedent and many precedents can come to constitute a right. We do not argue for a hostile policy toward our neighbor of the North, of whose greatness we are admirers, and not only for its richness and its power, but for its magnificent institutions, for its grandiose examples which it has given the world. Nevertheless, we certainly do advocate a more dignified policy which would evaluate us even in the eyes of the Americans, and which would influence them to treat us with more consideration—with the consideration to which one accredits a Nation zealous for its dignity and its honor. Those considerations constitute a force much more powerful than that of bayonets, because the right of force has lost its prestige considerably with the progress of civilization and many conflicts have been avoided through the respect which law imposes when it is supported with dignity and energy.

By treating no more than two points which lately have been debated between the two Republics we will recall that the Mexican Government permitted that of the United States to construct a large dam for storage of waters of the Rio Grande with the pretext that the American Government would supply the funds for construction of that colossal work and our neighbors would take the major part of the water, leaving us with a truly ridiculous quantity, if one considers that we have a right to half of it. The Mexican Government ought to have insisted that half the water should have been left for it to dispose of even in case that it should have had to pay the necessary cost for one-half the dam.

Lately, on the occasion of the visit of Sr. Root to Mexico, the question of the Magdalena Bay was raised. There would be much to say on this point, but we will limit ourselves to making the following very brief observation: What profit is there to the Mexican Republic with permitting the Government of the United States to send its squadrons to conduct exercises in blank firing in the Bay of Magdalena and to keep coaling ships there constantly? Undoubtedly, if the United States needs that Bay now, it will need it when the term which was granted to it shall terminate, and then it will be more difficult to deny them the permission, which, when repeated several times will come to constitute a servitude, and will be a constant threat for the national integrity.

On taking so important a step why did not General Diaz in a frank way consult the national will? Why did he so arrange it that the question should be treated in a secret session of the senate? If Root threatened, why did Diaz not issue a manifesto to the Nation explaining the outrage which was embodied in that threat and ask what attitude should be the be assumed? If Root stroked his own ego, he even did ill in rewarding his hosts with his brilliant discourse in which his vanity was so clearly revealed with a concession which he himself judged dangerous to the Fatherland, as the words of a high functionary of the Ministry of Foreign Relations show who, on being interviewed by a reporter of *El Tiempo* and on treating of his subject had said that "at the request of the American Government for the stationing of the coaling ships in Magdalena Bay for the term of five years, the Sr. President had replied that he would seek authorization of the Senate in order to grant it only for the remainder of this presidential term because he did not wish to leave for his successors commitments made by him."

At any rate public opinion did not approve that conduct and if its advice was not manifested in a hostile manner it was because all manifestation is that sense would have been a target of all sorts of persecutions. Furthermore, when the news was known in Mexico by telegram from Washington that the concession was an act already consummated, all protest would have been useless and also would have been highly dangerous. We ourselves knew of a protest supported by numerous signatures which was on the point of being published, but its authors understood the useless danger that was involved for them in such publication and they preferred to save all their strength for action in the next electoral campaign for the Presidency of the Republic and other federal officials. The electoral periods are those of true combat in democratic countries and although up to now those practices have not been acclimated on our soil, everything indicates that Mexicans will make a vigorous effort to do so very soon.

We will not end this question without citing the bad impression which the preparation of the Chapultepec Castle to receive Sr. Root caused as well as the very sumptuous celebrations with which he was received. The Castle of Chapultepec is the symbol of one of our purest glories, and the Republic considered as a profanation that the place which served as a glorious tomb of our young heroes should serve afterward as a lodging place for the representative of the people which occasioned in earlier days that sad war. We do not say this because we wish to perpetuate hatreds; no, such an idea is very far from us, but how did it come about to have so sumptuous a reception for the representative of a democracy?

Twice the Vice-President of our country has gone to the neighboring Republic (we say this because when Sr. Mariscal was alive he was vested with that rank), and never did they make such a sumptuous reception for him. Rather they indulged him in certain questionable matters, certain shameful situations took place for which some pretext has never been lacking. For all these reasons the reception of Sr. Root was humiliating for Mexico, especially if one considers the diplomatic mission which he knew how to fulfill so confidentially and with such success.

Also, at that time there was great misery among the people which contrasted sadly with the splendor of the celebrations, more than real, with which our illustrious visitor was received. In Europe, when a Sovereign visits another very seldom is such magnificence displayed, and we, a poor country, certainly do it for a guest who comes on more than a friendly mission, on one of self-interest. In Mexico City it was said with much insistence that Sr. Root himself had been surprised that they should prepare such a sumptuous reception for him.

What reasons would General Diaz have had for acting in this way? It appears that his policy has tended to avoid a conflict with our powerful neighbor to the North, but in truth he has only succeeded in postponing and each time making it more probable because he has been so complaisant with them, so that they day when another citizen with more energy may occupy his place and who does not wish to be so complaisant undoubtedly our diplomatic relations with the Republic of the North will be impaired. Yet not for that reason must there be a break, because that great Nation will not declare war against us for some foolish reason. It knows that a war with her would be considered here in Mexico as a national war and the resistance which they would stumble into would be very different from that which the French encountered during the war of Intervention and scarcely comparable to that which Napoleon I met in Spain and which he was never able to put down. Furthermore, the United States is a democratic people, and these if it is certain that they are lions when they undertake defense of their independence, they also have little interest in wars of conquest which benefit a certain number of capitalists to the prejudice of the immense majority of the people which is the segment that gives contributions of money and blood.

The noble attitude of the United States toward the Pearl of the Antilles which it occupied only temporarily in order to assure its regular functioning democracy presents us the most eloquent proof that they American is a magnanimous people and that we ought not to fear anything from it whenever our relations with it are loyal. Loyalty does not exclude dignity, but this will not happen without giving more luster to our friendly relations. It is possible that General Diaz may have another criteria, which is easily explained because a man who owes his fortune to brute force must have a special concept of it and must conserve a superstitious respect for it.

Passing now to study our relations with the sister republics of Central and South America we must lament that better efforts have not been made to make closer our relations with them. Wishing to apply the criteria of domestic policy to that outside the Republic, it has been considered that with those conventional phrases and with sumptuous receptions of the delegates of the Pan-American Congress it would be sufficient to maintain the prestige of Mexico among the sisters of the South.

Nothing could be more mistaken than such a belief, because nobody gives any credit to conventional expressions. Here in the interior of the country everybody is silent for fear of appearing to be dissatisfied with the administration, but abroad it is different and our international policy has been sharply criticized, as it deserves to be, by the press of those countries. Besides appearing to us to be quite inefficient, the effort which the Mexican Government has made to tighten the bonds which unite us to those people, we believe that it has committed two big errors. The first was to join with all the European powers when in a vast coalition they demanded of Venezuela the payment of bills which that nation owed to their nationals. It was not suitable for Mexico for any reason to assume that attitude, both for antecedents as well as for its own advantage. For antecedents, because through bitter experience we know how unjust such debts usually are; for convenience, because the only method of arriving at a possible equilibrium of forces in the American Continent is to unite all the Latin Republics so as to counter-balance the power of the Anglo-Saxon Republics.

Although we are of those who do not fear a war with this Nation for reasons already mentioned, prudence advises that we surround ourselves with elements which may augment our force, because as this force may become greater if diminishes the probabilities of a conflict. If, instead of Mexico being united to the claiming powers, it had interposed all its influence and even had assisted Venezuela with its credit, undoubtedly our situation in Latin America would be very different from what it is today: they would consider Mexico as their older brother and would be proud to say "our brothers." Whereas now they think of us with a little sadness on seeing a policy so little begun which we have followed with little dignity.

The other transcendental mistake has been not to dedicate all our efforts for promoting a union which the five Central-American Republics should form into one, single federative Republic, for in this way the interminable wars which agitate the area will be done away with; the hatreds which divide them will be erased and they would form a single powerful Nation that would have to be our natural ally, and that, with union and peace, it would be progress rapidly and would be steadily more strong, a force which would rebound equally in our benefit through the community of interests and of ideals.

Instead of that, while they are divided we run the danger that some of them may fall into the hands of an ambitious power as happened to Panama, and would constitute a serious threat for us to have such a dangerous neighbor. In order to succeed in bringing about such a federation, they would have been going about preparing all the threads of the warp in order to take advantage of the first opportunity which might present itself, such as the assassination of General Barillas. That event caused such effervescence in Central America which an intervention by Mexico at that time would be considered like a stroke of Providence because it would have provided for the downfall from power of the tyrant Cabrera, who, occupy the post of President of the Republic of Guatemala, was an insult to the human race.

Instead of that, and since our policy did not have a fixed orientation, we proceeded with vacillation, leaving us to carry on through impressions of the moment and left us in a ridiculous situation and winding up losing all the prestige which we had with our neighbors of the South *for having drawn the sword without reason, and then having sheathed it without honor,* a sentence in which in a very graphic way our previously cited and very good friend, Sr. Fernando Inglesis Calderon, summarized our policy in those circumstances.

We will not finish treating this point without saying that it seems highly impolitic to us for General Diaz to make a declaration to a reporter of *The Herald* in which he said, speaking of our army, that we needed it for repelling some future attack from our neighbors of the south because it in the North we were perfectly covered through friendship with the United States.

We approve of the second part of his statement but we do not approve of the first because it demonstrates a certain hostility for our brothers of the South and a certain arrogance for the weak, while toward the strong it is so condescending. Seeing that General Diaz is so competent in the art of remaining silent and of being impervious, he put his ability at risk in this situation.

Before proceeding further, we wish to make an important statement: It is not our purpose to attack Senor Mariscal, our very meritorious Secretary of Relations.

We have the very highest respect for his patriotism and for his integrity and we have learned that in the majority of the cases previously cited he has supported the policy which we have sketched as the most suitable for the Nation, but he has had to give away before the omnipotent opinion of General Diaz.

Since in this book we have proposed to speak the language of truth, it will be sufficient to say that since none ever knows what happens in the councils of the ministers, General Diaz easily arranges that there should fall on each one of them all the mistakes committed in the branch which he is responsible for, and on the other hand, all merit is attributed to what he has done. For this he is aided admirably by the salaried press, and by the minute divisions between the ministers which he knows how to foment so ably so as to have always an equilibrium between the forces so that none of them comes to dominate.

What happened with the famous mining bill shows us that General Diaz is the one who decides all those important subjects, even against the conviction of his ministers. In this case, the subject got a great deal of publicity through special circumstances, but undoubtedly, this situation is abnormal in the policy of General Diaz.

MATERIAL PROGRESS

The only thing that shows off the administration of General Diaz in his favor is our material progress. The official daily papers publish statistics and more statistics demonstrating that the increase in our commerce is fabulous, that the sources of public and private wealth have increased considerably, that our network of railroads is extending more and more, that in the ports magnificent works are being constructed in order to make them accessible to ships of deep draft, that in all the big cities drainage has been arranged for, the streets paved, and magnificent buildings have been constructed, etc., etc. * * *

All that is very certain; our economic progress, industrial, mercantile, agriculture, and mining is undeniable. As we have already said, General Diaz will do all the good that is possible for the country provided that it may be compatible with his indefinite re-election. And so it is clear that in the matter of liberties all of them were barriers for achieving his purposes, and for this reason he managed to finish them off. But the same thing does not happen with economic questions because the more developed may be the public wealth and with greater interests which may be created in his shadow, the greater will be the stability of his government. In order to bring this work to a crest, the two most important factors have been: peace and the wave of material progress which has brought to the world steam with its applications to transportation and to industry. We have seen the very skillful methods he has used to keep the peace, one of the principle ones being the construction of the great railroads, but these have served not only for keeping the peace, but they have brought about a marvelous development of the riches of the Nation.

General Diaz, with his great administrative gifts and as a consummate states-man, has known how to promote material progress by placing order in all that which touches his active participation. Nevertheless, a country as large as ours cannot be governed by one man and it is clear that he surrounded himself with competent persons and all that comes within his range of vision goes relatively well. But the same is not taking place in the States where the immense majority of the Governors are not concerned with anything except to increase their fortunes through, more or less, of good administration of the State because they do not devote their energies to the task.

The best proof of our material progress and that there is order in national finances is that the budgets for expenses are covered easily in spite of the interest on the national foreign debt which has increased considerably during the present administration. We will not publish figures to indicate our progress because the respective statistics are well known throughout the Nation. The only thing that we will say is that it is an error to attribute all the progress which we have enjoyed to General Diaz because in the same period of time many nations of the world have achieved a development which bears no relation with that of ours. We cite such nations as Japan, France, United States, Italy, Germany, and among our brothers of the South, Costa Rica, Argentina, Chile and Brazil. In all those countries has been noted, as among us, the beneficent influence steam which has revolutionized all industries and means of transportation.

In all those countries just mentioned, practical democracies exist; in those that are under the republican regime various citizens have alternated in power. And so it is not to General Diaz to whom we owe our economic well-being but to the great wave of material progress which has invaded the whole civilized world. If in place of an absolute government we would have had a democratic one, perhaps our material progress would have been greater; perhaps there would not have been so much pilfering in the States. And if it is certain that the government would not be so rich, then perhaps material works would have received greater impulses and most especially public instruction would have been attended to much more. But let us stop embroidering in a vacuum; we are studying what happened and not that which might have happened: nobody knows that.

AGRICULTURE

In this branch, so important for the wealth of the public, the government has done little for its development, because with the regime of government vested in on single person the result is that the only persons who take advantage of the concessions are those who surround him. More particularly in the present situation one of the means which General Diaz has used to reward his Tux-tepecan chieftains has been that of giving them great concessions of public lands. This action has constituted a hindrance in agriculture because it is well known that big proprietors rarely are occupied in cultivating their lands and generally specialize in cattle raising when they have not been abandoned in order to sell them to some foreign company, as has happened more and more frequently.

The concessions for use of water in the river has been thoughtless and always they have gone into the hands of a small group of favorites of the government, with the result that water has not been used as well as if it had been subdivided among many agriculturists on a small scale. The result of this policy has been that the country, in spite of its vast extension of cultivable lands, does not produce either cotton or wheat necessary for its consumption in normal years and in the dry years we have to import even the corn and beans, which are basis of food of the Mexican people.

What appears to have had the greatest development are the Maguey plantations, and although the sale of pulque provides fat profits to those who produce it, we should not for that reason consider its production as a part of the national wealth because, on the contrary, it is one of the causes of our decadence.

MINING AND INDUSTRY

These two branches certainly have received a portentous impulse with the railroads, especially the mining industry has had a surprising development, due both to the railroads as well as to the mining law which is so liberal. In reference to industry, it has received a positive impulse on the part of the government, granting to industry new exemptions from taxes and establishing legal protectionist laws.

Nevertheless, in certain cases the Government has been too lax in its desire to develop industry to benefit from the privileges. We refer especially to the factories making alcoholic drink of every sort and especially for those from corn because they transform that grain which is the basic food of the people into alcohol, which is one of the most pernicious poisons for the Nation. As a result, this industry has made the price of grain dearer and increased the poverty of the people in lean years.

On the issue of protectionist legislation, the Government has not always gone forward with assurance, and in order to decree the legislation a person has only to take into account the special interests of persons or friendly corporations whom it is desirous to protect without consulting the overall interests of the Nation which does not have any legitimate representative in those discussions. The result of this policy has been create the monopolies of paper and of dynamite and raise the price considerably of articles fabricated out of iron and steel to the prejudice of the whole Nation and the advantage of some special persons.

PUBLIC FINANCES

This is one of the branches of the administration most difficult to evaluate for a person who does not belong to the spheres of government because in order to issue judgments based on the majority of the subjects which concern him, comparative and detailed studies would be necessary, using data and statistics of every kind. For this reason, we will see ourselves limited to treating this subject very superficially.

Numerous statistics are published frequently, from which our material progress stands out as well as the moderate state of the Public Treasury. But on the other hand, material progress breaks into view and it is such that no one casts any doubt on that score. Our particular task is to ascertain, following the theme of this book, in what influences has the administration of General Diaz had upon our economic development. Immediately we can say that its influence has been enormous, but we repeat the principal cause of our progress is not a local cause, but worldwide because the Nineteenth century and the beginning of the Twentieth have been characterized by prodigious development of the sciences which have an application to industry and in general to material progress.

Nevertheless, the administration of General Diaz has the very great merit of having aided the nation to enter wholeheartedly into the road of material progress by promoting the construction of railroads, protecting industry, etc., etc. * * * Furthermore, we have said that General Diaz would promote all the good possible for the country provided that this should be compatible with his indefinite re-election. Let us see, then, these limitations which he has imposed on the Nation, and let us see how much these have been a factor in which the well-being was not greater. Immediately we must give credit to the present administration that has succeeded in balancing the National budget and even to show a surplus for the treasury in spite of the enormous service of the debt. That is, as we have said, the best proof of our economic situation, and that in the branch with which have been concerning ourselves, there exists a minutely precise order, an order which only managed to establish itself by cutting the roots of great abuses.

The immense debt contracted by the present administration has served to develop considerably our national wealth, and we do not believe that it is a great burden to the Nation from the moment that with pride the interest is paid and a part of the debt is being amortized. The financial crisis, which the country is undergoing currently, does not mean anything in contrast with the growth of the national wealth. Its causes are also worldwide because the crisis which the United States felt was reflected on us because they lowered considerably the price of our products for export and at the same time reduced the entrance of foreign money into the country.

The Sr. Minister of Treasury was alarmed by the crisis in the United States and he feared that it would reach us, seriously threatening the Banks of Emission because these institutions had acquired certain practices which were incompatible with institutions of that character because they had been converted practically from commercial banks. Furthermore, in some of them tremendous abuses had been committed by their advisers. In order to avert the evil Sr. Limantour convoked a meeting of bankers by which means of a circular in which he explained the modifications which, in his judgment, were necessary to make in the Banking Law. This circular made a deep impression in the financial circles and increased the financial crisis which had begun to be felt.

Nevertheless, the effect of this circular in augmenting the crisis has been much exaggerated because, as we have said, the principal cause which determined it were worldwide. Besides, we suffered the consequences of a well-known economic law according to which prosperous countries suffered periodic crisis.

We will not conclude the section on the Treasury without saying a few words on the merger of the rail lines and control of the nation over a great extension of the national lines. This important operation has been the basis of serious controversies in the press, but in spite of that we declare frankly that we consider it a great good for the country that the government should exercise control over the railroads because without that control we place ourselves under the coverture that some foreign trust should acquire them and exploit us, thus paralyzing all our sources of wealth.

The government will concern itself more with national interests than would a foreign company. Although at the present time some complaints are made known, they may not be well founded; but above all, it will be easy to remedy the evil and if the present administration does not do it, the following one will. One of these days the situation has to change! Another reason of real importance is that the acquisition frees the government from the pretext of international reclamation claims in the unfortunate event of internal troubles or of some international conflict.

And finally, very important reasons existed within the economic field and they caused the government to take that measure, as Senor Limantour indicated in his report. The great objection that is made to this operation is that it could have been made under conditions more advantageous to the Nation, because it is argued that the same operation served as a cover for fruitful speculations. That is very difficult to prove, but, as we have already said, the more unlikely they may be the more the public gives credit to all those rumors. It is indisputable that under the present regime of government they may commit very big abuses without it being easy to prove them because the control of the legislature and the independent press.

In spite of what has been said in the situation which now concerns us, the press has made great us of its freedom in order to challenge the actions of the Senor Minister of Hacienda. In general, this circumstance has not been appreciated duly and that action of Senor Limantour to give freedom of the press to attack him ought to cause them to extol him rather than to deprecate him. What occurs to us is that without us taking account of it, we work under the suggestion of General Diaz to whom it is not displeasing that the press should attack his ministers every now and then, especially when they begin to acquire a certain prestige. On the other hand, nobody can attack him; he is not the be blamed for any criticizable decision adopted by his secretaries, while to make him is attributed all the merit of good decisions which they make.

The result is that while one of his ministers is attacked because he has made some mistake in the branch for which he is responsible, every sort of adulation is lavished upon General Diaz, saying that with his great equity, his obvious talent, etc., they expect that he will remedy the evil. The people do not comprehend, that he is the one responsible for all the mistakes, both because the ministers are named by him and then make no important decision without his consent as well as the regime of absolute power which he has established and so he has paralyzed the influence which all citizens would be able to exercise if they should use one of the rights which the Constitution grants to them for engaging in public affairs.

FRANCISCO MADERO

"The Plan of San Luis Potosí," 1910

Francisco Madero took Porfirio Díaz at his word and formed a political party and started campaigning for the presidency of Mexico. Díaz later changed his mind and had Madero thrown in jail. After being bailed out, Madero fled to San Antonio, Texas, where he issued the Plan of San Luis Potosí calling for new elections and urging Mexicans to take up arms against the Díaz regime on November 20 at 6:00 P.M. The violence kicked off two days earlier in Puebla at the home of Aquiles Serdán, Madero ally.

SOURCE: *Francisco I. Madero, ed and trans.,* The Plan of San Luis Potosi, *(Joshua Hamill, 1999–2009).*

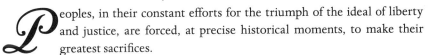

*P*eoples, in their constant efforts for the triumph of the ideal of liberty and justice, are forced, at precise historical moments, to make their greatest sacrifices.

Our beloved country has reached one of those moments. A force of tyranny which we Mexicans were not accustomed to suffer after we won our independence oppresses us in such a manner that it has become intolerable. In exchange for that tyranny we are offered peace, but peace full of shame for the Mexican nation, because its basis is not law, but force; because its object is not the aggrandizement and prosperity of the country, but to enrich a small group who, abusing their influence, have converted the public charges into fountains of exclusively personal benefit, unscrupulously exploiting the manner of lucrative concessions and contracts.

The legislative and judicial powers are completely subordinated to the executive; the division of powers, the sovereignty of the States, the liberty of the common councils, and the rights of the citizens exist only in writing in our great charter; but, as a fact, it may almost be said that martial law constantly exists in Mexico; the administration of justice, instead of imparting protection to the weak, merely serves to legalize the plunderings committed by the strong; the judges instead of being the representatives of justice, are the agents of the executive, whose interests they faithfully serve; the chambers of the union have no other will than that of the dictator; the governors of the States are designated by him and they in their turn designate and impose in like manner the municipal authorities.

From this it results that the whole administrative, judicial, and legislative machinery obeys a single will, the capriciousness of General Porfirio Diaz, who during his long administration has shown that the principal motive that guides him is to maintain himself in power and at any cost. For many years profound discontent has been felt throughout the Republic, due to such a system of government, but General Diaz with great cunning and perseverance, has succeeded in annihilating all independent elements, so that it was not possible to organize any sort of movement to take from him the power of which he made such bad use. The evil constantly became worse, and the decided eagerness of General Diaz to impose a successor upon the nations in the person of Mr. Ramon Corral carried that evil to its limit and caused many of us Mexicans, although lacking recognized political standing, since it had been impossible to acquire it during the 36 years of dictatorship, to throw ourselves into the struggle to recover the sovereignty of the people and their rights on purely democratic grounds. * * *

Along with other political parties that have the same purpose, the National Antireelectionist Party was organized, proclaiming the principles of EFFECTIVE SUFFRAGE AND NO REELECTION, as the only way capable of saving the Republic from the imminent danger that has threatened us due to the prolongation of the most onerous, most despotic, and most immoral dictatorship.

The Mexican people effectively supported this party, and responding to its call, sent representatives to a convention in which was also represented the National Democratic Party, that also received popular support. This convention designated its candidates for the presidency and the vice-presidency, choosing the nominations of Dr. Francisco Vázques Gómez for vice-president, and choosing me (Francisco Madero) to be president of the Republic (of Mexico).

We of course were at a great disadvantage, since our adversaries made up all of the electoral officials, who have supported Díaz without any scruples. But we believed in our cause * * * to serve the people * * * and we have spread our cry of EFFECTIVE SUFFRAGE AND NO REELECTION throughout the nation. Finally, the moment arrived when General Díaz realized what was going on and realized that he could not compete with me on the playing field of democracy * * * and as such he had me arrested and sent to prison prior to the elections, which took place and excluded the populace by means of violence, by filling the jails with independent citizens, and by means of the most shameless fraud imaginable.

In Mexico, as a democratic Republic, the public power can have no other origin nor other basis than the will of the people, and the latter can not be subordinated to formulas to be executed in a fraudulent manner. * * *

For this reason the Mexican people have protested against the illegality of the last election and, desiring to use successively all the recourses offered by the laws of the Republic, in due form asked for the nullification of the election by the Chamber of Deputies, notwithstanding they recognized no legal origin in said body and knew beforehand that, as its members were not the representatives of the people, they would carry out the will of General Diaz, to whom exclusively they owe their investiture. In such a state of affairs the people, who are the only sovereign, also protested energetically against the election in imposing manifestations in different parts of the Republic; and if the latter were not general throughout the national territory, It was due to the terrible pressure exercised by the Government, which always quenches in blood any democratic manifestation, as happened in Puebla, Vera Cruz, Tlaxcala, and in other places.

But this violent and illegal system can not go on any longer.

I have very well realized that if the people have designated me as their candidate for the Presidency it is not because they have had an opportunity to discover in me the qualities of a statesman or of a ruler, but the virility of the patriot determined to sacrifice himself, if need be, to obtain liberty and to help the people free themselves from the odious tyranny that oppresses them. From the moment I threw myself into the democratic struggle I very well knew that General Diaz would not bow to the will of the nation, and the noble Mexican people, in following me to the polls, also knew perfectly the outrage that awaited them; but in spite of it, the people gave the cause of liberty a numerous contingent of martyrs when they were necessary and with wonderful stoicism went to the polls and received every sort of molestation.

But such conduct was indispensable to show to the whole world that the Mexican people are fit for democracy, that they are thirsty for liberty, and that their present rulers do not measure up to their aspirations. Besides, the attitude of the people before and during the election, as well as afterwards, shows clearly that they reject with energy the Government of General Diaz and that, if those electoral rights had been respected, I would have been elected for President of the Republic.

Therefore, and in echo of the national will, I declare the late election illegal and, the Republic being accordingly without rulers, provisionally assume the Presidency of the Republic until the people designate their rulers pursuant to the law. In order to attain this end, it is necessary to eject from power the audacious usurpers whose only title of legality involves a scandalous and immoral fraud.

With all honesty I declare that it would be a weakness on my part and treason to the people, who have placed their confidence in me, not to put myself at the front of my fellow citizens, who anxiously call me from all parts of the country, to compel General Diaz by force of arms, to respect the national will.

The actual government, although rooted in violence and fraud for as long as it has been tolerated by the people, can continue to have certain legal titles in its relations with other countries until the 30th of next month * * * but after that date that government can no longer continue in power without the people taking up arms against it * * * as such I have designated SUNDAY, NOVEMBER 20th at 6:00 p.m. as the moment in which all of the peoples of the Republic are to rise up together, and take up arms (against Díaz).

THE PLAN

—The elections that took place in June and July of this year for president and vice-president are hereby declared null and void, as well as the elections for the Supreme Court magistrates and the Senate.

—We do not recognize the government of General Díaz, nor do we recognize the other government officials * * * that have been elected by means of fraudulent elections that are the most scandalous in Mexico's history. * * *

—Having been exploited by the laws regarding "idle lands," numerous small landowners (mostly the indigenous people) have been dispossessed of their land in accord with this government and the rulings of the courts. It is in the interest of justice to restore these lands to the original owners, and as such anyone who has acquired land by immoral and illegal means must return it to the original owners. * * *

—In accord with the Constitution * * * we declare under the laws of the Republic the principle of NO REELECTION of the President and the Vice-President of the Republic, of the Governors of the states, and of the municipal leaders. * * *

—I assume the role of Provisional President of the United States of Mexico, with the means necessary to wage war on the usurper government of General Díaz. As soon as the capital of the Republic and more than 1/2 of the states are in the power of the people, the provisional president will convene special general elections one month later and will turn over power to the newly elected president as soon as the results of the election are known.

—On the 20th of November, from 6:00 in the afternoon on, all of the citizens of the republic will take up arms to remove from power the authorities who currently govern.

—* * * Díaz himself justified the present revolution when he stated "that no citizen shall perpetuate the exercise of power * * * for that would result in the ultimate revolution." * * * If in the spirit of Díaz there had been more focus on the interests of the nation than the interests of his advisors (the científicos) we could have avoided this revolution, making concessions to the people, but since that did not happen, all the better! The change will be quick and radical, and the Mexican people, instead of lamenting like a coward will accept the challenge bravely. Given that General Díaz chooses to support himself by brute force and by imposing a yoke of oppression, the people will draw from this same strength to be freed from this yoke, to throw this corrupt man out of office, and to reconquer their liberty.

San Luis Potosí, 5 de octubre, 1910.
Fracisco I. Madero

DOLORES JIMÉNEZ Y MURO

"Down with the Dictatorship: The Political-Social Plan," 1911

Written in March 1911, the "Political-Social Plan" recognizes Madero as interim president and chief of the Revolution. The letter was written before the break between Madero and the anarchists. As can be seen in the document, Jiménez y Muro embraced some of the ideas of the 1906 PLM Plan and hoped Madero would be more liberal than he was when he took office.

SOURCE: *Chris Frazer, ed. and trans.,* Competing Voices from the Mexican Revolution *(Santa Barbara, CA, and Denver, CO: Greenwood Press, 2010), pp. 155–156.*

The situation that weighs on Mexicans is truly afflictive, for the rulers of Mexico have failed to quell the revolutionary movement which arose against their abuses. In order to shed the blood of more decent Mexicans, they have now suspended individual guarantees, abolishing the independent press, closing clubs, forbidding any expressions of public opinion and filling the prisons without regard for women or any other citizens who oppose tyranny.

From the beginning, these rulers were enthroned through deception, for they once proclaimed the same principle for which we are fighting today—Effective Suffrage and No Re-election. But instead of this principle, they established the most abject, abusive, and bloody dictatorship. And now, with the fraud of the last election, they stand accused of swindling the high posts they occupy, of betraying their own doctrines, and of abusing power.

In our political and social existence, there must be reforms and replacements of personnel. These are required by the needs of the contemporary generation, but are impossible to achieve at present under a plutocratic and dictatorial government.

The People are ultimately the only sovereign and supreme legislator, and we have been empowered by the people we represent—several groups, numbering more than 10,000 people in the states of Guerrero, Tlaxcala, Michoacan, Campeche, Puebla and in the Federal District, who have come together to proclaim the following plan and to invite our fellow citizens to adopt it if they agree that the nation needs reform and regeneration.

We repudiate the President and Vice-President, the senators and deputies, as well as all other elected officials, by virtue of the omissions, fraud and pressures that occurred in the last elections.

General Diaz, his Cabinet Ministers, and Sub-Secretary of the Interior Miguel Macedo—who unanimously voted to suspend guaranties—and the judges who unjustly sentenced so-called political prisoners, have violated the law and are traitors; all army chiefs will be judged according to the attitude they have taken towards the insurgents.

We recognize Francisco Madero as interim President and Supreme Chief of the Revolution.

We proclaim the Constitution of 1857 as the supreme law and uphold the principle of "Effective Suffrage and No Re-election."

The Press Law must be amended to clearly and precisely determine the instances where a person can rightly complain of defamation, as well as instances where infractions actually disrupt public order, and that properly punish the offender, if and when the act is really a crime.

The rights of suppressed municipalities must be restored.

The centralization of education must be abolished and replaced with a federative system.

The indigenous race must be protected in every way, obtaining by every means their dignity and prosperity.

All properties usurped under the current administration must be returned to their former and rightful owners.

Wages must be increased for rural and urban workers of both sexes, fixed to the rates of return on capital, as determined by a commission responsible for reviewing the data.

The hours of a work-day must not be less than eight or more than nine.

Mexican nationals must compromise no less than half of the workers employed by foreign companies in the Republic, in both subordinate and superior positions, with the same salaries, considerations and privileges granted to foreign employees.

When circumstances permit, the value of urban properties must be reviewed in order to establish fair rents, subject to additional work to create hygienic and comfortable accommodations for the working classes.

All proprietors who own more lands than they need or want to cultivate must be obliged to give uncultivated land to those who need it, receiving for their part a return of 6 per cent per year, corresponding to the fiscal value of the lands.

Monopolies of every kind must be abolished.

Down with the Dictatorship! Effective Suffrage and No Re-Election!

JUSTO SIERRA

"Reservations," 1878

A liberal who served as the secretary of public education for Porfirio Díaz and later as ambassador to Spain for Madero, Sierra here explains why Mexicans cannot simply ignore the constitution. He points out its inherent flaws and connects them to the heightened tensions at the moment it was written. Despite its flaws, he argues that it must be followed and amended if Mexico is to progress as a nation.

SOURCE: *José Antonio Aguilar Rivera, ed., Janet M. Burke and Ted Humphrey, trans.,* Liberty in Mexico: Writings on Liberalism from the Early Republican Period to the Second Half of the Twentieth Century *(Indianapolis, IN: Liberty Fund, 2012), pp. 385–387.*

W)hen we speak of the Constitution, when we demand respect and honor for it, when we assign this as the first of our political duties, we do not claim that constitutional principles should be accepted as articles of faith; nor do we believe they are a perfect work, no. In our judgment, the Constitution of '57 is a fine liberal utopia but destined, by the prodigious amount of political *lyricism* it contains, to be realized only slowly and painfully. The same thing happens with it that has happened with all laws made to transform customs that permeate the social masses, provoking conflicts and incessant struggles, and sometimes society suffers, other times the law is discredited until, when the definitive work of amalgamation has occurred, society and the Constitution are transformed.

The principles of political emancipation, the bright prospects for liberty and regeneration, and more than all that, the destruction of clerical rule, fired up the enthusiasm of our fathers for that code promulgated as a new Decalogue in the name of God. That was yesterday; today, principles, dreams, and theories are coming to the discussion anew. All the precepts of the fundamental law are destined, because of the fatal demands of history, to suffer severe revision before the tribunal of new ideas. This could not be done in a moment of storm and struggle, so it was necessary to affirm, from the stormy summits of the liberal party, our religious dogma (constitutional dogmas are nothing other than that) and point out from the seats of the Constituent [Congress], in the loftiest and purest region of the heavens, our ideal of citizens and men.

Our fathers believed they had made a work profoundly practical because they took our institutions from a practical people, and this idea was radically erroneous. What the practical consists of in American people is not having consigned in the federal code such and such principles, but rather that those principles are perfectly appropriate to the social medium in which they had to unfold.

We believe that, in copying the principles, we are imitating their practical sense, and this was not true; what we should have done, what would have been true imitation, was to give ourselves institutions that could unfold not in the heart of our corrupted habits, but of those habits that our history, our material necessities, our climate, and even our geographical conformation imposed on us. This examination was impossible, we recognize, in the epoch of passion and combat that was present at the advent of the Constitution.

We do not reason without proof. An induction based on the cruelest experiments can take us gradually to these conclusions, and we claimed those experiments in the saddest hours of our history, from '57 until now. Our fundamental law, created by men of the Latin race who believe that something is certain and realizable to the degree it is logical, who tend to humanize brusquely and through violence any ideal, who pass in one day from the rule of the absolute to that of the relative without transition, without nuances, and wishing to obligate the people to practice what is true in the region of pure reason; these men, we are among them, perhaps, who confuse the heavens with the earth, made us a lofty and noble code of union, but one in which everything tends to differentiation, to individual autonomy carried to its *maximum*; that is to say, to the level at which the action of social duties stops and everything is converted into individual rights.

Thus each one of the political powers tends to include the sphere of action of the others, basing itself on the Constitution; each state tends to weaken, to nullify, the federal bond, based also on the Constitution; it tends to declare its absolute independence from the social group in which it lives. But as, in order to carry out each one of those ideas, we find ourselves with a nation at two or three centuries' distance from the constitutional ideal, everything miscarries into political convulsions, into muffled tremblings of the unsettled society, and into that unconquerable apprehension that puts in the depths of all our consciousnesses I do not know what vague and tenacious skepticism with respect to the next day.

But why, then, do we demand respect for the Constitution? If we do not believe it to be good, why have we made it our standard? Why yesterday in its name have we battled a government that had begun by calling us its friends and today we embrace another government that began by treating us as enemies? Here is the reason: the Constitution is a rule, it is a law, it is the impersonal authority of a precept, supreme guarantee of human liberty; beyond it, there is nothing but arbitrariness, personal despotism, and, in a word, the rule of one man over the others. And as we believe that, given our present mode of being, there is nothing worse than the absence of rule and limits; as we believe that what is established in this way, although it might be a marvel, will remain established on a crumbly base of sand and will be destroyed, not only for our love of liberty—which is, in the last analysis, human dignity—but also for our love of order, a principal factor of progress, we have to maintain that it is necessary to place the Constitution above everything else. It will be a bad law, but it is a law; let us reform it tomorrow; let us obey it always.

JUSTO SIERRA

"Liberals and Conservatives," 1878

Here, Sierra calls generally on people representing differing political ideas to come together. He argues for the need for progress, for which he considers himself a liberal; but he does not want that progress to come only through violence, for which he considers himself conservative. It is a call for both liberty and order within Mexico.

SOURCE: *José Antonio Aguilar Rivera, ed., Janet M. Burke and Ted Humphrey, trans.,* Liberty in Mexico: Writings on Liberalism from the Early Republican Period to the Second Half of the Twentieth Century *(Indianapolis, IN: Liberty Fund, 2012), pp. 388–390.*

*I*n our country there have been neither liberals nor conservatives, but rather only revolutionaries and reactionaries. This refers to the factions, not the men. The revolutionary faction, to be liberal, has lacked the knowledge that liberty considered as a right cannot be realized outside of the moral development of a people, which is order; and the reactionaries, to be conservatives, lacked even the instinct for progress characteristic of our epoch, outside of which order is only immobility and death. In large part this has not been their fault, and it is absurd to demand of a country born and raised in conditions so unsuitable for social life what people better endowed with long experience and the dissemination of scientific instruction demand today, not always with good success.

Our existence has gravitated toward two extremes. The colonial system based on isolation is one extreme; the other is the constitutional regime based on this dogma: this individual is an absolute sovereign. The first gave us a reality without an ideal; the second offers us an ideal without reality; and this is an error, because it is necessary to be concerned simultaneously with the power of attraction that an idea exercises on a people and with the conditions in which that people live and up to what point those conditions permit the people to approach that ideal.

When our fathers promulgated the Charter of 1857, they believed themselves called to exercise a function more priestly than political; that time has passed. New ideas gain ground every day over the old verbal principles of liberty, and these ideas are inflexible because they are scientific laws. They teach us that the individual and society are two large organic realities that cannot be separated without destroying them. These laws teach us that nothing is definitively improved by revolutions because inevitable reactions follow them, and that the result of this oscillation is precisely to attain a progress equal to the progress that would have been obtained by the regular activity of peaceful means. So it is that there is always too much blood shed and vitality wasted.

What is it, then, that we want? To alienate forever from the mind of our country the idea that it can be regenerated by violence; to study the conditions in which we live, the obstacles placed in our advance, with such a desire to arrive at the truth, with such a profound determination to speak it, that we might manage, even at the risk of being victims of the rhetoric of fools, to find what our true needs might be and try to resolve them; thus it might be necessary to pass over a principle in our path or erase an ideal from our heavens.

Liberty! And where is the social force that secures us sufficiently against the violence of others? Democracy! And where are the people who govern, where is the enlightenment that directs their vote? Where is the faithful mandatory who collects it? Is our democracy perhaps something other than a shattered ballot box into which only fraud puts its hand? Who would be able to prevent it? The sovereign. We do not know it. This sovereign is a word. It is not a man. And how will it come to be? With work, with peace, with instruction.

Can this be a living fact, here where individual initiative is null except for the efficient action of the public authority of the state? Can this action be exercised without subjecting the strength of the state's momentum to rules, without giving it the right to do good where today it does evil, because it does it arbitrarily? To this study we consecrate ourselves.

We are young and we arrived at public life yesterday, still filled with dreams. We have been returned to reality by the spectacle of our disgraced country, which, however much it has inscribed beautiful ideas in its laws, continues along as disgraced as always; the spectacle of the other people who, not wishing to lose their prosperity, withdraw into themselves and create what suits them, what is useful to them, without worrying about political dogmas; the voice of science that tells us that nothing absolute is given to man to realize, man being subject irremissibly to the inflexible laws of nature; and the voice of our conscience that compels us to sacrifice a world of illusions in order to obtain an atom of well-being for our country.

We declare, consequently, not to understand liberty if it is not realized within order, and for that we are conservatives; nor order if it is not the normal impulse toward progress, and we are, therefore, liberals.

Immense is the seriousness of our social and political problems. We do not presume to present a solution; certainly, we have the assurance of advancing along the only road by which it can be found.

JUSTO SIERRA

"Our Battle Plan," 1879

Written in 1879 in support of Porfirio Díaz's reelection to the presidency against the candidacy of Justo Benítez. Sierra calls on the people of Mexico to support Díaz and to avoid taking up revolutionary arms. He argues that people need to follow the decisions of congress. This piece serves, in many ways, as a call for order.

SOURCE: *José Antonio Aguilar Rivera, ed., Janet M. Burke and Ted Humphrey, trans.,* Liberty in Mexico: Writings on Liberalism from the Early Republican Period to the Second Half of the Twentieth Century *(Indianapolis, IN: Liberty Fund, 2012), pp. 406–407.*

*N*o one is in a better situation than we to choose positions in the face of future events. We have maintained, supported by the good sense of the country (of this we have more conclusive proofs every day), that it was necessary to reform the Constitution in the sense of creating elements of governmental energy in order to preserve social interests. Political events subsequent to our first affirmations have demonstrated that we were right when, in a society that is unsettled, we maintained that it was necessary to strengthen the center of cohesion.

A legitimate consequence of the principles in which we have believed, that every effective attempt at political reconstruction must be supported, has been this, which we hold as an incontrovertible truth: there is nothing to hope from revolutions now; every revolution essentially antipatriotic and criminal.

Two laws derive from this for us: to support at all costs the present administration against revolutionary attacks; to combat those attacks in whatever form they present themselves. For that reason, we fight at all costs against the candidacy of Mr. Benítez. He was a man who had the unanimous abhorrence of the country; everything that might be done in his favor had t be artificial; to put official resources at his disposal was to solicit boldly an uncontainable revolution, because it gave him, more than a pretext, a reason for being.

Thanks to the good sense shown this time by the president of the Republic, Mr. Benítez has given up his candidacy, and this relinquishment, even though it might not be sincere, the circumstances will make irremediable. The new tendencies that start, if not from the center, certainly from the circle that immediately surrounds it, seem to us to show that the idea of creating a candidacy with official means, without the support of opinion, has not been abandoned.

We do not delude ourselves. We know perfectly that the country will not take part in the election; that our parties are not political groups but rather personal factions; that our country needs them to wait on its table; what is necessary, and in this the eternal error of Mexican governments has consisted, is to serve the country a meal it likes. This is the secret: a question of cuisine, like the majority of political questions. For that we have requested in all the annotations of the registry of supplications [*registro deprecatorio*] to the gentleman president, that he settle on one citizen that the country accepts, and he will see how, without appeals to force, the election, or what is called such, deserves the applause of all honorable citizens.

It is not hidden from us that the profound work of decomposition that undermines and wears down this society, not now muffled but rather visibly, necessitates in the crises in which the latent anarchy will rather visibly, necessitates in the crises in which the latent anarchy will rise from the muck heap to the street, men of extreme energy, incapable of tyrannizing but trained to repress. So as much for the country as for the future president, the effective collaboration of General Díaz would be very fortunate, and all these circumstances increase greatly the responsibility of the current leader of the executive. Men have little influence on the current of human events, ruled by inevitable laws; but a man can hold back or hasten the advice of this current, and General Díaz is in that situation.

Our role in the future is, then, very simple. To support the administration; to combat the official efforts on behalf of candidates not accepted by opinion. If these efforts continue, we will contribute with all our strength to the consolidation of a group of unofficial parties that might bring to the electoral field the possible struggle against the forces of the government.

Nonetheless, and even if this is equivalent to the most serious of admissions, subject to making it more explicit in a subsequent article, we declare that, in any case, we will fight against the revolution and we will bow before the resolutions of Congress, be they in agreement with our aspirations or not, because outside of this we do not see salvation.

EMILIANO ZAPATA, OTILIO MONTAÑO, AND OTHERS

"The Plan de Ayala," 1911

After the initial outbreak of violence in 1910, the Zapatistas sided with Francisco Madero. Their proximity to Mexico City was central to the eventual defeat of Porfirio Díaz because the federal army could not deploy all its forces to northern Mexico to confront forces under the leadership of Pascual Orozco and Pancho Villa. However, after the peace treaty was signed the interim president, Francisco de la Barra, ordered Victoriano Huerta to disarm the Zapatistas, who refused. Madero himself went to talk to the Zapatistas, but the rebels did not trust the interim government and refused. Instead they went into hiding. After the election, the Zapatistas, still frustrated by the government's appeals for patience, issued the Plan de Ayala.

SOURCE: *John Womack Jr.,* Zapata and the Mexican Revolution *(New York: Vintage, 1968), pp. 400–404.*

*L*iberating Plan of the sons of the State of Morelos, affiliated with the Insurgent Army which defends the fulfillment of the Plan of San Luis, with the reforms which it has believed proper to add in benefit of the Mexican Fatherland.

We who undersign, constituted in a revolutionary junta to sustain and carry out the promises which the revolution of November 20, 1910 just past, made to the country, declare solemnly before the face of the civilized world which judges us and before the nation to which we belong and which we call [*sic, llamamos,* misprint for *amamos,* "love"], propositions which we have formulated to end the tyranny which oppresses us and redeem the fatherland from the dictatorships which are imposed on us, which [propositions] are determined in the following plan:

1. Taking into consideration that the Mexican people led by Don Francisco I. Madero went to shed their blood to reconquer liberties and recover their rights which had been trampled on, and not for a man to take possession of power, violating the sacred principles which he took an oath to defend under the slogan "Effective Suffrage and No Reelection," outraging thus the faith, the cause, the justice, and the liberties of the people: taking into consideration that that man to whom we refer is Don Francisco I. Madero, the same who initiated the above-cited revolution, who imposed his will and influence as a governing norm on the Provisional Government of the ex-President of the Republic Attorney Francisco L. de Barra [sic], causing with this deed repeated sheddings of blood and multiplicate misfortunes for the fatherland in a manner deceitful and ridiculous, having no intentions other than satisfying his personal ambitions, his boundless instincts as a tyrant, and his profound disrespect for the fulfillment of the preexisting laws emanating from the immortal code of '57, written with the revolutionary blood of Ayutla.

Taking into account that the so-called Chief of the Liberating Revolution of Mexico, Don Francisco I. Madero, through lack of integrity and the highest weakness, did not carry to a happy end the revolution which gloriously he initiated with the help of God and the people, since he left standing most of the governing powers and corrupted elements of oppression of the dictatorial government of Porfirio Díaz, which are not nor can in any way be the representation of National Sovereignty, and which, for being most bitter adversaries of ours and of the principles which even now we defend, are provoking the discomfort of the country and opening new wounds in the bosom of the fatherland, to give it its own blood to drink; taking also into account that the aforementioned Sr. Francisco I. Madero, present President of the Republic, tries to avoid the fulfillment of the promises which he made to the Nation in the Plan of San Luis Potosí, being [sic, siendo, misprint for ciñendo, "restricting"] the above-cited promises to the agreements of Ciudad Juárez, by means of false promises and numerous intrigues against the Nation nullifying, pursuing, jailing, or killing revolutionary elements who helped him to occupy the high post of President of the Republic; Taking into consideration that the so-often-repeated Francisco I. Madero has tried with the brute force of bayonets to shut up and to drown in blood the pueblos who ask, solicit, or demand from him the fulfillment of the promises of the revolution, calling them bandits and rebels, condemning them to a war of extermination without conceding or granting a single one of the guarantees which reason, justice, and the law prescribe; taking equally into consideration that the President of the Republic Francisco I. Madero has made of Effective Suffrage a bloody trick on the people, already against the will of the same people imposing Attorney José M. Pino Suárez in the Vice-Presidency of the Republic, or [imposing as] Governors of the States [men] designated by him, like the so-called General Ambrosio Figueroa, scourge and tyrant of the people of Morelos, or entering into scandalous cooperation with the científico party, feudal landlords, and oppressive bosses, enemies of the revolution proclaimed by him, so as to forge new chains and follow the pattern of a new dictatorship more shameful and more terrible than that of Porfirio Díaz, for it has been clear and patent that he has outraged the sovereignty of the States, trampling on the laws without any respect for lives or interests, as has happened in the State of Morelos, and others, leading them to the most horrendous anarchy which contemporary history registers.

For these considerations we declare the aforementioned Francisco I. Madero inept at realizing the promises of the revolution of which he was the author, because he has betrayed the principles with which he tricked the will of the people and was able to get into power: incapable of governing, because he has no respect for the law and justice of the pueblos, and a traitor to the fatherland, because he is humiliating in blood and fire Mexicans who want liberties, so as to please the científicos, landlords, and bosses who enslave us, and from today on we begin to continue the revolution begun by him, until we achieve the overthrow of the dictatorial powers which exist.

2. Recognition is withdrawn from Sr. Francisco I. Madero as Chief of the Revolution and as President of the Republic, for the reasons which before were expressed, it being attempted to overthrow this official.

3. Recognized as Chief of the Liberating Revolution is the illustrious General Pascual Orozco, the second of the Leader Don Francisco I. Madero, and in case he does not accept this delicate post, recognition as Chief of the Revolution will go to General Don Emiliano Zapata.

4. The Revolutionary Junta of the State of Morelos manifests to the Nation under formal oath: that it makes its own the plan of San Luis Potosí, with the additions which are expressed below in benefit of the oppressed pueblos, and it will make itself the defender of the principles it defends until victory or death.

5. The Revolutionary Junta of the State of Morelos will admit no transactions or compromises until it achieves the overthrow of the dictatorial elements of Porfirio Díaz and Francisco I. Madero, for the nation is tired of false men and traitors who make promises like liberators and who on arriving in power forget them and constitute themselves as tyrants.

6. As an additional part of the plan we invoke, we give notice: that [regarding] the fields, timber, and water which the landlords, científicos, or bosses have usurped, the pueblos or citizens who have the titles corresponding to those properties will immediately enter into possession of that real estate of which they have been despoiled by the bad faith of our oppressors, maintaining at any cost with arms in hand the mentioned possession; and the usurpers who consider themselves with a right to them [those properties] will deduce it before the special tribunals which will be established on the triumph of the revolution.

7. In virtue of the fact that the immense majority of Mexican pueblos and citizens are owners of no more than the land they walk on, suffering the horrors of poverty without being able to improve their social condition in any way or to dedicate themselves to Industry or Agriculture, because lands, timber, and water are monopolized in a few hands, for this cause there will be expropriated the third part of those monopolies from the powerful proprietors of them, with prior indemnization, in order that the pueblos and citizens of Mexico may obtain ejidos, colonies, and foundations for pueblos, or fields for sowing or laboring, and the Mexicans' lack of prosperity and wellbeing may improve in all and for all.

8. [Regarding] the landlords, científicos, or bosses who oppose the present plan directly or indirectly, their goods will be nationalized and the two third parts which [otherwise would] belong to them will go for indemnizations of war, pensions for widows and orphans of the victims who succumb in the struggle for the present plan.

9. In order to execute the procedures regarding the properties aforementioned, the laws of disamortization and nationalization will be applied as they fit, for serving us as norm and example can be those laws put in force by the immortal Juárez on ecclesiastical properties, which punished the despots and conservatives who in every time have tried to impose on us the ignominious yoke of oppression and backwardness.

10. The insurgent military chiefs of the Republic who rose up with arms in hand at the voice of Don Francisco I. Madero to defend the plan of San Luis Potosí, and who oppose with armed force the present plan, will be judged traitors to the cause which they defended and to the fatherland, since at present many of them, to humor the tyrants, for a fistful of coins, or for bribes or connivance, are shedding the blood of their brothers who claim the fulfillment of the promises which Don Francisco I. Madero made to the nation.

11. The expenses of war will be taken in conformity with Article II of the Plan of San Luis Potosí, and all procedures employed in the revolution we undertake will be in conformity with the same instructions which the said plan determines.

12. Once triumphant the revolution which we carry into the path of reality, a Junta of the principal revolutionary chiefs from the different States will name or designate an interim President of the Republic, who will convoke elections for the organization of the federal powers.

13. The principal revolutionary chiefs of each State will designate in Junta the Governor of the State to which they belong, and this appointed official will convoke elections for the due organization of the public powers, the object being to avoid compulsory appointments which work the misfortune of the pueblos, like the so-well-known appointment of Ambrosio Figueroa in the State of Morelos and others who drive us to the precipice of bloody conflicts,

sustained by the caprice of the dictator Madero and the circle of científicos and landlords who have influenced him.

14. If President Madero and other dictatorial elements of the present and former regime want to avoid the immense misfortunes which afflict the fatherland, and [if they] possess true sentiments of love for it, let them make immediate renunciation of the posts they occupy and with that they will with something staunch the grave wounds which they have opened in the bosom of the fatherland, since, if they do not do so, on their heads will fall the blood and the anathema of our brothers.

15. Mexicans: consider that the cunning and bad faith of one man is shedding blood in a scandalous manner, because he is incapable of governing; consider that his system of government is choking the fatherland and trampling with the brute force of bayonets on our institutions; and thus, as we raised up our weapons to elevate him to power, we again raise them up against him for defaulting on his promises to the Mexican people and for having betrayed the revolution initiated by him, we are not personalists, we are partisans of principles and not of men!

Mexican People, support this plan with arms in hand and you will make the prosperity and well-being of the fatherland.

Ayala, November 25, 1911

Liberty, Justice, and Law

Signed, General in Chief Emiliano Zapata * * * Otilio Montaño, * * * [et al.]. Camp in the Mountains of Puebla, December 11, 1911.

MANUEL PALAFOX, OTILIO MONTAÑO, AND OTHERS

"The Agrarian Law," 1915

Written in 1915, the Agrarian Law is influenced by many of the events that unfold over the course of the Revolution. While it is still an indigenous-authored document, like that of the "Plan de Ayala," the presence of urban intellectuals, especially Manuel Palafox, is evident. Despite its later date, this piece is included in the game to show the ideas that many indigenous people in southern Mexico were looking for in terms of land reform. A few elements, such as references to the presidency of Victoriano Huerta have been redacted for the purposes of the game.

The Agrarian Law was issued in 1915, postdating the start of the game by three years; however, because it is important to understanding agrarismo, it is included here as a key text. This document and its introduction have been adapted from the

John Womack version for the purposes of the game to avoid references to events that occurred after 1911. References to Womack's paging are included to aid in citations and for anyone interested in reading the original.

SOURCE: *John Womack Jr.*, Zapata and the Mexican Revolution *(New York: Vintage Books, 1968), pp. 405–411.*

nited Mexican States
 Executive Council of the Republic
 AGRARIAN LAW

The Executive Council, in use of the faculties invested in it, makes known to the inhabitants of the Mexican Republic

Considering that in the Plan de Ayala are condensed the longings of the people risen in arms, especially in regard to agrarian recoveries, the intimate reason and supreme goal of the Revolution, there it is of necessary urgency to regulate duly the principles confirmed in said Plan in such a form that they can forthwith be carried into practice as general laws of immediate application.

Considering that the people have shown in various ways their wish to destroy at the roots and forever the unjust monopoly of land in order to realize a social state which guarantees fully the natural right which every man has to an extension of land necessary for his own subsistence and that of his family, it is a duty of Revolutionary Authorities to respect that popular wish, expediting all those laws, which, like the present, satisfy fully those legitimate aspirations of the people.

Considering that not a few authorities, far from fulfilling the sacred duty of doing revolutionary work, which the exercise of any and every public responsibility imposes in the present times, giving thereby proofs of not being identified with the Revolution, refuse to second the steps taken to obtain the economic and social emancipation of the people, making common cause the with reactionaries, landlords, and other exploiters of the working classes, therefore it becomes necessary, to define attitudes, that the Government declare definitively that it will consider disaffected from the cause and will hold responsible all those authorities who, forgetting their character as organs of the Revolution, do not assist effectively in the triumph of the Revolution's ideals.

For the preceding considerations, and taking into account that the Executive Council is the supreme authority of the Revolution, since the Sovereign Revolutionary Convention is not at present in session, [the Council] decrees:

ARTICLE 1. To communities and to individuals the fields, timber, and water of which they were despoiled are [hereby] restored, it being sufficient that they possess legal titles dated before the year 1856, in order that they enter immediately into possession of their properties.

ARTICLE 2. Individuals or groups who believe themselves entitled to the recovered properties of which the previous article speaks will have to adduce [the title] before commissions designated by the Department of Agriculture, within the year following the date of recovery, and subject to respective regulation.

ARTICLE 3. The Nation recognizes the traditional and historic right which the pueblos, ranchos, and communities of the Republic have of possessing and administering their fields of communal distribution [*común repartimiento*] and communal use [*ejidos*] in the form which they judge proper.

ARTICLE 4. The Nation recognizes the unquestionable right which belongs to every Mexican of possessing and cultivating an extension of land, the products of which permit him to cover his needs and those of his family; consequently and in order to create small property, there will be expropriated, by reason of public utility and by means of the corresponding indemnization, and the lands of the country, with the sole exception of the fields belonging to pueblos, rancherías, and communities, and those farms which, because they do not exceed the maximum which this law fixes, must remain in the power of their present proprietors.

ARTICLE 5. Proprietors who are not enemies of the Revolution will keep as inexpropriable terrain portions which do not exceed the area which, as a maximum, the following table fixes:

CLIMATE	QUALITY OF LAND	WATER	ACREAGE
Hot	Prime	Irrigated	247.1
Hot	Prime	Seasonal	345.9
Hot	Secondary	Irrigated	296.5
Hot	Secondary	Seasonal	445.8
Temperate	Prime	Irrigated	296.5
Temperate	Prime	Seasonal	535.4
Temperate	Poor	Irrigated	345.9
Temperate	Poor	Seasonal	494.2
Cold	Prime	Irrigated	345.9
Cold	Prime	Seasonal	445.8
Cold	Poor	Irrigated	445.8
Cold	Poor	Seasonal	543.6
Rich fields of pasture			1,235.5
Poor fields of pasture			2,471.0
Rich fields of rubber shrub			741.3
Poor fields of rubber shrub			1,235.5
Henequen fields			741.3
Untilled fields in the North of the Republic—Coahuila, Chihuahua, Durango, the North of Zacatecas and the North of San Luis Potosi			3,3706.5

ARTICLE 6. Declared as national property are the rural properties of the enemies of the Revolution. Enemies of the Revolution are, for the effects of the present Law:

a. Individuals who under the regime of Porfirio Díaz formed part of the group of politicians and financiers which public opinion designated with the name of "Científico Party."

b. Governors and other officials of the States who during the administrations of Porfirio Díaz [or any other anti-Revolutionary administration] acquired properties by fraudulent or immoral means, taking unfair advantage of their official position, appealing to violence or sacking the public treasury.

c. Politicians, public employees, and businessmen who, without having belonged to the "Científico Party," made fortunes, having recourse to criminal procedures or [operating] under the protection of concessions notoriously costly to the country.

* * *

f. High members of the Clergy who [help] to sustain [Díaz or any other anti-Revolutionary government], by financial means or by propaganda among the faithful; and

g. Those who directly or indirectly helped the dictatorial governments of Díaz * * * and other governments hostile to the Revolution in their struggle against the same.

Included in this clause are those who provided said governments funds or subsidies for war, supported or subventioned newspapers to combat the Revolution, attacked or denounced the supporters of the same, carried on divisive activity among revolutionary elements, or in any other manner entered into complicity with the governments who fought against the revolutionary cause.

ARTICLE 7. Fields which exceed the extension mentioned in Article 5 will be expropriated by reason of public utility, through due indemnization, * * * and in the time and form which regulation designates.

ARTICLE 8. The Department of Agriculture and Colonization will name commissions which, in the various State of the Republic and on the basis of the information in the case, will judge who are the persons who, according to Article 6, must be considered as enemies of the Revolution and subject therefore to the penalty of confiscation in reference, which will be applied immediately.

ARTICLE 9. Decisions delivered by the commissions mentioned remain subject to the definitive ruling delivered by special Land Tribunals which, in conformity with the disposition of Article 6 of the Plan de Ayala, must be instituted, and whose organization will be a matter for another law.

ARTICLE 10. The total area of lands which are obtained in virtue of the confiscation decreed against the enemies of the revolutionary cause, and in virtue of the expropriation which must be made of the fractions of farms which exceed the maximum fixed in Article 5, will be divided in lots of which will be distributed among Mexicans who solicit them, preference being given in every case to country people. Each lot will have an extension such that it permits the satisfaction of a family's needs.

ARTICLE 11. To those presently sharecroppers or renters of small farms, these [farms] will be adjudicated as property, with absolute preference [to the present sharecroppers and renters] over any other solicitant, so long as those properties do not exceed the extension which each lot has to have in conformity with the disposition of the previous article.

ARTICLE 12. In order to fix the area which the said lots must have, the Department of Agriculture and Colonization will name technical commissions composed of engineers, who will locate and duly survey said lots, respecting in every case the fields belonging to the pueblos and those which are exempt from expropriation according to Article 5.

ARTICLE 13. To carry out their works of survey and subdivision, the said commissions will decide on the claims which are made before them by small proprietors who consider themselves despoiled by virtue of usurious contracts, by abuses or complicity of political bosses, or by seizures, or by usurpations committed by great landlords.

The decisions which are thereby delivered will be reviewed by the special Land Tribunals, which Article 9 mentions.

ARTICLE 14. The farms which the Government cedes to communities or individuals are not alienable, nor can they be mortgaged in any form, all contracts which tend to go against this disposition being null.

ARTICLE 15. The rights of property to fields subdivided and ceded by the Government to farmers can transmitted only by legitimate inheritance.

ARTICLE 16. In order that the execution of this law be as rapid and complete as possible, there is conceded to the Department of Agriculture and Colonization the exclusive power to inculcate the agrarian principles confirmed in the same, and to hear and resolve in all affairs of the [agrarian] branch, without this disposition involving an attack on the sovereignty of the States, since the point is only the speedy realization of the ideals of the Revolution in regards to the improvement of the disinherited farmers of the Republic.

ARTICLE 17. The foundation, administration, and inspection of agricultural colonies, whatever be the nature of these, as well as the recruitment of colonists, is of the exclusive competence of the Department of Agriculture and Colonization.

ARTICLE 18. The Department of Agriculture and Colonization will set up an [office of] technical inspection to execute works which will be called the "National Service of Irrigation and Construction," which will depend on the said Department.

ARTICLE 19. Stands of timber are declared national property, and their inspection will be made by the Department of Agriculture in the form in which [the

Department] regulates it, and they will be exploited by the pueblos in whose jurisdiction they belong, employed for that the communal system.

ARTICLE 20. The Department of Agriculture and Colonization is authorized to establish a Mexican agricultural bank in accord with the special regulation which the said Department will make.

ARTICLE 21. It is of the exclusive competence of the Department of Agriculture and Colonization to administer the banking institution of which the previous article speaks, in accord with the administrative bases which the same Department establishes.

ARTICLE 22. For the purposes of Article 20, the Department of Agriculture and Colonization is authorized to confiscate or nationalize urban property, the material works of national or expropriated property, or works of whatever kind, including furniture, machinery, and all the objects [those properties] contain, so long as they belong to enemies of the Revolution.

ARTICLE 23. Declared void are all concessions furnished in contracts celebrated by the Department of Public Works and related to the branch of Agriculture, or [those celebrated] by this [Department of Agriculture] in the time it existed up to [now], it remaining to the judgment of the Department of Agriculture and Colonization to revalidate those [contracts] which it judges beneficial for the people and the Government, after scrupulous and conscientious review.

ARTICLE 24. The Department of Agriculture and Colonization is authorized to establish in the Republic regional agricultural [and] forestry schools and experimental stations.

ARTICLE 25. Persons to whom are adjudicated lots in virtue of the distribution of lands, to which Articles 10, 11, and 12 to the present law refer, remain subject to the obligations and prohibitions which the following article confirms.

ARTICLE 26. The proprietor of a lot is obliged to cultivate it duly, and if for two consecutive years he abandons this cultivation without justified cause, he will be deprived of his lot, which will go to he who solicits it.

ARTICLE 27. Twenty per cent of the income from the nationalized properties of which Article 22 speaks will be destined for the payment of indemnizations of expropriated properties. * * *

ARTICLE 28. Proprietors of two or more lots will be able to unite to form Cooperative Societies with the object of exploiting their properties or selling the produce from these in common, but without those associations being able to take the form of joint-stock companies or be constituted among persons who are not directly or exclusively dedicated to the cultivation of the lots. Societies which are formed in violation of the disposition of this article will be totally null in law, and there will be popular action to denounce them.

ARTICLE 29. The Federal Government will expedite laws which regulate the constitution and functioning of the cooperative societies in reference.

ARTICLE 30. The Department of Agriculture and Colonization will expedite all regulations which may be necessary for the due application and execution of the present law.

ARTICLE 31. The fiscal value presently assigned to property does not prejudice at all future evaluations which the national treasury will have a right to make as a basis for taxes which in the future may weigh on the property.

ARTICLE 32. Declared national property are all waters utilizable and utilized for whatever use, even those which were considered as in the jurisdiction of the States, without there being reason for indemnization of any kind.

ARTICLE 33. In every use of waters preference will always be given to the demands of agriculture, and only when these are satisfied will the waters be used for power and other uses.

ARTICLE 34. It is of the exclusive competence of the Department of Agriculture and Colonization to expedite regulations on the use of waters.

ARTICLE 35. * * * [A]ll contracts relative to the alienation of goods belonging to enemies of the Revolution are declared to complete nullity.

ENABLING ARTICLES—

First: All Municipal Authorities of the Republic are obliged to carry out and have carried out, without loss of time and without any excuse or pretext, the dispositions of the present Law, it being their duty to put pueblos and individuals immediately in possession of the lands and other properties which, in conformity with the same Law, correspond to them, without prejudice to the fact that in their own time the Agrarian Commissions which the Department of Agriculture and Colonization will designate will make the rectifications which may arise, in the knowledge that said Authorities who are remiss or negligent in the fulfillment of their duty will be considered enemies of the Revolution and severely castigated.

Second: It is declared that the present Law forms part of the fundamental [laws] of the Republic, its observance therefore being general and all those constitutive or secondary laws which in any way are opposed to it being abolished.

Granted in the hall of pleadings and proceedings of the Municipal Building, on the twenty-second day of the month of October of nineteen hundred and fifteen.

Therefore, we order that it be published, circulated, and be given its due fulfillment.

REFORM, LIBERTY, JUSTICE AND LAW

Cuernavaca, October 26, 1915

Manuel Palafox

Secretary of Agriculture and Colonization

Otilio E. Montaño

Secretary of Public Education and Fine Arts

* * *

United Mexican States

Executive Council

RICARDO POZAS

"Juan the Chamula," 1952

The introduction to Pozas's text comes from Joseph and Henderson and explains the importance of the document to the game. While this document was published in 1952, decades after the events in this game, it is included here to provide a perspective of the Revolution that is otherwise missed in the political documents.

SOURCE: *Gilbert M. Joseph and Timothy J. Henderson, eds.,* The Mexico Reader: History, Culture, Politics, *(Durham, NC: Duke University Press, 2002), pp. 387–397.*

Few accounts of the revolution better illustrate its intensely factionalized nature and the shallowness of the allegiances of common footsoldiers than the following "ethnological re-creation" of the life of a Chamula Indian by Ricardo Pozas, one of Mexico's most distinguished anthropologists. Pozas based his account on fieldwork conducted in the 1940s and 1950s among the Chamulas of Chiapas, a group of about sixteen thousand people who spoke the Tzotzil Maya language and who lived in rural settlements in the highlands around the regional center of San Cristobal de las Casas. Even today many Chamulas live principally from subsistence farming, supplemented by contract labor on lowland coffee plantations. They practice a culture that still owes much to pre-Columbian traditions.

The principal character in this account, Juan Perez Jolote, first leaves home in order to escape the wrath of his abusive father. He is clearly puzzled by the world outside his village and has little understanding of the meaning of revolution or aims of the various factions he fights for. In short order, however, the revolution revamps his identity and redirects his fortunes.

They were looking for people to work on a farm called La Flor. I contracted to go, and when I got to La Flor the patron told me: "I'm going to give you your meals and you'll sleep there next to the henhouse, so you can scare away the animals that try to steal the chickens at night." I slept there, and woke up when I heard a noise. Then I shouted so that the animals would run away. I worked at La Flor for about three months, and got to know three men from Comitan who had women with them to cook their meals. One of them asked me, "Are you going to keep on working here, Jose?" "Yes," I said. "Then don't eat over there in the kitchen. You better eat here with my woman," he said. ⋆ ⋆ ⋆

The men from Comitan used to get drunk every payday. When they were drunk they exchanged their women among themselves, but the next day they were jealous.

"You, you cabron!" one of them said. "You're screwing my wife."

"And you're screwing mine."

Then the fight began:

"Why don't we ask Jose Perez if it isn't true?"

"He doesn't drink, and anyway I saw you, cabron." * * *

They asked me if it was true.

"I don't know * * * I don't sleep here, so I don't see what happens at night." * * *

"You mean you don't want to tell us."

That was right. I didn't want to tell them because I knew what would happen, but I'd seen the whole thing and the woman who cooked for me told me about it in the morning.

They fought with their machetes. The women and I were frightened and we just watched them. One of them was killed, and the other two and the three women ran way.

I didn't know what to do. "If I run way," I thought, "they'll say I killed him." So I stayed there, watching the blood run out of his wounds.

As soon as they knew that a man from Comitan had been killed, they went to tell the authorities in Mapa. The police came out to the farm to find out what happened, and they saw me there near the corpse.

"Who killed him?"

"I don't know"

"What do you mean, you don't know! You were right here with the rest of them. If you don't tell us we'll have to take you in."

"I don't know" I said. And without another word they fastened my hands with a rope and tied me a post. * * *

They took the dead man way, and they took me to Mapa as a prisoner and I slept there in the jail.

Early the next morning we went on to Tapachula and they put me in the jail there. I was a prisoner for eleven months and two weeks. I wove palm leaves and they paid me one centavo for each armful. A man from San Cristobal named Procopio de la Rosa advised me not to sell the woven palm but to make sombreros out of it. "If you weave five armfuls, that's only five centavos. But if you'll make the brims of the sombreros I'll pay you three centavos apiece." I could finish two brims a day, and I earned six centavos. * * *

Later on, Don Procopio told me, "I'm going to give you your palm from now on, so you can work on account." He was the one who sold the palm to everybody. He delivered the finished sombreros by the dozen to be sold outside. Then he taught me how to make sombreros that sold for a peso and a half. * * * I didn't suffer in jail because I learned how to make all these things. * * *

When they first put me in jail I could understand Spanish well enough but I couldn't pronounce the words. I learned how to make things by watching because there wasn't anybody who knew how to speak my language, and little by little I began to speak Spanish.

While I was in jail we learned that the Government [Huerta's] was in danger of losing because they killed the President [Madero]. It was looking for people for the army so it could defend itself. Two prisoners wrote letter to the Government, and it told them if they wanted to be soldiers they could put in a request. The rest of us didn't say anything, because we didn't know if we wanted to be soldiers or not, but the government didn't accept just the two who wrote letters, it accepted everybody in the jail. Even the invalids got out along with the others.

The soldiers came for us at four in the morning, and the man in charge said, "All prisoners get their belongings together. You're all going to be free." But they took us to the station and put us into a boxcar, the kind that's used for cattle and bananas. The soldiers guarded us on all sides, and two of them stood at the door of the car, poking us with their pistols and saying, "Come on, get in."

I brought five new sombreros along with me to sell on the way. We arrived at San Jeronimo and they took us off the train and put us in a barracks. They took my sombreros away from me to start a fire so they could make coffee. They gave a close haircut to everyone who had long hair. They took our extra clothing away if we had any, and gave us coats with long sleeves.

The next day we went on toward Mexico City. I could hear them naming the different places we passed: Orizaba, Puebla. * * * We arrived at San Antonio, where there was firewood. They took us out of the cars to rest and built a fire so we could warm ourselves. It was the season when the corn is ripe. After we ate, they put us back in the cars and we went on until we reached the Mexico City station. They took us to the army post called La Canoa, and the next day they signed us up. * * *

They took us to a different barracks and made us take off all our clothes. Then they examined us. Those who had ringworm * * * weren't any use as soldiers because the Government didn't want them. It also didn't want anyone with boils or tumors. They only ones they kept were the ones with clean skins, and since I've always had a clean skin, without any sores, they didn't let me go free.

They began to pay wages to those of us who were left: twenty-five centavos a day and our meals. After a few days they gave each of us a pair of huaraches, and then a pair of shoes. Later they gave us kepis, and Mausers with wooden bullets, and now that we were in uniform they paid us fifty centavos a day and our meals.

The training started at four in the morning. The corporals, sergeants, lieutenants, and captains made us form ranks and learn how to march. At six o'clock we all drank coffee. There were a hundred and twenty-five of us, and we were from many different villages because there's a jail every village. They called us the 89th Battalion.

A few days later they taught us how to handle our guns and how to shoot. We formed ranks, some of us in front and the rest behind, and when they shouted the command we had to throw ourselves flat on the ground. At other times they ordered some of us to kneel and the others to remain standing. They lined up some of our own men in front of us, and said, "This is the enemy. We're going to practice what you'll have to do in battle. Ready! Aim! Fire!" We pulled the triggers, there was a loud noise, and the little pieces of soft wood popped out of the Mausers. We were training, so the bullets weren't real. * * *

Finally they gave us real bullets, fifty to each man, and we began to earn a peso a day. After they gave us the real bullets we didn't fire any more, we just practiced the way they taught us before.

A little later we went out to fight Carranza. Before we left, a priest came to the post and they told us to form ranks. He stood up on a chair, we all knelt down, and he said, "Well, men, I'm here to tell you that we're going into battle tomorrow or the day after, because the enemy is getting close. When you're out there fighting, I don't want you to mention the devil or the demons. I just want you to repeat day and night the words I'm going to tell you: *Long live the Virgin of Guadalupe!* Because she's the patron saint of every Mexican, the Queen of Mexico, and she'll protect us against our enemies when we go into battle."

We left the next day. They loaded us into boxcars with our weapons, and told us we were going to Aquascalientes. We could hear artillery along the way, and when we looked out through the cracks we could see people running across the mountains. My comrades said, "It's going to be wonderful!" Some of them had guitars with them, and they played and sang because they were so happy.

We stopped in Aquascalientes, and then went on to Zacatecas. Then we just stayed there, because the train couldn't go any farther. They took us out of the cars and put us in a big house that was like a fort. We stayed there for several days. They got us up at four o'clock every morning and gave us a drink of aguardiente with gunpowder in it, to make us brave, and then gave us our breakfast. Those that had women with them were contented, they laughed and sang and played their guitars. "We're doing all right," they said, "and tomorrow we're going to the fiesta."

The time came to go out to fight. There was a mountain near Zacatecas with a little hill in front of it, and the artillery faced the mountain. The artillerymen dug a cave near their guns and cooked their meals in it.

At nine in the morning we crossed a wide field to climb up the mountain, and while we were crossing it we heard the General shout, "Spread out!" The bugle blew and we scattered across the field. The enemy was up there on the top of the mountain because the bullets came down at us from above. We started to shoot too, but since we couldn't see where they were, and they could get a good aim at us, a lot of our men were killed. The Artillery was firing at the mountains, and some other soldiers ran forward and climbed up the mountain from the side, and the enemy retreated a little.

That night we had to bring in the wounded, without even having drunk any water all day. Once of them said to me, "Take me back to the artillery positions. I can't walk. And bring my Mauser. "I got him to the artillery. My throat began to hurt, and when I tried to drink some water it wouldn't go down. I couldn't eat anything, either, and I was deaf from the noise of the cannons.

They sent me to the post at Zacatecas, and then to Aquascalientes. I was in the hospital there for two days, and on the third day I was sent to the hospital in Mexico City, where I almost died from my earaches. First blood came out, then pus. I was in the hospital for several months, because they wouldn't let me leave until I was well again.

The people who were taking care of us began to say, "Who knows what'll happen to us, because they're going to come here to eat people, and we don't know what kind of people they like to eat."

The sick and wounded began to cry because they couldn't leave the hospital and run away, and those others were going to eat them. We heard it was the Carrancistas that were eating people.

A little later Carranza entered Mexico City. We could hear his troops go by in the street, shooting off their guns and shouting: "Long live Venustiano Carranza! Down with Victoriano Huerta! Death to Francisco Villa! Death to Emiliano Zapata!" They only cheered for Carranza. And we just looked at each other, there in the hospital, without being able to leave.

The next day the Carrancistas came to the hospital to visit the sick and wounded. They arrived with their officers, and after greeting us they asked, "How are you? What happened to you? Are you getting better? We're all friends now, that's why we've come to see you."

The men that had been crying spoke first: "They told us the Carrancistas eat people."

"What? * * * No, we're not cannibals."

"Then it isn't true that you're going to eat us?"

"Of course not!"

So the sick and wounded were happy. "Here's two pesos," the Carrancistas said, "and stop being afraid." They gave two pesos to each one of us.

I stayed in the hospital until I was cured. As soon as they let me go I went to Puebla and worked as a mason's helper, carrying lime and bricks. I also worked for some butchers, bringing the goats and sheep in from the haciendas to be slaughtered. They gave me my meals and a place to sleep, but they didn't pay me anything.

After two weeks I left Puebla and walked to Tehuacan de las Granadas. A butcher let me live in his house there. I'd already worked for butchers in Puebla, so I knew they were good people. I worked for butchers in Puebla, so I knew they were good people. I worked for him for five months.

The butcher's father used to go to the butcher shop at two in the morning to cut up the meat, and he always took me with him because he was deaf. When we went past the army post he couldn't hear the guard shout, "Who goes there!" and he was afraid they'd shoot him if he didn't answer. I had to answer; "Carranza!" and they'd let us go past without stopping us. * * *

All they gave me was my clothing and my meals. I wanted to earn some money, so I went to the army post to talk with the captain. I said: "Captain, sir, I'd like to be a soldier."

"Good, Good! What's your name?"

"Jose Perez."

They gave me a shirt, a pair of trousers, and a kepis, and paid me a peso and half.

When the old [deaf] ditcher found out I was a soldier, he came looking for me the next day. "Don't take him away from me," he begged the captain, "because I need him to help me. I've been good to him, too * * * I don't even criticize him. Ask him yourself."

"Is that true?" the captain asked me.

"Yes," I said. "I only left because I wanted to earn some money, but he's good to me and gives me food and clothing."

"Well, if he feeds you and clothes you and doesn't hit you or anything, you ought to go back with him. What more do you want? Good food, good clothes * * * he's practically your father. You've got a home now. We don't know when we'll be called out to fight. Maybe we'll all be killed. I feel sorry for the old man because he was crying when he came in here. Go back home with him, hombre." The captain gave me five pesos, and I went back with the deaf man.

But I only stayed in him house another week, because one day I met a woman who lived with one of my friends while we were fighting for Victoriano Huerta. She saw me in the street and said, "Jose, it's you! What are you doing here?"

"I'm just living here. Where's Daví?"

"He was killed in the battle. I'm going back home. I'll take you with me if you want. I've got enough money to pay your fare."

I went with her to Oaxaca. She told me she was going to stop there and not go any farther, but she told me I could get home from there without any trouble. We arrived at Oaxaca in the train and she took me to her house to spend the night.

I left the next morning, to go home. I started asking the way to San Cristobal de las Casas, but nobody could tell me. I must have asked a hundred people at least, but they all told me they didn't know. Finally I got tired of walking around the city, so I went to the army post to sign up. They asked me my name and wrote it down, and I was a Carrancista again.

After I'd been in Oaxaca for about a week they sent all the soldiers in the post to Mexico City, and I had to go with them. First they sent us out to Cordoba, and then to a little village where the Zapatistas had come in to rob the houses. We stayed there for six months, guarding the village, and that's where I first had a woman.

They assigned me to a lieutenant, and when I was off duty I went to the plaza to drink pulque. It was sold by an old woman with white hair, and one day she asked me, "Do you have a woman?"

"No, senora, I don't."

"Then why don't you find one? This village is full of pretty girls."

"I know * * * but I don't know what to say to them."

"But you do want a woman?"

"Yes."

"And you've never had one?"

"No, senora, not yet."

"Let's go to my house."

"Good, let's go."

She gathered her things and took me to her house. She gave me something to eat, and after we finished eating she led me to her bed.

I went back to the barracks after we were all done. "Now that you know where my house is, you can come here whenever you want." ⋆ ⋆ ⋆

She used to come to the post when she wanted me to go home with her. She'd ask the maid who worked in the kitchen, "Is Jose in?"

"I don't know. Go in and look for him."

She'd go in and as soon as I noticed her I'd raise my hand to stop her, so she wouldn't speak to me in front of my friends. I was ashamed to have them see how old she was. I'd get up and go over to speak to her, and she'd say, "I'll be waiting for you tonight." And at night I'd go there.

At the end of six months they sent us to another village. The old woman who sold pulque stayed at home.

We went back to Cordoba and stayed there for a month, and then we went to Pachuca and stayed for two months. Next they sent us to Real del Monte, but we were only there for twenty days because the weather was too cold for us. We returned to Pachuca again and went out to another village, where the Villistas attacked us.

They entered the village at daybreak. We were all asleep, even the sentry, when the sound of gunfire woke us up. We all ran out and they started shooting at us. We had sixty-five men. Some of them were killed, some ran away, and twenty-five of us were taken prisoner by the General Villa. They asked us why we'd become Carrancistas, and I said: "The Huertistas made us go with them, and when Carranza started winning we had to change sides."

"Where are you from?"

"I'm a Chamula."

The man who was questioning me, a lieutenant, turned to General Almazan and said, "These poor men were forced into service."

An old man with a big mustache said: "Well, what do they want to do now?"

I said, "I just want to be on your side."

"What about the rest of you?" they asked.

"Just what our friend said, to be on your side."

"All right, but if you have any tricks we'll shoot you."

"No, senor, we're telling you the truth."

"We'll see about that. We're going to send you straight into battle, to find out if you're really men."

They signed us up and gave us weapons and five pesos each, and that made us Villistas. ⋆ ⋆ ⋆

The officers paid us all the money that they had with them so we could buy what we needed, and when it ran out they began paying us with stamped slips of paper. These slips were only good in the village itself, and nobody else would accept them because they weren't worth anything. The leaders kept saying, "The money will get here in a day or two," but finally there wasn't anything left to eat in the village, and we couldn't buy anything outside because they wouldn't take the stamped slips.

General Almazan got us all together, private and lieutenants and captains, and told us: "The Carrancistas have captured all the villages and haciendas. I'm leaving, because there aren't any more villages we can stay in. You can leave too, or stay here. Or if you want to join up with the Carranza forces in Tehuacan, you can do that."

We decided to go to Tehuacan, and left the village at night. We traveled across the mountains all night long, and when it was daylight we got some sleep and let the animals graze. The next night we started out again. We came to a hacienda near Tehuacan, and the leaders sent a note to the Carrancistas who were in the village. The note said that we wanted to join them, that we were a hundred and fifty Villistas who wanted to go over to Carranza. General Almazan had accomplished us as far as the hacienda, but when the messenger came back from Tehuacan with the answer, the General said to us: "Go ahead and give yourselves up, but I'm not going with you. If I did, they'd probably wring my neck." He left us that night, and in the morning we went on toward the village.

The Carrancistas came out to meet us, and we ran into them about a league outside of Tehuacan. They all had their Mausers in their hands, aiming them at us, and we carried our own Mausers butt first to show we were surrendering. They marched us ahead of them to the barracks and took our rifles away from us at the gate, although they let us keep the rest of our things. Inside, they asked us where we'd been and we told them about the different places we stayed at.

The next day they got us together and said; "Now that you've surrendered, what do you want to do? Do you want to be Carrancistas? If you don't, we'll let you go free, so you can go home and farm your land."

I said, "I want to leave, I want to work in the fields."

"Where do you want to go?"

"To Veracruz," I said. Now that I could go free, I wanted to visit that town, and to be a free man, not a soldier.

"You can go there, you can take the train. It won't cost you anything."

They gave me my ticket and twenty-five pesos, and above all they gave me my freedom…

I worked [in Veracruz] for nine months. * * * When I got tired of working there I went to a different farm called San Cristobal, where I worked for three months in the cornfields. I didn't like it there either, so I came back home. * * *

I went into the house and greeted my father, but he didn't recognize me. I'd almost forgotten how to speak Tzotzil, and he couldn't understand what I was saying. He asked me who I was and where I came from.

"You still don't know me? I'm Juan!"

"What? ＊ ＊ ＊ You're still alive! But if you're Juan, where have you been? ＊ ＊ ＊ I went to the farm twice looking for you."

"I left the farm and went to Mexico City to be a soldier." I was kneeling down as I said this.

"Did you really become a soldier?"

"Yes, papacito."

"Well, I'll be damned! But how come you didn't get killed?"

"Because God took care of me."

Then he called my mother: "Come here and see your son Juan! The cabron has come back to life!"…

And I stayed here, I lived in my own village again. The first night I woke up when my father started blowing on the embers of the cooking fire. I was afraid he'd come over and wake me up by kicking me. But he didn't because I was a man now!

"Corrido of Tomochic"

This corrido celebrates the resistance of the Tomochitecos (people of Tomochic) against the Mexican government in December 1891. They declared that only God had authority over them. In many ways they fought the "progress" that Porfirio Díaz and the científicos were working to bring to Mexico. The Tomochitecos continued to route federal soldiers for almost a year. The embarrassment was such that when the government finally defeated them, they executed the final six survivors. As is called out in the song, the Tomochitecos were devotees of Teresa Urrea, also known as the Saint of Cabora, venerated by both Yaqui and Mayo natives during a period of intense conflict between the native groups and the Mexican and American governments. Because of the Tomochiteco attempt to consult with her and their belief in her healing abilities, she was accused of supporting them and exiled to the United States.

This ballad provides a perspective of the events and of the diversity of religious beliefs in Mexico. While local communities believed in Santa Teresa Urrea, she was not recognized by the Catholic Church. As the song spread through the communities, it continually reminded people of the Tomochitecos' ability to resist the government.

SOURCE: *Chris Frazer, ed. and trans.,* Competing Voices from the Mexican Revolution *(Santa Barbara, CA, and Denver, CO: Greenwood Press, 2010), pp. 6–7.*

Señores, keep in mind that I am going to sing
the Corrido of Tomochic, and it's a popular song.

The government decided to finish the Tomochis.
But day and night—it was a fight for the 11th and the Ninth Battalions.

Rangel took the summit with five hundred men
Oh! They were not well-prepared, and they soon met their match.

The Tomochis starting shooting from the hill of the Cross;
those ragged Tomochis were ready to fight.

Cruz Chavez told the soldiers: "It is not easy baldies,
whatever you think; we are ready for the 11th and Ninth Battalion."

The Tomochis were brave; they knew how to die in the sun.
They defied deadly shrapnel, and defended their land and their homes.

Eight Tomochis were brave came out and formed pairs, two by two.
They shouted to the baldies: "Long live the power of God!"

How fine the soldiers look, with a general at their side.
But Cruz Chavez cried out: "We'll die with the 11th and Ninth Battalion."

Love for Santa Teresita of Cabora, rang out in Cruz Chavez's voice.
But no baldies were inspired to fight and die with honor.

A brave young Tomochi cried out: "The holy Mother inspires me;
She is right here beside me as I fight Don Lorenzo Torres."

In Cabora is grace; in Tomochic, power. But the arrogant Government
had no understanding, so it sent the 11th and Ninth Battalions.

Now the history has been written of this fierce, bloody war;
the baldies fell dead like flies defending their governor.

Women in the church tower were also sharpshooters;
they shed their own blood as they fought for their freedom.

But the Tomochis were done for the baldies died too.
Yet God's power lives on as the Supreme Good.

The Tomochis were brave; they knew how to die in the sun.
They defied deadly shrapnel and defended their homes and their land.

JOSÉ MUÑOZ COTA

"Corrido of the Meeting between Zapata and Madero"

This corrido commemorates the meeting between Zapata and Madero after the defeat of Porfirio Díaz. The meeting occurred in Mexico City, not Cuautla as the song claims. Written by a Zapatista, the ballad shows the integrity of Zapata and acknowledges that Madero's actions were, at least initially, viewed with respect by the Zapatistas. However, it also shows that Madero did not understand the Zapatistas desires and convictions.

SOURCE: *Chris Frazer, ed. and trans.,* Competing Voices from the Mexican Revolution *(Santa Barbara, CA and Denver, CO: Greenwood Press, 2010), pp. 53–55.*

On June 8, 1911, Madero, the chief of the rebellion
against the dictatorship came to the town of Cuautla.

On that morning Zapata had a meeting with Madero.
Madero was from the North; Zapata was from the South.

We know about their meeting, and we know what they said
for Gildardo Magana is the witness who told us.

Madero was a good man who loved the revolution.
He was a man of conviction, but he lost our trust.

They spoke of Figueroa and Zapata accused him of
trying to betray him during the attack on Jojutla.

But Madero patiently asked that Zapata submit;
Zapata replies: "Only time will tell who is right."

But Madero insisted: "The Revolution is over
for we have defeated Porfirio Diaz."

"So disband the people who fought at your side.
For peace is assured now; that's my point of view."

Zapata was disciplined when he answered Madero:
"I am sure in my heart that would be a mistake,

"until we get what we want"; the General insisted.
"the return of our lands, just as you promised.

"The Indian rebelled for nothing but the land * * *
to take back the lands the hecendados usurped."

Zapata was Chief of the South, the apostle of conviction.
He was the voice of the land, the voice of liberation.

The good apostle Madero, the man who dreamed, who
just counseled patience and faith in law and order.

But Zapata the ranchero had learned to be weary.
He saw danger for Madero, and so he insisted:

"I don't think that the federals will support you Senor;
So take every precaution against their betrayal."

Madero replied: "You must disband your troops,
for I already agreed in the treaty I signed."

Magana told us that Zapata stood up
with his carbine in hand—his constant companion.

He stood before Madero and demanded his watch,
and gave him a lesson that astonished us all:

"if I have my carbine, I can steal your watch,
but if you have a weapon the next time we meet,

"would you take it back, Senor Madero?" he asked.
"Not only that," said Madero, "but with indemnity too."

"Well, that's what we want," Zapata concluded.
"Morelos want the land the hacendados have stolen.

"My armed campesinos, with respect but with strength
have told me to ask you for fair restitution."

Madero agreed this was righteous and promised once more
to fulfill the promise that he made in his Plan.

But he still hoped Zapata would surrender to a bribe,
so he offered a ranchito to Emiliano Zapata.

The Chief of the South could not hide his disgust,
so he slapped his carbine and indignantly replied:

"I beg your pardon, Senor Madero,
but I didn't rebel to be a landowner or a boss.

"I am fighting for justice for the miserable peon;
I won't abandon the people without winning their demand.

"And if we do not fulfill what we already promised,
they will rise up again in a new armed rebellion."

So Gildardo Magana, who fought with Zapata,
witnessed this meeting and told us the story.

"The Corrido of the Soldadera"

Women have been involved in battles in Mexico since before Spaniards arrived in 1492. As mentioned in the Corrido of Tomóchic, women fought alongside men. In contrast to the women fighters, this song acknowledges the place of women in the military encampments. While wars are regularly associated with male soldiers, women as fighters and as caretakers were present as well.

SOURCE: *Chris Frazer, ed. and trans.,* Competing Voices from the Mexican Revolution *(Santa Barbara, CA and Denver, CO: Greenwood Press, 2010), pp. 171–172.*

LA SOLDADERA (FEMALE VERSION)

I am a soldadera and I have my Juan; he is my first one and everyone knows it.
When he is drunk, everybody respects him: and when he is sober, they all imitate him.

As the Sergeant of the company, they keep him inside all day long.
They do not want him out on the street, since they do not want to guard him.

The Second Lieutenant told me one day, that I would be his assistant,
But what I will do in exchange I do not know, for he did not explain.

Since that day, night by night, I am happy to travel in the coaches,
for the captain and even the majors are very gallant and offer me flowers.

I make them happy because my Juan will someday be promoted to Captain.

In the trenches and the line of fire, I am the queen and I go there with courage.
I am soldadera and I have my Juan; he is my first one and everyone knows it.

LA SOLDADERA (MALE VERSION)

I have my Juana, my Juana comes with me, and the campaign is going to begin.
Your eyes will be my only shelter and they know how to kill the enemy.

My Juana, can you hear the trumpets; how they vibrantly call us together?
The manes of the horses are flying and prayers are filling my heart.

With pride, I will follow my flag and I assure you that I will succeed,
if cartridge belt is full and if my soldadera cheers me on.

If I go into the battle and if your sapper is killed,
recover my soul, look for my ribbon, while you killed the wicked enemy.

But when my victory has been decided and if my battalion has won,
look for my body and if I am alive, put your heart into my wound.

But if the bullets are accurate, just my soul and courage will remain.
Make some skirts or whatever you want with the flags of the invader.

And when victory is determined, afterwards, do what you want.
Make some earrings with their medals, and see if they give you pleasure.

"Corrido de la Cucaracha"

The recognizable song "La Cucaracha" dates to this time period. Like many corridos, it has multiple versions, one of which was printed in 1915 with engravings by José Guadalupe Posada (shown here). Often Posada's artwork was recycled in multiple contexts, with or without his permission, such as the case here. To enlarge the image, see www.loc.gov/pictures/item/99615844.

SOURCE: *Caroline and Erwin Swann collection of caricature and cartoon, U.S. Library of Congress*

CORRIDO DE LA CUCARACHA

QUE NO HA SALIDO A PASEAR,
PORQUE NO TIENE

CARTONCITOS

QUE GASTAR.

La Cucaracha, la Cucaracha,
ya no quiere caminar
porque no tiene, porque no tiene
dinero para gastar.
  Pobre de la Cucaracha,
se queja de corazón,
de no usar ropa planchada
por la escaces del carbón.
  La ropa sin almidón,
se pone todos los días
y sin esas boberías
se me figura melón
  La Cucaracha ya suprimió
el bisteff y la remolacha,
por lo caro de la carne;
¡pobre de la Cucaracha!
  Ahora, come en salada,
verdolaga y quintonil,
porque no tiene dinero
para comprar metlapil.
  También suprimió el candil
de petróleo que tenía,
y todo va suprimiendo
por la horrible carestía.
  Que fea te vez Cucaracha,
con tu enagua desaguada
y ántes, ¡ay! qué bonita
me parecías una ada
  La Cucaracha en cuestión
cargaba muy buena plata,
ahora con tanto cartón
anda bailando en la reata.
  Se queja la Cucaracha,
de lo caro del jabón.
ue no encuentra combustible
  toda la población.
  a Cucaracha antes era
  hacha simpaticona
  meneaba la cadera,
como cualquiera española.
  Era la gran vivandera
y mujer de corazón,
tenía pimienta y canela
y por ning uno ilusión.

Gastaba muchos meneos,
cuando bailaba boleros,
y era muy aficionada
al amor de los toreros.
  Muchas veces á la calle,
salía con grande mantón
y los pollos de la esquina,
le decían: adios corazón.

IMPRENTA
de Antonio Vanegas Arroyo,
Segunda Sta. Teresa 40.
1915.

  A los toros no faltaba
en la lumbrera de Sol,
y ahora no va ni á la esquina
por no tener ni un cartón.
  Yo sé que á la Villa fué,
á jugar á la partida
y tanto alargó la mano,
que encontró la olla podrida.
  Pero vá al Cinematógrafo,
es donde dan más barato
y allí está la Cucaracha,
hasta arrita como gato.
  Pobre de la Cucaracha,
en qué triste situación
se encuentra esa muchacha,
pues su Juan se fué al Pantéon.
  La Cucaracha ya no es,
la antigua mocetona,
ahora se ve muy flaca
vieja, viehoca y pelona.
  Antes tan sólo á Gambrinus,
se le miraba llegar
y ahora con esta miseria,
á la piquera va á dar.
  Ya se acabó ese tiempo,
Cucarachita mía,
en que gastábamos pesos
en cualquiera pulquería.
  ¿Qué te pasó Cucaracha
que estás bebiendo agua pura?
bebe pulque colorado
y si no, á la sepultura.
  No llores Cucarachita,
que ya la carne bajó,
y muy pronto ya diremos
la miseria se acabó.
  Y me vengo á despedir
Cucaracha, Cucaracha,
que voy pronto á visitar
á mi adorada muchacha.
  Adios Cucaracha mía,
te dejo mi corazón
trátalo con cariño
haslo por compasión.

EMILIO RABASA

"The Election," 1912

Writing after the defeat of Porfirio Díaz, Rabasa calls into question the idea of universal suffrage. Looking at both U.S. and Mexican democracy, he points to problems in both historically. Without directly calling out Madero, he questions Madero's election because of the rebellion against Díaz.

SOURCE: *José Antoniom Aguilar Rivera, ed., Janet M. Burke and Ted Humphrey, trans.,* Liberty in Mexico: Writings on Liberalism from the Early Republican Period to the Second Half of the Twentieth Century *(Indianapolis, IN: Liberty Fund, 2012), pp. 468–485.*

When an adolescent first becomes aware of what popular election is and the goal it has, the idea presents itself to his spirit in its simplest form; it is like a revelation of justice that seduces him and wins over his will. The idea is annoying mainly because of its simplicity, the simplicity of the immaculate theory. On the eve of the election, each citizen reflects on the individual most suitable for the position with which the election is concerned, rejects some, puts other aside, chooses, and classifies until fixing his preference on that one who combines the greatest talents and offers the most because of his civic and private virtues. How could one not do it in this way, when good judgment affects his own interest and error his own liability? When the hour of action arrives, the citizens file in before the ballot box, depositing their ballots; the inspectors read and count; the president makes the numbers known and proclaims the one elected by the people. Nothing more just, nothing more natural, nothing more simple.

Although this idea assumes a great number of virtues in practice, much greater still is the number its consequences assume. The innocence of the adolescent, developing the theory of government emanating from the people from the theory of election, believes that each elected person, already virtuous in himself, feels the force of public opinion, simultaneously his strength and his menace, and he will be unable to be less than a zealous guardian of general interests and an active promoter of the common good. The man invested with the dignity that election confers on him and elevated by the delegation of popular power, which is the only legitimate power, divests himself of common passions, gets inspiration from justice, forgets or does not know from the beginning who gave him their vote, who rejected him, and, with only the fulfillment of duty and the subordination of his acts to the laws, he satisfies the broadest program of good in the government and equity in the administration. This it has to be; but if it were not thus, if, through an error very remote from the electors, the one designated by the majority should disappoint public confidence, the force of opinion or the action of the law put into practice will dismiss him from the post to replace him with another more worthy.

It is not an innovation that has need of proof that, as the peoples are cultured, they resemble children more in their way of thinking. Between them they have in common a simple spirit without malice that, in good faith, falls into error and innocently produces failure in the individual and catastrophes in the peoples. Uniformity, for which an embryonic logic is sufficient, seems typical of the state of nature; children conjugate all the verbs as regular, and in new peoples, all political ideas are turned into syllogisms. The former would take us, if we would permit it, to the most solid *Esperanto*, as the latter have gone, whenever they have been able to dominate, to the most disastrous Jacobinism.

The way of conceiving of an election and calculating its consequences that we have shown in the adolescent is also the way of our people, the way of the limited part of the nation capable of perceiving its electoral right, if we deduct from it the very scant number of citizens with specific education who reflect on the problems of our political existence. The summary of this idea is contained in two entirely false suppositions: the first, that popular election is easily realizable; the second, that the actual election will instill order in the whole political organism. And if the number of those who, because exceptional, do not accept the first is very small to begin with, there are still among them many who believe in the extraordinary virtue of the actual election.

The common conception to which we first alluded produces, as a great error, serious consequences. If there is the conviction that citizens will carry out the election with order, with disinterest, and even with wisdom if only the liberty of suffrage is not obstructed, and that such an election certainly produces the public good, every intervention that obstructs that liberty must correctly be considered a criminal offense that has neither extenuations nor other explanation than the despotic egoism of whoever has the elements of force at his disposal. When, from a false premise, a logical inference is made, the legitimacy of the consequence gives to this consequence glints of truth sufficient to dazzle the common people, and the common people are the great majority. Any badly thought out and poorly written newspaper, generally a work of noxious tendencies, makes use of the logic of the consequences applied to principles invoked from the fundamental law in order to acquire, through the voice of anonymous writers on public affairs, because little known, greater prestige among the masses than the most sensible government with the greater proven patriotism. But as the false premise is nothing less than a constitutional precept that bases a right in the democratic system established by the Constitution, the accusation appear legally reasonable, however much satisfying them might bring the country to greater danger.

This situation causes the perpetual conflict between popular aspiration and the action of governments, which must be guided by needs rather than principles, because principles do not obey needs, nor were they inspired by the realities that in the end dominate in spite of all the chimeras. All revolts have invoked electoral right, seeking to base their action in the propensities of the masses and to cause the men in power to lose prestige; but all revolts, in becoming government, have responded to the supreme need for stability and have had to thwart the aspiration of the people, which, realized, would make national life impossible. As long as the people have the right to do what the government has the need to resist, the country will remain in a state of latent revolution, capable of showing itself in any moment of weakness in the organism.

It is useless to attempt the reconciliation of two contradictory extremes. For this reason all effort dedicated to calming the public conscience is wasted, that is to say, all effort to make the only true peace neither by election nor by repression. If, in Mexico, should there be an election realized by universal suffrage, the first concern of the government emanating from it (if it can endure) would be to prevent such a phenomenon from repeating itself, for universal suffrage is necessarily the enemy of all established government, the disorganizer of every ordered mechanism, because of a need that springs from the articles of our Constitution that created the incompatibility. As for repression, it can make peace but not constitute it, because something can be constituted even on a movable sediment provided it is permanent, and repression is a condition but not a substance, and this condition is, if one permits the image, the troubled result of two variable forces.

All the conservative elements of a society are on the side of the government that ensures order because they live from order; they prefer authority to the exercise of rights that, at most, would lead them to the tranquility they now enjoy without the need of securing it or putting it in danger. But the conservative elements, which are always found in the highest strata of the people, if they are excellent with respect to passivity and resistance, they are less than useless in the activity of political struggles, in which they have much to lose end little or nothing to gain. So general is this truth that, among people as intensely democratic and as broadly institutional as the North American, the electoral corruption that perverts the parliament and decays the tribunals is owed principally to the abstention of the higher classes who feign disdain to hide their egoism.

On the other hand, the appeal to right and to absolute truths, which are held out as ideals to arouse the people, move and exalt the conscientious majority, which lives on aspirations because the realities of existence make the impatient ones incline toward a new condition that always assumes better.

Here one discovers a new unhappiness: the social field is divided into two parts that should have the same interests and that do not collide in well-constituted countries, at least regarding the general idea of suffrage as a foundation for the stability of the nation. The remedy consists of making of the election not a threat to the order, but rather the foundation of security. In this way the conservative elements and those who proclaim the right will have a common interest in guaranteeing the suffrage. And as for the governments, they will have relief from duties when, proceeding from the election, they know that, in the popular suffrage, they find the release from many responsibilities and, in the strength of the parties, a solid foundation of support.

II

Far from being easy and simple, the electoral act is the most difficult step for peoples ruled by a system more or less democratic, or that aspires to that government. The honest and simple election we have assumed in the preceding section is impossible in any society, because in any human social unit, great or small, there are distinct interests that soon become antagonistic, fight to prevail, and come inevitably to dispute and struggle. When there are no opposing ideas of government, the interests that act are, at least, tendencies to put authority in favorable hands, and, lacking parties of programs, one arrives at parties of persons, which are fruitless for the good. The struggle of opposing interests does not occur without winning over partisans, convincing, seducing, imposing, and bribing, that is to say, denying to as many as it can the absolute and paradisiacal liberty pure theory gives them. Among the sought after, some resist because they have personal ideas, which are blank ballots in the dispute; others yield; the timid hide; the arrogant abstain; and the few who initiated or took the active and effective part of the movement have thus designed the political parties, although only in a temporary and transitory way. When the repetition of successive electoral events and the results of the government they establish characterize the ideas of both sides and define the limits of their propensities; when, in addition, the directing groups classify themselves and acquire a genuine individuality, each faction is a system and each system an organized party. Having arrived at this point, the ideal liberty of the citizen in the election is reduced practically to the liberty of choosing the party in which he would like to register and to whom he has to submit himself. He preserves the right to vote, but he has lost the right to choose.

The creation of parties is a necessity that arises from the nature of things; it is not an invention of ingenuity, but rather a natural and inevitable product of electoral liberty. For this reason, to invent political parties that are simply electoral, to arrive through them at the liberty of elections, is to claim that nature inverts its processes, and nature does not lend itself to such inversions. If the general principle that necessity creates the organ can still be doubtful, it is not doubtful that there is absurdity in creating the organ to produce the necessity for the function. The invention of the railroad would be impossible if commerce had not existed before; and in the social order, it is useless to create the Central American union, which, nonetheless, would be constituted spontaneously if Colombia or Mexico tried to absorb the five little republics by violence.

The works realized as a result of natural forces are impossible for human effort; the intervention of man is useful, in such cases, only to put natural forces in working condition. Thus, for example, if an elevated temperature is required for two bodies to combine chemically, it is useless to *force* the phenomenon, but this phenomenon will be realized inevitably if the chemist intervenes, heating the flask to make possible the action of the mysterious forces of the atom.

To create a party for electoral purposes in Mexico is pure political *dilettantism*. What is important is making the election possible, suppressing disruptive causes that make impossible the spontaneous action of social forces. These social forces are responsible for producing the parties, creating their mechanism for them, giving them moment, and arming them for the efficacy of their functions. The disruptive causes are in the very Constitution that one is trying to carry out and not in the governments that have always been blamed.

The organization of political parties in democratic countries is very complicated, even in those countries where it seems simpler, only because the weft of the thread is not immediately apparent at a mere glance during the election; and it cannot be otherwise, given that all uniform action of multiple and complex elements suppose subordinations and disciplines that are not acquired except by processes, established rules, recognized sanctions, and they require unity that necessitates directors and even almost renouncing personal ideas.

No organization has been created without an evolutionary process and without it being urgent for the operational need of the parties. Let us take the most characteristic, the one we, for powerful reasons, incline to imitate—that of the North American parties.

It is known that, when Washington retired from public life, the great lines of the two national parties were marked out: the Federalist (today Republican) and the Republican (today Democrat); the first, with Hamilton, aspiring to federal unity to give strength to the nation; the second, with Jefferson, defending local independence against an absorption dangerous to the state and to the lofty right of the individual. It is also known that these two elements, representing the centripetal and centrifugal forces that create balance in the system and that so marvelously served to constitute the nation on its constitutional principles, have managed to blur their differences when the federal equilibrium, definitively established, made them disappear as if by automatic action; but the life of the two parties remained as an integral part of the institutions, and [the parties] are maintained, despite the evolution that has come to blend their dogmas, because of the simple need to renew the power, with the primarily personal aims of their followers, but in the end, and above all, as indispensable wheels of the political machinery. So necessary thus is the establishment of parties for constitutional life!

In 1796 Adams and Jefferson were candidates of both parties by a spontaneous sentiment that did not require express declarations. Four years later, the then Republicans, unanimous in the candidacy of Jefferson, were not unanimous with the respect to the designation of vice president, and to agree upon it, the deputies and senators of the party met in the first nominating caucus. This system continued without any great obstacle until 1816. In 1820 the nominating caucus of deputies and senators, which came under attack as usurpers of the right of the people, although it met, did not dare *nominate* a candidate; and in 1824 the one nominated came in third in the polls, which ended up discrediting the system. The system had to change, and so in 1828 the candidacy of Jackson was recommended by the Tennessee legislature and by meetings of the people, giving rise to the practice that, one year before the next election, conventions would meet, composed, for both parties, of delegations from the states; and for the same election, a convention of young people, accepting the nomination of the new national Republicans, adopted ten resolutions that constituted the first party *platform*. In 1836 only the Democratic party had a convention, but in 1840 there was a convention of both parties and the process was regularized. Bryce, whom we follow in this account, adds: "This precedent has been followed in all subsequent contests, so the national nominating conventions of the major parties are today as much a part of the regular political machinery as the rules the Constitution prescribes for the election. The establishment of the system coincides with (and represents) the complete social democratization of politics in the time of Jackson."

Forty-four years were consumed and twelve electoral exercises spent to arrive at the organization of the system that prepares each party and brings at the organization of the system that prepares each party and brings it into agreement for the campaign; this for a Saxon people who were preparing themselves for democratic life since before thinking about their independence. One sees, then, in what was just expounded, the complexity of the mechanism, and we have confined ourselves only to the presidential election, assuming the nominating convention created; but for the convention to meet, a mechanism prepared in each party is needed, and as, besides the deputies, the officials of the state, those of the district, those of the county, and those of the city must be elected, all of which put the mechanism into action very frequently, this requires having a permanent committee in every locality and a perfectly defined process, commonly practiced, better known even than the electoral laws of public order, so that the foundation of every election and, consequently, of every nomination of candidates might be the will of the primary electors.

The permanent committee convokes in each case the primary caucus, which in theory is composed of all citizens qualified to vote in the smallest electoral district. The primary caucus selects the candidates of the party as officials of their own locality and names delegates to gather in their delegation at larger electoral district conventions that include delegates of various primaries; this convention of secondary electors must designate candidates for higher posts of the state. But there is still more; the secondary convention has, at times, the task of naming new delegates to a third and higher convention, the national convention, which nominates candidates for the presidency and vice presidency of the Republic. Consider the complexity of this mechanism with all the details each stage requires, and bear in mind that the work begins in the meeting of the primary assembly, in which is discussed the right of each person in attendance to vote, his status as party member, his conduct toward the party in preceding elections, labors that provide occasion for the danger of fraud, bribery, the influence of the professionals to commence from the beginning, and the alienation of men of good faith who do not wish to expose their electoral district to such a game.

This system is not rigorously uniform in the entire country, but the local modifications do not alter its essence. It was not created, but rather was formed over a half century by experiences and efforts at accommodation. It is not an emanation of race, for all that the conditions of race helped its development, but rather a derivation of the vitality of parties. But the parties were started and strengthened because there was, from the beginning, respect for electoral right and a field of free action.

This is where we need to start. When there is confidence in electoral liberty, one will think about going to the polls; one will go to them. It will be necessary to report the misfortunes of the first attempts, which would not be trivial. The parties will be established in the American way because there will be no other, given out form of government, and the parties will rest on a mechanism as complex, difficult, and exposed to fraud and corruption as that of the United States. Democracy and federal government are very difficult. Their fundamental foundation, popular election, is very far from responding to the dream of purity of the adolescent and the childlike people.

III

When liberty in the election is ensured, in the sense that the public power does not restrict it with persecutions or obstruct it with critical influences, citizens go spontaneously to the polls, and soon with growing interest, but with the help of two conditions: that they have an awareness of the purpose of the event, and that they surmise a real value in their vote to the results of the election. Against both conditions, the Constitution established, in deference to French handbooks of democracy, universal suffrage and the indirect vote, the first because all the sons of the country have a right to take part in naming their mandataries, given that all are equal, and the second because Mexican citizens, with that universality, are incapable of electing well, and even of electing poorly.

The Drafting Committee of '57 had not committed such an error; with the good sense that always placed it so much above Congress as a whole, it ended the article that expressed the conditions of citizenship with this sentence: "From the year 1860 forward, besides the conditions expressed, knowing how to read and write will be required." But the deputy Peña y Ramírez "declares himself against the requirement of knowing how to read and write, because it does not seem to him to conform very well with *democratic principles*, and because *the indigent and needy classes are not to blame*, but rather the governments that have overseen public instruction with such carelessness." [Ponciano] Arriaga, to whom it seems that the continuous attacks of his own coreligionists since the meetings of the commission have cast doubt on his own criteria, responded "that he did not agree to answer the objections of the previous speaker," met with his fellow committee members, and this committee withdrew the final sentence of the article.[‡] Thus, so simply and briefly, without awareness of the seriousness of the resolution and by a unanimous vote, Congress closed the doors on possible democracy in the name of theoretical democracy. The government was guilty of the fact that indigents did not know how to read or write—that government, which in thirty-five years of independence, revolts, and penury, had not disseminated instruction to all parts—and the exclusion of the illiterate was unanimously seen by the deputies not as a measure of political order but rather as an article of penal code that punished ignorance unjustly.

Suffrage is not simply a right; it is a function, and it requires, as such, conditions of aptitude that society has the right to demand, because the function is nothing less than the primordial function for the ordered life of the Republic. It is as much a function as that of the inhabitant who serves as a juror, and who, within free institutions, has the right to be registered on the lists of judges of the people; but for the task to be given to him, he must meet certain conditions that ensure his suitability. The vote is not exercised to the detriment of the citizen, but rather at the expense of the destiny of the social body, and only an incomprehensible aberration of criteria and common sense can have placed the right of each man above the interests of the nation to oppress it, to stifle it, and to overwhelm it.

Universal suffrage produces in all countries the appearance of *disruptive elements*, that is to say, elements that obstruct the genuine expression of the conscious will in popular election. But in advanced countries, although such elements are harmful, they are dominated by the actively free population, which is the majority, or they cause, in the end, a tolerable misfortune. In the United States the black people and the new and poor immigrants are electors that are won by the bribes of political professionals or by the trickery of the jongleurs at the polls; they are a minority, but all American treatise writers still regard them as very dangerous. In England the influence of the great landowners creates a disruptive element in the tenants and farmers. In France the disruptive element is the workers in the great factories, through the intervention of the well-liked employers. But these subordinate groups do not generally manage to prevail in the election, and therefore they are simply disruptors. For us, seventy percent of illiterates is not a disruptive element in the expression of the will of the people, but rather destroyer of the election itself. If the cities of importance are excepted, which are very few, the rest of the country has electoral districts in which the great majority is unlettered, completely ignorant of the system of government; and it is not venturesome to maintain that, in a fifth of the total electoral districts the greater number of the so-called citizens belong to the indigenous race and do not have the slightest notions of the law, nation, president, Congress, or state. That there be the will of the people, which is the obligatory

---

[‡] Zarco, *Historia del congreso constituyente 7*, Session of September 1.

phrase of all known theorizers, each citizen must have will, and will is impossible without knowledge of the matter that must activate it.

In these conditions, seventy percent of the electors are nothing but material on hand for the violation of the will of the citizens who do actually have a will; and as those citizens are, because of an age-old flaw, submissive and obedient to an authority that commands them from close by, they have been, without exception of place or time, the force with which governments have served themselves in order to avoid free elections and make the election benefit their purposes. The weapon is a double-edged sword: when the central power employs it, it subdues the states; when the local government uses it, the federal government does not have the opinion of its partisans in the state to balance or bring down the aggressive force of the rebellious local power. The election has always been (with very rare exceptions that occur only in revolutionary periods) in the hands of the general government or those of the governor; but still today theories of democracy are invoked to sustain this shameful and lamentable condition; and one blames the power for using such a process, without considering that it is the least unfortunate process that can result from the absurd institution, given that it would be much worse for the country if greed agitators, always of a mean disposition, replaced the power in the privilege of making and unmaking governments, congresses, and tribunals.

The truly democratic principle of universal suffrage consists of extending the right to vote to the greatest number of members of the social body qualified by their fitness, and without making exclusions by reasons of birth, social or pecuniary condition, or any other that constitutes privilege. As there are no external signs that reveal electoral suitability, and laws must provide general rules, qualities have been sought that presume the probability of fitness, with not only knowledge of the act and its objective being considered within the condition of suitability, but also interest in carrying it out well. In France the general culture and the democratic spirit have extended the law up to the suffrage of all adult men; the limited number of illiterate people cannot appreciably influence the election. In England, which had elections during five centuries before arriving at the nineteenth century in its present democratic state, social status based on income is required; but this is so low that the United Kingdom has around seven million electors. In the United States the constitutional amendment that gave the vote to black people is still considered by the native and foreign treatise writers as a grave error that will threaten the great nation with very serious dangers, and has certainly imposed on southern politicians the need to resort to games of intrigue in order to deceive people of color and make a joke of their right to elect.

The requirement of knowing how to read and write does not guarantee knowledge of the electoral act, but it gives probabilities of it and abilities for acquiring it; and at any rate the electors are encouraged and the politicians animated by the assurance that the fight to exclude the ignorant masses, in whom only the action of force can work for carrying out their mechanical function, is possible. When free and possible elections give birth to parties, even if they might be at heart parties of personality, they will be charged with instructing the elector by means of publications that not only bring the elector up to date on the function and its objective, but also bring to him through their discussions, even if exaggerated and intense, information about their purposes, knowledge of their methods, and features of their men.

No restrictive quality more liberal than this to which we refer, given that it can be acquired with ease and in some months; and if we should not expect, in a people apathetic about the existence of political right, that each man would intend to learn to read and write out of eagerness to be an elector, it is not an illusion to suppose that interest in increasing the number of votes might induce the parties to increase the number of schools for adults in the regions where they have followers. The progress of instruction, which in the last twenty years has been notable, will increase the elector body from day to day and will expand the democratic system naturally and spontaneously. Thus it happened in England with the income requirement, much less dependent on the will of the individual: in the fifteenth century, the amount of required annual income was twenty shillings; but the increase of wealth in currency and the development of agriculture and industries lowered the value of money gradually and constantly, and the income of twenty shillings was becoming less significant and ended by being laughable, making the number of electors who were persons of independent means grow notably. English writers maintain that twenty shillings in the fifteenth century meant at that time as much as eighty pounds now.

The expression "universal suffrage" is one of the many hyperboles that political language has invented, to the detriment of the health of democracies; the word "universal" was chosen because another of greater breadth was lacking, and, nonetheless, in all countries, requirements for the elector are established that do not permit, for the suffrage, the less promising adjective of "general." Words like that, like "sovereignty" of the sate-divisions within the federal state, make people ill with hallucination, bring them to the disorderly trembling of delirium, and damage the discernment even of the good part of the directing class of the country. The suffrage that democratic principles imply is not *right-of-man* suffrage, attributed to all the inhabitants, nor to all the natives, or even to all men, or, finally, to all the adult men; but rather *political-right-and-function* suffrage, guarantee of the community, which must be extended to all those, and only those, who have sufficient knowledge of the function to perceive the responsibility of exercising it. To this condition, the restriction of knowing how to read and write, which has the advantage of opening the doors of current citizenship to all who would like to pass through them, approaches the possible; this is not exclude anyone or to establish a suffrage less universal than that of the most democratic peoples.

The preceding arguments will seem pointless, if they are not seen as foolish, to anyone who might be a stranger to the way our political ideas develop. It will seem unbelievable that it is necessary to discuss exclusion from the polls of men who are, because of their ignorance, as incapable of voting as crazy people and idiots; of men who have not entered into the community of conscious life; for whom there is no epoch; who have no sense of evolution at all, whether or not the government is at fault; that there are, among those, entire peoples who, not knowing the national language, have not yet even been put in contact with the civilized world, and they have today the same notion of national government as they had in the sixteenth century of the privileges of the crown. And nothing, nonetheless, more urgent than the need for this discussion, because men of government, persons called to exercise influence in the order of political ideas, still declare themselves, either because of Jacobin vices or because of conventional democratism or because of malevolent mumbo-jumbo, maintainers of good faith of universal suffrage, whose modification they see as an outrage on the rights of the people.

Democracy has no worse enemies than men of the upper classes who, courtiers of the errors of the people, court common fears that are the means of trading in applause and obedience. Thus, religious faith has no more harmful enemy than the priest without a conscience, who, to ensure the faith of the humblest followers, nourishes, instead of fighting, the most miserable worries and preaches words he does not believe but that contribute to ensuring him the dull submission he cultivates.

The true citizen should mistrust any public man who fights against, and any government that objects to restriction of, the suffrage. Defense of universality of the vote reveals the underhanded purpose of excluding all people from the public interests.

IV

Succession in the highest power has been the primary problem in constituting peoples, including primitive peoples. Wandering tribes, nomadic peoples, recognize as leader the one who leads them in war and devotes himself to victory; conquered, they submit to the rule of the conquering leader. Succession is determined by the murder of the *caudillo* or by his defeat in the daring rebellion of a conspiratorial group, and then the people have as general and king the murderer or rebel who imposes himself and who is acclaimed because of admiration and fear, and because his very action shows that he meets the conditions of valor and fierceness that are the ones the horde needs in its captain. When the leader arrives at the level of prestige sufficient to elevate himself over his tribes until coming to be seen as of superior lineage, he establishes hereditary succession, which is the first form of peaceful transmission of power; the rebel, to supplant him, kills him and also puts an end to his sons, but by doing so he confirms the right of succession in popular sentiment, because he makes the heirs disappear in order to establish his right, now secondary to ferociousness and strength.

Later nationalities are begun, and the conquering and prestigious leaders link their authority and their right to rule with the religious principle, which gives it a new prestige and a sacred origin. The succession takes place in the laws of the people, and ruling families begin. Rebellions are not now made against a man, nor is disappearance of the direct descendants sufficient; it is necessary to overthrow the dynasty. At any rate, the establishment of political societies has entered a new stage that means an important advance. The succession is legal; the usurper makes use of the law, avails himself of the religious principle, and bases his own dynasty on both. The evolution that operates since with respect to the royal power, until arriving at the limitations of modern monarchies, gives no importance for purposes of succession to the supreme leader, who continues to be merely and purely legal, given that the only obeys preestablished rules to find title to the crown.

In the third and final stage, the supreme power is conferred by popular election and for a determinate period; the law does not provides rules to define on whom the succession of the power falls, but rather to establish by whom and in what form the successor should be designated. The succession enters into a new period that the constitutional system perfects, leading it to secure the advantages of renewal and the stability that public opinion, which has authorized and must sustain him, should give to the leader of the government.

Such has been, in the general movement of the world, the successional evolution of the power, and although human history has many centuries now, the forms of succession are reduced essentially to those that characterized the three great stages: usurpation by force, designation by law, election by the people.

As happens with all general classifications that arise from the analytical observation of history, what has been expounded is not uniform in all epochs or among all the peoples of the world if, in attempting to find the pure type of each stage, it is sought in particular cases. There are in antiquity peoples of elective rule, but incomplete and above all fleeting, and which is lost later, as if in order for the exceptional people to obey the inevitable law of progressive evolution.

In modern times what happens with all the great classifications happens also with the law of progressive evolution: there is hybridization, like that of languages on the borders of peoples who speak different ones; there are shades, like those of the colors in contact with one another; finally, there are confusions between the laws and the practices, between the supposed and the realized, and between the temporary and permanent that mislead the criteria of analysis. Careful and calm observation always discovers the essential character of the stage.

Among the Latin peoples of America, who did not develop spontaneously, but rather were influenced by others more advanced in history and saw themselves subject to an anomalous form of government not produced by their own evolution, forward movement suffered disruptions that still persist after having them break the orderly advance of the model peoples of Europe. During the centuries of the viceroyalty, they did not pass to the second stage, but rather, their growth force nullified, they remained without evolutionary action, and, upon gaining their independence, found themselves filled with the most advanced ideas of the transformed peoples, but lacking the harmonious development that gives strength and equilibrium to whomever has exercised, in the normal struggles of nature, all the muscles of the body and all the psychic faculties. From this arises the fact that the Latin nations of the continent have laws from the last stage and have not yet emerged, for the realization of the succession of the government, from the period of primitive peoples.

Argentina, Brazil, and Chile are barely managing to provide, to their transmission of power, a character less similar to the first stage, because the changes owing to violence are less frequent in the three nations. An abrupt modification, and for that reason little deserving of confidence, has shown in Peru the legitimate succession of recent presidents, not without attempts at revolt that threaten the constitutional order. Only the little republic of Costa Rica, for reasons that for us do not have sufficient explanation, presents an exception that could not be taken into account without studying in depth its history and the internal process of its political practices and customs.

As for Mexico, it is clearly and fully in the first stage. In order not to go to the confusion of the epoch of daily revolution, let us take the series of governments from [18]55 to now: Santa Anna was thrown out by the Revolution of Ayutla; Comonfort was defeated by the Revolution of Tacubaya; Juárez attacked by the Revolution of the Noria, which failed; Lerdo de Tejada deposed by the Revolution of Tuxtepec; General Díaz deposed by the Revolution of the North. After each triumphant revolution, the leader of the rebellion becomes the president of the Republic. Although the processes have changed during the time that has elapsed since the Christian era, the fact is, at heart, the same that occurred more than twenty centuries ago in the forest of the north of Europe. In the succession of power, the people does not express its will to elect a new president, but rather to depose the one who governs, and expresses it by taking up arms and fighting. Once the victory is obtained, the election is unnecessary because there is no candidate other than the leader of the subversive movement. In these cases the election is free of physical coercion precisely because no one has moral liberty.

The man who assumes power in those cases, not because they give it to him but rather because he takes it, does not come to his rule with strong ideas of democracy, nor less does he think of them as rules of government. The defects of origin continually extend to mentality and conduct, because of the necessity that it appear logical and that only a spirit more than superior, exceptional, capable of infringing laws of human nature can break.

He who overthrows a president and imposes himself in his place does not feel himself to be mandatary or leader of the government; he feels himself master of the laws and leader of the nation, because it is not natural that he would superimpose juridical theories on the deep impression left by the events from which his authority is derived. The imposition having sprung spontaneously from him, he does not tolerate obstacles; limitations irritate him, and, as a consequence, he subordinates to his will all elements that must intervene in managing public affairs, and before long he arrives, if it did not begin with a dictatorship, at a dictatorship so much less benevolent the more resistance is opposed to it. Perpetuity comes right away, which is the highest condition of dictatorial force and, consequently, its necessary company, and with perpetuity established without law, the succession of power can be operated only through violence. Here we are, then, in the first stage of successional theory, condemned to have dictatorship as a form of government, and as an end for each dictatorship a revolution.

We are not trying to deny in an absolute manner the charges made against our race and our education as being the cause of our deplorable and backward political condition. Perhaps it might be true that we put "in the conquest of power the same ardor free of scruples that the companions of Pizarro put into the conquest of gold,"** obeying hereditary impulses, but there is less observation and clemency in condemning us without extenuation when we are within the historical laws which the old peoples of Europe have obeyed over long centuries.

We are going to arrive at the third stage of the successional evolution without having prepared ourselves in the second; it obliges us to force the law of gradual development, and the violation of natural laws has inevitable and harsh sanctions. Every effort of public men of patriotic conscience must be consecrated with loyalty and disinterest to helping the evolutionary movement so that it might be realized in practice, since it is operating in theories and in public sentiment. The perspective of the Republic presents itself in this simple and hard dilemma: *Either election or revolution.*

* * *

EMILIO RABASA

"Supremacy of Legislative Power," 1912

Writing in 1912, Rabasa compares European and American systems. Following the disruption of the overthrow of Porfirio Díaz, he is considering the divisions of power within various governments and the electoral process. He acknowledges the challenges ahead for Mexico as it determines the role government should play in Mexico.

SOURCE: *José Antonio Aguilar Rivera, ed., Janet M. Burke and Ted Humphrey, trans.,* Liberty in Mexico: Writings on Liberalism from the Early Republican Period to the Second Half of the Twentieth Century *(Indianapolis, IN: Liberty Fund, 2012), pp. 486–498.*

** Barthélemy, *Le Rôle du pouvoir exécutif dans les république moderns*, p. 204.

*T*he actual election establishes the government but does not regulate it, and precisely in the harmonious operation of the branches created by the Constitution lies the secret of the stability of the government, the guarantee of liberties, and the foundation of the tranquility and success of the nation. The peoples who have already passed their political infancy and have liberated themselves from fear of usurpations, because they have the disposition sufficiently superior not to tolerate them, take up the real problem of government organization, which consists of the balance among the powers that constitute it in order that the superiority of one not come to destroy the others, degenerating into an oppressive power. Each of those peoples has given, to the complex problems of political organization, the solution to which their history, their idiosyncrasy, and their needs have led them, in such a way that, if well within the general common principles founded in human nature and analyzed by reason, each has found the special solution it has consecrated in its laws and embodied in its customs. For this reason, no two nations have equal institutions in practice, despite the fact that, besides general common principles, some among them certainly have similar histories and origins, and despite the fact that commerce in ideas and study of foreign experience have also caused reciprocal imitation.

The old classification of systems, which could have had scientific merit one hundred years ago, reveals today only the external appearance of the governments, but it misleads with respect to the intrinsic reality. There is greater similarity between the governments of the North American republic and the German empire than between the republics of the United States and Switzerland or between the empires of Germany and Russia. The essence of the classification takes root in the strength and constitution of the executive power, which directs and regulates the community's interior and exterior life, and which varies from absolute rule in Russia to the balance of powers in North America and the almost complete abrogation of powers in Switzerland.

But in order to speak only about the type of government in which the popular element participates by means of the suffrage, a type to which all peoples of the world are tending to accommodate themselves, we focus on the great division between parliamentary governments (the English model) and the balance of powers (North American model). The first is based in the theory that national sovereignty resides in the assembly elected by the people, whose will it represents exclusively; the second rests on the principle of a plurality of powers, to which the people delegates its sovereignty (executive and legislative), giving them jurisdictions that should keep their activities separate and in a balance that guarantees against omnipotence that not even the people themselves should have. European experts in public law attribute great superiority to the parliamentary system, which predominates in the Old Continent, but the grand model of the American type does not permit them to condemn, or even declare the system of the New Continent definitively inferior.

With the intent of speaking about parliamentarianism later, we confine our-selves, in order to limit our subject matter, to the system that, with reference to republics, is now called "presidential."

The presidential system establishes power and national sovereignty in its three departments: legislative, executive, and judicial, with jurisdictions and limitations that ensure their independent, balanced, and harmonious action. The first two rep-resent the will of the people and have authority to interpret it in order to "require" in the name of the constituent and determine according to suggestions of the nation or according to their own ideas that they have because of ideas from the nation; as a consequence, the officials who represent those agencies must necessarily originate from popular election. The judicial is an organ of the nation that enters into certain elevated functions as a great equalizer of elements, but, limited to applying the law (declaration already made by the will of the people), it cannot "require" in the name of the people because, in the administration of justice, the people itself is inferior to the law and must subject itself to it; consequently, to appoint the holders of this function, public election is not only not necessary, it is not logical.

In every constitution of this system, what is essential and delicate lies in the balance of the two powers that represent the will of the people; the theory of parlia-mentarianism rejects precisely that double representation of a single and indivisible will. But, leaving to theoretical conceptions the limited value that falls to them in the practical sciences, it is necessary to recognize that in the fact of two distinct agencies sharing the representation of the will of the people creates between them an inevi-table antagonism and causes the major difficulty of keeping them constantly within established limits. Each one fighting to expand its activity at the expense of the other, the legislative tends toward converting the government into congressional anarchy, and the executive toward taking it to dictatorship; and if neither of the two extremes is reached, at the very least the expansion of one of the two powers deforms the constitution that the country has desired, and always with the danger of going fur-ther. The president of the French Senate reproached a member of the chamber, interrupting him with applause from his colleagues, because the member alluded to the constitutional power of the executive to have reconsidered a project voted by the chambers. The allusion seemed to dishonor the sovereignty of the assembly, when in reality it was the Senate that disrespected the constitution. In France the legislative has gained such ground on the executive that, in official acts, the legitimate powers of the executive are not recognized.[‡‡]

In the United States the succession of presidents without great character made the constitutional balance vacillate in favor of Congress, in the opinion of Wilson, to the point that the distinguished writer considered that the nation was threatened by parliamentarianism[§] and later, Berthélemy, writing in 1906 after the administration

---

[‡‡] Barthélemy, *Le Rôle du pouvoir exécutif dans les républiques modernes*, p. 678.

[§] Wilson, *Congressional Government*.

of MacKinley [*sic*] and during that of Roosevelt, saw, on the contrary, the already insuperable tendency of the American government toward the personal influence of the holder of the executive. It is certain that, in the events of 1906 until now, neither the American people nor President Taft has permitted the confirmation of this tendency, which seems not to have shown itself except in specific circumstances.

Outside the legal order, the president possesses elements of strength that give him superiority in the struggle with Congress. He has the public force materially at his disposal, has the army of employees who depend on him, has on his side the interest of those who hope for this favors, and generally attracts popular sympathies, which, only in moments of intense unrest, the collective and almost anonymous personality of a legislative assembly gains. But, within the constitutional order, which is what we must take into account in examining the makeup of the government, the superiority of the Congress is unquestionable because of its sole power to prescribe the laws to which the entire nation and even the executive power must submit. The danger, then, of encroachment that alters the stability of the institutions is principally in the abuse Congress can make of its legitimate powers, for all that this seems paradoxical in our country because we have never lived under the constitutional system, and, consequently, the preponderance has been on the side of the executive.

The complete separation of the two powers would not ensure their balance. It would give them an antagonistic independence in which each would exert itself to reach the maximum expanse, and both would become unbearable for the governed. It is required, on the contrary, that one serve as a limitation to the other by means of specific intervention in their activities; and, as the legislative already has as its specific function the great means of prescribing laws in order to regulate the course of public affairs, the attention of the fundamental law directs itself primarily to arming the executive against the encroachments and excesses of the legislative power, strong because of its faculties, immune because of its absolute lack of responsibility, bold because of its nature as representative of the people that it wants exclusively to claim for itself, and impassioned because of its crowdlike nature, which subjects it more to oratorical efforts than to the value of reasoning.

In the form of government the Mexican Constitution adopted, there is another element of complication and another force to take into account for the balance of the whole: the legal status of the independent states, which confers on them a freedom of internal activity to which has been given the improper name of sovereignty, which we use in this specific sense for the sake of brevity. The federal powers are limited, by local independence, to everything that, and to only what concerns the interest of the nation, leaving to the governments of the federal divisions the care and management of the interests of each, which assumes for them the characteristics of an autonomous people. A new distribution of jurisdiction is added to what the division of powers entails and demands, and in this distribution, the fundamental law again seeks the counterweights that might guarantee, of course, the liberty of the federal entities, but in the end, and most important, all the liberties of the people against tyrannical power and the never-ending tendency to absolutism; because the federal system, if it was created with the goal of preserving their rights for the English colonies that formed the North American Republic, proves to be in every instance excellent for reducing the power of the government, with advantages for the security of public liberties, always in danger before a formidable power.

The legal status of the states is manifest in two forms to limit the omnipotence of the national government. The first is their internal independence, which puts local interests beyond the authority of the national government; the second is their status as political entities, which, on the one hand, gives them the right to constitute a chamber of Congress, with an equal number of representatives for all, and, on the other, gives them the right of voting as units for the highest laws, those that modify the fundamental pact of the nation.

The liberty of action of the states, as electors of the federal chamber and as legislative agency in constitutional matters, depends on their strength and their independence, and it cannot give cause for legal conflicts; not so their liberty of internal rule, which can be violated by laws or acts that encroach upon or restrict it. The agency of equilibrium is, for those situations, the judicial department of the nation, which, without abandoning the forms of procedure appropriate to the administration of justice, without general declarations that would convert it into the omnipotent power it is trying to combat, prevents the execution of every act of violence and defends the independence of the state or division from every threat. If the balance is broken by the state to the detriment of the federal jurisdiction, the judicial agency of the nation reestablishes it by the same procedure, limited to preventing the simple execution of isolated acts.

Such is the coordination of powers and the mechanism of balances on which the American system of government is based, established with simplicity and mastery in the Constitution of Philadelphia, "the most admirable work," according to Gladstone, "that human understanding has produced." From it, our [Constitution] took an organization that our constituents managed to improve on certain points, but that proved to be profoundly modified by the very different criteria it used for the work of adaptation.

Did the modifications made in that work leave the balance that is the goal of the presidential system ensured in our political organization? Certainly not. The elimination of the Senate broke it, as much by increasing the power of the unitary chamber as by depriving the states of their equal representation in an assembly of the legislative power.[§§] With the Senate established in a subsequent epoch, some errors remain in the supreme law that, in the free practice of its precepts, will cause serious conflicts among the powers; the preponderance of the legislative over executive remains, which will result in any of the extremes to which the omnipotence of

---

[§§] The 1857 constitution suppressed the Senate, but a constitutional amendment restored it in 1874.

Congress leads: the submission of the executive, which establishes the dictatorship of an assembly, or the coup d'état, which enthrones the dictatorship of the president. And after any of these dictatorships, revolution again. We do not yet know what the outcome of our Constitution will be in full practice because we have never realized it, and foresight is insufficient for calculating it in the complexity of elements that enters into the physiology of a people that lives by its agencies. The machinery constructed to make a new product is not free from danger of malfunctioning at the moment of connecting it to the motor that must set all its parts in motion, and only the flying asunder of a part will reveal the error of calculation that must be corrected so that the entire mechanism meets its objective. Our political organization, written in the Charter of '57, needs to be connected to the actual suffrage, which is the force that must set it in motion. Only then will we know which is the work that produces and the effort that provides, but through the experience of other similar mechanisms we already know what parts are going to fly asunder if they are not adjusted beforehand.

There is only another reason why the Constitution might, for the most part, be an enigma as long as it is not put into free practice, to which it arrives are not possible, neither the interpretation nor the adaptation. The interpretation, which determines the scope that must be granted to each precept, is not possible as long as the constitutional agencies are not free to use their judgment, to discuss with the others their limits of activity, and to establish their sovereignty as an insurmountable barrier to disruptive encroachment.

For the interpretation, the adaptation is made first; but the adaptation is essentially evolutionary and, in our judgment, as inevitable as useful. If two peoples of analogous origins and situations were to adopt identical written constitutions, ten years after putting them into practice with equal liberty, they would have different actual constitutions, and fifty years later, it is probable they would have totally distinct ones. Not only has the English common-law constitution made the admirable evolution from ruling aristocracy to broad democracy in a century without altering the visible organization of its government, but also the inflexible (written) constitutions, have, without modifying their texts, changed their principal ideas through slow transformation. The American Constitution was established on the greatest respect for the independence and for the almost real sovereignty of the states, which the states required to accept it. Jefferson, the zealous sustainer of such a principle, dedicated eight years of government to its development, and nonetheless, at the end of separatist war, the absolute and sole sovereignty of the nation remained the unquestionable foundation of the federal union, and this new principle has produced the effect of giving the central government a preponderance that is neither written in the law nor would have been accepted by the free colonies. The French Constitution of 1875 was voted by a Congress with monarchical tendencies and with the view to a restoration, and it tried to preserve in the president of the Republic the prerogatives that should not be denied a monarch. It was based on the division of powers and on the limitations of balance, and nonetheless, keeping to its texts, it has permitted the transition to the most complete parliamentary government, with a near nullification of the executive under the unlimited sovereignty of the popular assembly.

The persistent action of the social constitution imposes little by little and day by day its characteristics forms and makes the political constitution, which always has much of the artificial and mathematical, yield. The modifications that, in general ideas, produce the changing needs of life, the progress of ideas, and all the forces of national growth do not adjust themselves conveniently to the unchanging mold that a past generation forged, and it is preferable that the mold yield slowly and permit less rectilinear forms than that the mold shatter in pieces under the strength of irresistible forces.

II

To Congress can be applied, in the abstract, the expansions of Wilson, "Congress is the aggressive spirit," and of Bagehot: "Congress is a despot that has unlimited time, that has unlimited vanity, that has or believes it has an unlimited ability, whose pleasure is in action and whose life is work." *** So that, having faculties superior to those of the other branches of the power, an instinct for attack, and not only capacity but organic need to work, it brings together the most complete conditions for disturbing the harmony of the government and frustrating the best calculated precautionary measures of the fundamental law. But there is more that Bagehot in his phrases, cited and written for comparison with the limitations that fatigue, pleasures, sociability, and his individual psychology impose on the president, should not take into account: the lack of responsibility of the Congress (especially the most numerous chamber) makes it bold and careless; its method of election, in which demagogic elements play more than any other, give it, generally, a majority inferior to the task; individually, its members do not have an opinion on the matters submitted to their vote; together, it lets itself be carried off by the coarse eloquence that fascinates it with greater docility than by the serious reasoning suitable for persuading it.

In the House of the Representatives of Washington, the representatives frequently request that, at the moment of the vote, the session be suspended, because they do not know what to do and they need to go to the people best informed about the matter to orient themselves. Their personal opinion is null, the work abundant and rapid, and thus made impossible for the deliberation of a body whose value depends precisely on the fact it is constituted to deliberate. The discussion, and even the vote of the chamber, has been replaced by the discussion and vote of the permanent committees, about which it should not be said that they give an opinion, but rather that they themselves alone resolve the affairs of the state. In each committee

---

*** Ibid.; and Bagehot, *Principles of Constitutional Law.*

the "chairman" who presides over it prevails, and notwithstanding the transcendental importance of his exceptional functions, the "chairmen" are named directly and exclusively by the Speaker of the House, who thus assumes an enormous power in the functions of the state. If we have to speak of being guided by general cases, we must say that the sole serious and reliable function of the House is exercised in the election of the Speaker, which is done through the majority of votes * * * of the party that dominates in the assembly.

Thus we refer to the most learned democracy of those that have adopted the presidential system of government.

Among those subject to the parliamentary system, the most numerous chamber is of a much higher intellectuality because the prominent participation that it takes in the government of the nation makes of the election of the deputies the act of greatest importance for the country, and the subject matter of the participation attracts persons from the serious elements of society and especially of the political world. In the chambers of representatives of England and France are seated many men of the first order, deep thinking in political science, masters of diplomacy, consummate jurists, famous soldiers and sailors, eloquent orators. Personal opinion can be, if not entirely general, in the great majority, but subject to the needs of the party and, within the party, to the group, to the factions, which in France, above all, give to the deliberations of the assembly its particular appearance and to the votes their definitive direction. The importance of the vote that in one day changes the government and determines all the acts of the executive—that is to say, all the daily life of the nation—makes the discussion impassioned, intense, more of a dispute than a deliberation, and arrives at the moment of deciding with the "yes" or the "no" of the sovereignty of the people in an atmosphere charged with ill will and threats, that still vibrates with the rude words of the interrupters and the strikes of the president's gavel, and maybe a raised fist agitated in order to slap a face or some inkwells hurled some distance in order to wound.

There is no way to choose between an assembly like the American, which is more or less satisfied by mediocrities and incompetents, in which the custom of speaking is deteriorating more and more, which, subject to the committees, is at the point of completely abdicating its functions as a deliberating body, and another assembly like the French, in which there are representatives of great quality by talent and knowledge, but who are ceaselessly stirred up in the struggle against the government and make of it the preferred, almost only, occupation, turning discussion into a combat of eloquence, at times drowned out by clamors, insults, and affronts. The American nation tolerates and rewards the unhappiness with the strength that it takes from its incomparable and healthy youth, as well-nourished and vigorous body supports and restores the local illness of a member. The French superimposes its well-being of accumulated wealth, its superior culture, and the patriotism that constitutes its saving virtue upon constant threats from reaction and from international complexities. But neither the one nor the other nation has the assembly conceived by the constituent legislator for the loftiest functions that popular sovereignty confers, and each one on its path follows a course that does not yet give signs of stopping or deviating and that can lead the country to profound alterations in the system of government.

What will be the tendency in Mexico of a Congress freed from controls by the actual election from the electoral districts? What its influence in the specific system of government that will have to arise from the letter of the Constitution combined with our character, our education, and our idiosyncrasy? It is not possible to conjecture correctly in the responses, if what is desired is to determine details with the precision or nuances with subtlety, but the most serious dangers can indeed be determined with the certainty of not erring greatly on the side of foreboding, and consequently suggesting the means of preventing the greatest and most certain ills so as to minimize the influence of possible surprises from experience.

The natural reaction the unfortunate effects of a current situation cause in the public spirit make it see poorly the good effects that it also carries with it and incline it completely in favor of a situation diametrically contrary, whose unsuitable aspects it refrains from perceiving. The absolute preponderance of the executive in our political system raises hope in the legislative and fills it with the prejudice of all saviors in waiting. The nation aspires to a system in which Congress predominates, and by shaking the omnipotence from the president of the Republic, it does not fear his nullification, because it does not see it as an evil, nor does it assume the omnipotence of the chambers, of which it has no experience whatsoever. This support of public opinion, which a free Congress would suddenly have, is what makes it most dangerous for the balance of national powers and stability of institutions.

If the country is lacking electoral agencies, which only the exercise of the suffrage creates and perfects, one cannot expect in the first elections that the conservative elements, which are the masters of wealth, culture, and the good judgment there is in the entire nation, would vigorously take part; but it is even difficult for such agents to be very useful for the good designation of representatives, because in countries of the presidential system interest is in the election of the president, and, as in the United States, the election of deputies is left officially to the politicians, who are generally men of second order if one classifies by learning and patriotism. Our Congresses (the first ones without any doubt) will be made up, in their majority, of men gathered through the spell of small localities or by clever intrigues in which a local competence triumphs; of politicians from the states who usually become confident and seize great opportunities in the broad and favorable medium of the capital; of some experienced in legislative tasks by some previous service, ready to use a liberty they did not have before, and who it is probable owe their credentials to the influence, that will not come to be null, of the governors. A Congress composed of such personalities will probably have qualities of good faith, of interest in the states, and of preferential dedication to their tasks, and it will provide moreover the advantage of bringing to light men who renew the ranks of politics, owing to the spontaneity of the medium, which is the great revealer of characters and talents.

On the other hand, even when it has men of note, the common intellectual standard in such assemblies will be very narrow, and the instruction in political science and in the various types of knowledge that enrich and support it, very scarce.

Skeptics will say that this Congress will subject itself to the executive, like the previous ones, through promises or habit; we will not assert the contrary, but in such a case, the assumption of independence chambers would not hold, and we will not have advanced at all in the development of the institutions. No danger, but no progress!

The free Congress is one that takes note of its important role, that studies its faculties, that senses itself the first of the powers and immediately makes itself invader, provoker, and aggressor. If its general culture is low, as in what we have foreseen, hostility is impulsive because it proceeds from erroneous ideas that give it, as its first and even as its only conviction, that of its own omnipotence and the feeling of its lack of responsibility. The resistance of the executive to the invasion of its jurisdictional ground seems to it rebelliousness, and the eloquence of the orators overflows, always convincing for the mute benches. And after some time of burdening itself with excitements of pride, stimulants of greed, it ends up by being persuaded that it must unconditionally subjugate the leader of the executive power or compel him to resign.

* * *

Earlier we spoke of the legislative power of the Congress, because the two assemblies that form it take part in the enactment of the laws in exercising almost all the faculties in the scope of their powers. At times the Senate will also be able to be, in its specific faculties, invader and oppressor of the executive, but it is an unalterable fact that the predominance of the Congress is summed up in the specific supremacy of the Chamber of Deputies. In parliamentary governments it is the popular chamber that makes and unmakes governments; the Senate, reduced to the mere status of reviewer, rarely dares to reshape a project the other chamber sent it, and little by little cedes its most important prerogatives. In France the Senate has a first-line role; in England the House of Lords has been ceding the terrain to the democratic advances of the Commons for a century, and recently it surrendered to it, subjected by force, the right of veto in the budgets voted by the lower chamber.

The danger of the single chamber is thus implicated in the predominance of the Congress, threatening by all the evils inherent in it and with the violation of the constitutional system. Perhaps the subordination of the Senate, in the European countries ruled by cabinet governments, depends greatly on the hereditary or less popular origin of their members, but that is not the only nor probably the main reason. The primary cause is that the more numerous a body, the more imprudent, bold, and responsible it becomes; the Senate must take refuge in prudence to avoid clashes of serious consequences, and prudence is always on the frontier of weakness.

PASCUAL OROZCO

"Plan de Santa Rosa," 1912

At the beginning of 1912, just over a year after Madero became president, Pascual Orozco went into open rebellion in the north. The following plan sought to redress grievances felt by Orozco and Zapata, thus the statement of "Land and Justice." While Zapata's open rebellion against Madero happened first, Orozco's rebellion in the north brought back a two-front war. The division in Madero's initial supporters showed that the frustrations of the various social and economic classes were different and not mutually reconcilable.

SOURCE: *Román Iglesias González, introducción y recopilación,* Planes políticos, proclamas, manifiestos y otros documentos de la Independencia al México moderno, 1812–1940. *Universidad Nacional Autónoma de México. Instituto de Investigaciones Jurídicas. Serie C. Estudios Históricos, Núm. 74. Edición y formación en computadora al cuidado de Isidro Saucedo. México, 1998, p. 637. Translation by Stephany Slaughter.*

February 2, 1912

On the second day of February, 1912, at 10 p.m., at the southeast corner of the Santa Rosa Cemetary, in the suburbs of the capital of the state of Chihuahua, we, the undersigned, vow to achieve, by means of arms, the definitive triumph of the Plan de San Luis Potosí, betrayed by "maderismo científico," adding the following articles to said plan:

1st—The slogan of our flag is "Land and Justice."

2nd—It is declared, for the benefit of public use prior to legal formalities, the expropriation of national territory, with the exception of the area occupied by urban farms, the buildings that constitute what is generally known as the hacienda compound, factories and ranches, and railroad lines.

The government will forever be the exclusive owner of lands and will rent them only to those whose request is proportional to what they can personally cultivate with family members.

Pasture lands will also be rented to individuals, ensuring that its distribution corresponds with the goal of equity proposed by the previous paragraph.

3rd—Civil and penal codes will be reformed in order to impart justice rapidly.

4th—The electoral law will penalize, with prison and fines, the town councils that do not distribute electoral ballots with due opportunity, or that in any way defraud suffrage; and will penalize with prison those citizens who use trickery to flout the voting process.

5th—States will have their militias and the Federation will not be able to send its forces to the states unless their respective Executives request it with the previous approval of local Legislatures. The Houses of the Union will determine the places where forts or quartering of the Federal Army will be established.

6th—From now on, the Federation will not receive what is now known as the 20% federal contribution, rather, the states will dedicate it to the promotion of the construction of the indigenous race; this contribution will be named the 20% indigenous school.

7th—The state secretaries of the president of the Republic will be named by him and will be personally and financially responsible under the law.

8th—All government employees with be personally and financially responsible under the law.

9th—Penal action against official crimes is non-lapsable.

10th—Only in the evident case of the disruption of public peace can extraordinary authority be conceded to executives.

PASCUAL OROZCO

"Plan Orozquista," 1912

After his open revolt, Orozco issued a follow-up plan. Whereas the first one stated the aims for his rebellion, this one specifically took aim at Francisco Madero and his family. He especially calls into question Madero's integrity and the legality of the elections that raised him to the presidency.

SOURCE: *Román Iglesias González, introducción y recopilación,* Planes políticos, proclamas, manifiestos y otros documentos de la Independencia al México moderno, 1812–1940. *Universidad Nacional Autónoma de México. Instituto de Investigaciones Jurídicas. Serie C. Estudios Históricos, Núm. 74. Edición y formación en computadora al cuidado de Isidro Saucedo, 1998, p. 655. Available at www.biblioteca.tv/artman2/publish/1912_213/Plan_Orozquista_o_Pacto_de_la_Empacadora_1835 .shtml. Translation by Stephany Slaughter.*

March 9, 1912

Notice is hereby given of the protest by General Pascual Orozco to fight for the triumph of the ideals of the Plan de San Luis, reformed in Tacubaya in compliance with the relating part of the Plan de Ayala.

It is declared:

I. The initiator of the Revolution, Francisco I. Madero, falsified and violated the Plan de San Luis.

II. Francisco I. Madero made the Revolution with money from American millionaires and with the indirect and covert support of the U.S. government.

III. Francisco I. Madero counted freebooters among his ranks from the U.S. and other nationalities to assassinate Mexicans.

IV. Francisco I. Madero robbed the Nation, with the pretext of armed forces in the elections that raised him and José María Pino Suárez to the presidency and vice presidency.[†††]

V. He imposed himself through military force together with interim governors and was elected through fraud, violating the sovereignty of the States.[‡‡‡]

VI. Within two days of taking usurped power, he contracted and received 14 million dollars from Wall Street with the pretext of expanding services of national rail lines.

VII. For these offenses and crimes, Francisco I. Madero and his accomplices are declared traitors to the Fatherland, and outlaws.

VIII. Since fraud and armed forces interceded in the elections of October 1911, the elections of President and Vice president are declared null and void.

IX. The Revolution does not recognize and will nullify all concessions and contracts made by the usurping government to members of the Madero family, by blood or by marriage, and to the so-called ministers of his Government.

FÉLIX DÍAZ

"Plan Felicista," 1912

In October 1912, Félix Díaz raised his flag in revolt against the presidency of Francisco Madero. Díaz justifies his plan based on the revolts of both Orozco and Zapata. He also supports the notion of Madero's corruption and the illegality of his election to office. For the purposes of the game, this plan considered to already be public knowledge.

SOURCE: *Peter V. N. Henderson,* Félix Díaz, the Porfirians, and the Mexican Revolution *(Lincoln: University of Nebraska Press, 1981), pp. 151–153.*

††† This is a literal translation of the original Spanish that could be interpreted multiple ways: "Francisco I. Madero robó a la Nación, con el pretexto de la fuerza armada en las elecciones que lo llevaron a él y a José María Pino Suárez a la presidencia y a la vicepresidencia."

‡‡‡ The original Spanish reads, "Se impuso por las fuerzas de las armas junto con Gobernadores interinos e hizo elegir por medio del fraude de los propietarios, violando la soberanía de los Estados."

Mexicans: In a moment of extreme anguish for the fatherland, I come to raise my voice to request support from all men of good will who desire to contribute to the rebirth of an era of peace and harmony.

It is no longer possible to support silently all the evil that has been forced upon the Republic by the nefarious administration which sprouted from the Revolution of 1910.

The President has already cast aside his mask of democracy and altruism, which he used to deceive villainously the people to the point of forcing them into an armed movement. Now the man who has no legitimacy shows his true face, for while others have been the true soul of the Revolution, he proclaims himself the chief of the movement and thus rises, aided by a moment of national insanity. This man is eager for riches for himself and his numerous family; he is lacking any natural talents of a man of government, and is cruel and cold-blooded like all men who are feeble and faint-hearted. Even the state of his mind causes concern when one sees the lack of conscience with which he guards the responsibilities of the high post he occupies.

Fire, slaughter, pillage are the weapons which the government uses, not to defend itself against aggression, but rather to quiet the voices of some former party-members who shout: Fill your promises! And slaughter, pillage, and fire are the means by which the deceived ones carry out their reprisals. Raised to the height of rage, faced with the impotence of their complaints, only one way remaind; that of fighting and dying with arms in their hands rather than perishing like wild animals. These people are hunted over the ashes of their razed villages, and over the corpses of their brothers, sons, wives, and mothers who were uselessly and ignominiously sacrificed.

What everyone knows and cannot doubt is that the Madero Revolution, although a provoked revolt, has exercised the most cruel abuses of authority, and attacked property, honor, and life.

In order for the Republic to be prosperous and happy as the nation deserves, it is necessary to make a supreme effort and destroy the evil at its source, taking power from the inept and bloody hands of those who abuse it.

It is to this noble end that I am dedicating my life and those of the valiant men who have clustered around me. If we die, it will be with the satisfaction of having indended the best for our country. If success favors us, the provisional government which we will install will be composed of men of known honesty, intelligence, and prestige without distinction as to political connections of beliefs, and this government will work without rest to realize the ideal recorded on the flag of rebellion that we now raise, "Impose Peace by Means of Justice."

When the country returns ot order, the government will call elections which will be respected, and it will support the popular mandate of "Free Suffrage and No Reelection," now so vilely mocked. The government promises that it will not repeat the cruel hoax of a false election, like the fraudulent and illegal one used to choose the vice-president.

Noble Army, to which I have had the honor of belonging since my youth until recently when I suffered the sadness of separation as a violent protest against taking commands from criminals snatched from the scaffold and foreign adventurers who are now our equals or superiors, you, my brothers, are the sons of the glorious Military College. Discipline has a limit, as I clearly expressed before the supreme authorities who ruled this country on August 21, 1908. In a discourse that I pronounced on that date on the occasion of the commencement of our Association's conference, I stated, and I repeat here, that discipline has as its limit the ultimate welfare of the state. The arms that the nation has given us for its defense have been transformed by the present government into executioners' axes to impose tyranny. I summon you to unite with us to do the work of justice.

Good sons of the present Revolution, let us gather together so that our action can be more effective, as I offer you, along with my life, my name. This, I assure you, has always served patriotism and honor.

Mexicans all: lend me your moral and material strength fo rhte work of securing peace, which will begin with this war. I do not present you with promises impossible to fulfill, nor am I appealing to you to deceive you or take you unawares in your good faith, as the men of the last Revolution did. I promise you only peace: I will work and struggle for peace. When this deed is accomplished we will have eliminated those who provoke war to benefit themselves with the public treasury despite their countrymen's rivers of blood. You will see to your benefit that justice and the practice of liberty can come by this means alone, as a natural fruit of the peace and order established by a serene and impartial justice for call.

Let our theme be the motto with my signature—Peace and Justice—Félix Díaz.

FÉLIX DÍAZ

"Félix Díaz's Political Program," 1913

Written in April 1913, Díaz's political program outlines what he would seek to accomplish if he were to become president. His list was not new, but consideration of several of the topics demonstrates a realization by some of Porfirio Díaz's old supporters that a shift needed to happen in some areas. Exactly how those problems would be solved is not mentioned.

SOURCE: *Peter V. N. Henderson,* Félix Díaz, the Porfirians, and the Mexican Revolution *(Lincoln: University of Nebraska Press, 1981), pp. 154–156.*

Dear Friends,

I am grateful for your memo of March 28, and the ideas therein. Now I am answering it, explaining my political ideas which will guide my future administration, should I be favored by the votes of my fellow citizens for the First Office of the Republic.

My convictions have been revealed by my conduct from the moment I intervened in the present state of affairs. I procured, in agreement with the present President of Mexico, the creation of a Ministry of Agriculture, which will resolve the troublesome question that threatens our national existence, the happiness of our people, and our integrity. Also, because of my liberal convictions, I cannot accept the radicalism which has transformed basically tolerant liberal theories into a weapon of systematic opposition to religion itself. I judge, on the contrary, that it is time to quench the echoes of this new struggle, elevating Mexico to the ranks of the highest cultured nations, in which religious beliefs are respected by all. Thus, inequalities will disappear, but in accordance with our fundamental laws.

In synthesis, in translating the bases of these revolutionary activities in which I am involved to the solution that I will secure to the political problem which presented itself at the downfall of the defeated government, and from the beliefs which inspire me, I show here my aspirations for my country:

I. To implant order and public peace energetically before anything else; these are the indispensable bases of our national prosperity.

II. To establish the effectiveness of justice, the only thing that can assure a definitive peace as a natural product of the self-respect of every right and completion of every obligation.

III. To propagate public instruction in the land, especially elementary education, and to raise thereby the intellectual and moral level of our people.

IV. To make certain that the powers of government function in a way that best serves the needs of society.

V. To facilitate the development of the states, so that all the states will advance under the auspices of our constitutional regime.

VI. To organize national defense in the largest and most noble sense, to democratize the country and at the same time to fortify it, by means of a prudent regime which will make each soldier a citizen and each citizen a soldier.

VII. To inspire a vigorous morality in all departments of government, and to avoid the present problem of functionaries confusing their political duties with their personal interests.

VIII. That public finance be managed with as much skill as honesty, without losing sight of the influence of finance over our national independence.

IX. That the government be always responsive to public opinion, whether it be through the replacement, alternation, or by direct responsibility of the functionaries, or by any other prudent means.

X. The formation of a civic virtue which will revive economic interests and the personal conscience of individuals, and thus will resolve the problems of labor, agriculture, and education.

XI. To solve the agrarian question by adequate and prudent means, but always keeping in mind the absolute respect for private property which was legitimately acquired.

XII. Consequently, as an indispensable means of solving the agrarian problem, we must multiply the number of communication links so that the wealth of the country can be developed and can circulate freely.

XIII. That the radical problems can be solved with a spirit of protection and humanitarianism.

XIV. Mexico in this way will attain a role of stature in Latin America, and will work in full harmony with the nations of the world.

The consequences of the practice of the previous principles would be that the government would cease to be the exclusive tool of a circle or party, or any personal interest. Instead, it would become the center of national cohesion, and could be constantly pondering the social forces in the Republic.

These are, in brief exposition, the principles in which I believe. Some of these have been sustained by diverse political parties, among them the Republican party, formed for the candidacy of the now deceased Bernardo Reyes. It is hoped, not only because of this program, but also because the party desires peace and concord, which is also the general basis of my program, that this party will attract the sympathy and adherence of a great number of fellow citizens. Let it be understood that without hatred or unjust prejudice, the aspirations of all Mexicans, despite their diverse political programs, will be fulfilled. Many have struggled without respite for elevated ideals with the hope of realizing these ideals some day. They will find, surely, that the balance of our forces favor living in true progress, and favor the welfare of our people.

To conclude, I express my firm convictions that, as I have said in general terms, there must be an honest politician to manifest the people's aspirations. To make promises to a nation beyond the means of realizing them, or to formulate a government depending on those unrealizable principles, would be tragic. Therefore I, who am a decided believer that telling the truth is the best policy, have spoken truthfully to the Republic.

I remain your friend and servant,

Félix Díaz

ERNESTO MADERO

"Economic Outlook Bright in Mexico," 1912

Writing in January 1912, before Pascual Orozco's revolt, Ernesto Madero was concerned with assuring the world that Mexico was still a viable place to invest. This letter to the Bankers' Magazine *was a call to the international public to continue investing in Mexico. To convince them of the country's viability he details where resources in mining and banking remained strong. At the end there is a brief nod to the on-going unrest of the Zapatistas, though the faction is not mentioned specifically.*

SOURCE: Bankers' Magazine *Vol. 84, Iss. 1 (Cambridge: January 1912): pp. 81–83.*

*I*f, a year ago, it had been predicted that Mexico would pass through a severe revolution; that she would witness a change in her high governing personnel; that she would have experience of a provisional Government and a new period of electoral agitation, and all this without producing intense economic upheavals, the author of such statements would have been regarded as unduly optimistic and his forecasts would have been characterized almost as day-dreams. Yet all this has come to pass and despite the many factors that might have been expected to cause a sharp break in the economic and financial activities of Mexico, the development of the country's resources has continued and the Nation has met its obligations and paid its way, almost as if the year 1910–1911 had been a normal year.

The volume of the public revenue may serve as an index of the Nation's economic strength, for, naturally, when conditions are straitened and difficult, the Government's receipts undergo a shrinkage. But, at the end of a year of revolution, provisional Government and new elections, Meixco had a surplus of more than eight million pesos and the public revenues amounted to $111,000,000 in round numbers. There were increases in all branches of the revenue, with the single exception of the stamp tax, the yield of which shows a very slight diminution.

All the public services were, therefore, defrayed with strict punctuality. The interest and sinking fund service of the Public Debt has been met with religious regularity, nor has it been necessary to make unusual retrenchments. The expenses of the revolution and the indemnities for damage occasioned by it have been and are being paid out of the funds accumulated during the long series of years in which the revenue has exceeded expenditures and the Nation still possesses cash reserves exceeding $23,000,000 gold (U.S. Cy.)

Let us now take a brief survey of the showing of the different branches of public wealth.

The mineral output of the Republic continues to expand. In the year 1910–1911, the production of gold was more than $600,000, U.S. Cy., in excess of the previous year's production; and the increase in the production of silver was $2,000,000, U.S. Cy. The gold mined in the Republic during the year under review mounted to $23,000,000, U.S. Cy., and the silver to more than $40,000,000, U.S. Cy. There was an increase, also, in the output of other metals though on a lesser scale.

The imports, far from diminishing, increased by more than five and half million dollars, gold, and the increase took place in items so important as machinery, textiles and textile goods, and vehicles. The total imports exceeded one hundred million dollars, gold, thus demonstrating the country's increased purchasing power.

The same healthy activity is to be noted in the export trade. The total exports amounted to one hundred and fifty million dollars, gold, and they exceeded the exports of the preceding year by more than sixteen million, gold. There were gains in almost all lines of exportation and the excess of exports over imports was nearly forty-four million dollars, gold, which is the largest balance in favor of exports for years past.

It is true that the exports include a shipment of about four million dollars, gold, in Mexican and foreign gold specie, which only proves that, though the products of our mines, our farms and our factories sufficed to meet our foreign indebtedness, the investment of foreign capital as it had been in former years.

It was natural that a revolution, so severe and widespread as that of 1910–1911, should inspire foreign capital with some distrust, producing a consequent stringency in the exchange market and starting a movement—which was soon checked—in the shipment of gold specie abroad.

The Exchange and Currency Commission which studies all the phenomena connected with foreign exchange and is the channel through which the Government exerts an influence on the exchange market, this commission, I repeat, seconded by the banks and energetically backed by the Government's credit, succeeded in bringing into the country for investment ten million dollars, gold, of foreign capital and in this way easily warded off the exchange crisis. The major part of Mexico's stock of gold was retained in the country and the rate of the exchange stood and continues to stand firm without ever going beyond the gold point.

The situation of our railways is excellent. The National Railways of Mexico, whose lines cover a large portion of the National territory, extending, as they do, from out frontier with the United States, on the north, to our frontier with Guatemala on the south, had an extremely prosperous year. Their earnings approached thirty-one million dollars, gold, while their disbursements were only twenty millions. Their net earnings enabled them to meet fixed charges with the utmost ease. Betterments are constantly being effected in the company's system, and its credit in the United States and Europe is unimpaired, as is proved by the fact that all along a ready market has been found for its bonds.

Our banks of issue, mortgage banks and banks of encouragement have also enjoyed continued prosperity, and their credit tokens are amply guaranteed by their cash holdings which exceed forty million dollars, gold. The note circulation is fifty-eight million dollars, gold, in round numbers, and is guaranteed by cash holdings of forty million dollars, gold. Last year there was an increase of more than two million dollars, gold, in the notes outstanding. The mortgage bonds outstanding amount to more than twenty-four million dollars, gold.

All or the greater part of the various operations of the banks showed increased activity during the year under review, proving that, in spite of the country's unusual state, credit facilities have been extended for the promotion of new enterprises and the expansion of old ones.

The foregoing data are very significant, for none but a strong and solid Nation could pass through so severe a crisis without suffering serious financial perturbations. Peace has been restores and the unimportant foci of disorder that still remain are being eliminated, thanks to the Government's energetic action. Very soon it will be possible to say that all traces of a political character, of the late revolution have been completely effaced. The Republic will then move forward under a more vigorous impetus than before and the Government, which is maturing large plans for irrigation, for the better tillage of the land and the development of agricultural credit, will welcome the coming of the foreign capital to Mexico on a greater scale than ever to cooperate in the promotion of our civilization and progress.

ERNESTO MADERO

"Secretaría de Hacienda's Report to Congress," 1911

The secretaría de hacienda is expected to present an annual report to congress. Ernesto Madero explains that his report, submitted on December 14, 1911, includes a study of the current economic condition of the country, an estimate of income from each source, and an explanation of changes to the proposed expenditure budget for the upcoming year. At the time of his writing, he is optimistic that Mexico is entering a period of peace and prosperity. This following excerpt highlights topics central to the game's debate. While this report is similar to his letter in the Bankers' *Magazine, it provides greater specificity and diversity within the various topics.*

SOURCE: *Translation by Stephany Slaughter and Jonathan Truitt.*

rnesto Madero
December 14, 1911

"SECRETARY OF FINANCE'S REPORT TO CONGRESS FOR THE 1912–1913 FISCAL YEAR"[§§§]

Explanatory Memorandum of the Federal Revenue Law and Federal Expenditure Budget Drafts and of the Budget Initiative for the 1912–1913 Fiscal Year.

*J*t is an important sign, that demonstrates the great vitality of our country, the fact that the consequences of the great revolutionary movement of 1910–1911 have not been felt more deeply thus far in the economic progress of the Nation. In effect: the recently passed fiscal year, despite the development of the revolution, closed with a surplus of income over expenditures, above ten million pesos; it is possible to say as well that the current fiscal year has begun under relatively unfavorable auspices, considering that if we examine the revenue from the two principle assets of the country, which are import duties and taxes that are brought about in Stamp form, we will only note a reduction of 20% in round numbers, during the first four months of the current fiscal year; and for Stamp taxes, the reduction is less than 10%, also in round numbers, in the first three months of the same fiscal year. * * *

* * *

[Madero goes on to suggest that the economy is solid and that in 1912–1913] as long as no new complications arise, very probably the economic consequences of the revolution will have disappeared almost totally. [p. 301]

Conviction of national economic power makes the undersigned Secretary permeate the present study, if cautiously, at the same time without pessimism. In doing so, he knows that for now the State should principally rely on the resources that proceed from taxes already established and experienced over time. The longing for progress and improvement in public services that form part of the way of being of all good Mexicans and especially those individuals who make up the Government, have to restrain themselves in the face of the idea that, at the current moment, it would be inopportune to raise the burden of the tax payers; even though there's no reason to reject the possibility that in the future it seems advisable to modify some of the existing taxes, and even create others intended to affect certain branches of public wealth that are reaching great development and until now have not contributed, or contribute very little, to federal expenses. It is necessary, therefore, in order to institute a significant increase in our budget, to wait for the sources of income to recover

---

[§§§] *Full title: "Exposición de Motivos de los Proyectos de Ley de Ingresos y de presupuesto de egresos e iniviativa de presupuestos para el año económico de 1912–1913," p. 298–374, written by Ernesto Madero in* Memoria dé la secretaria de haciendá y crédito publico: 25 de mayo de 1911–22 de febrero de 1913 *(Mexico: Secretaria de Hacienda y Crédito Público Publicaciones Históricas, 1949).*

their ascending tendencies. Nevertheless, there is one branch of this budget where it is impossible to not introduce considerable increases because it would be counterproductive to the economy: I refer to the branch of war and marine, deserving of priority, because linked with it is the reestablishment of order throughout national territory; neither would it be just to make great savings in branches that, like that of Justice, Public Instruction, and Development, demand, for their importance to social life, preferential attention. If economy and prudence are always recommendable in the calculation of budgets, undoubtedly they now command with greater cause; but under no circumstances should such an economy reach the extreme that the country move backwards or that services vital for the defense of the nation or the security of its citizens be neglected. In this respect, it will be necessary, more than economizing, to contain for now the natural growth of public services so that the increase in expenses not exceed that absolutely necessary, nor pass the possibilities indicated for the provision of income, made with prudence, it is true, but with no prejudice.

3. *Agricultural production.* Repeatedly in budget initiatives the insuperable difficulty that exists to be able to estimate by numbers, and above all by numbers of comparative character, the results of our agricultural production, has been discussed. Consequently, in analogous occasions to the current one, the Secretary has had to lament the existence of these difficulties that impede his contemplation with perfectly clear vision the progress of our agriculture and that, therefore, do not allow him to obtain abundant and reliable data relative to that which one can expect each year from the situation of our sowing and harvesting. Such deficiencies have been substituted by pure generalized, and to a certain point vague, deductions, based on the exterior appearance of the crops and in the importation numbers of certain primary need goods. In the present initiative, nothing else will be able to be done. It is also known that the conditions of national agriculture are, in a sense, precarious, be it for perfectly palpable defects in land distribution, be it for insufficiency of our water system and our system of irrigation; be it, finally, for the scant development that agricultural credit reaches among us. Due to these vices, agricultural production does not have a constant tendency, but rather it often offers strong inflections. [p. 302]

[The report goes on to discuss importation of corn and wheat.]

* * * [I]n the past fiscal year, it was necessary to bring more than $11,000,000 in corn from abroad, however the request for wheat was ceased at a sum that can approximately be estimated at six or seven million pesos, and this circumstance compensates the expense of importing corn. Nevertheless, we must keep in mind that, in terms of the welfare of the popular classes, corn assumes a much greater importance than wheat, since that grain is the one that individuals with few resources consume the most, from whence it follows that the result of the corn harvest has a great influence over transactions in general, and especially over those involving workers and poor people, who constitute the most considerable nucleus of consumers; and we must not forget that the reduction in orders for wheat is explained, in great part, by the existence of numerous reserves from the previous year, 1909–1910. With reference to the aspect of corn crops, the information that has arrived at this ministry, without manifesting a completely idyllic situation, principally in the northern part of the Republic, does reflect a state which on average can be considered favorable. It should be taken into consideration that in the current calendar year, the rainy season was considerably prolonged and there were no premature frosts that damage crops; which explains why the central region has obtained brilliant results, deserving very special mention [are] those achieved in the states of Jalisco, México, Michoacán, Guanajuato and Puebla, and in the Federal District. The same cannot be said of the wheat crop. Importation of this grain is growing again, reproducing a phenomenon, that can be qualified as constant, by virtue of which the Republic does not manage to produce enough wheat for interior consumption and must be imported from abroad; nevertheless, it does not seem that this phenomenon is destined to last much longer, since the Ministry in my charge has reliable news that in the last months, the sowing of wheat has grown considerably in the North as in the Center of the Republic. If the immediate prediction is not completely favorable, however in the future there is reason to believe that things will improve.

* * *

Summarizing: to the point that it is possible to foresee in this subject, whose obscurity has never been hidden, we can venture the idea that given the situation of current crops, probably in the year 1911–1912 our agriculture will continue favorable progress; and therefore, a larger quantity than that obtained in 1910–1911 will remain in the hands of the mass of consumers.

With respect to the future, the National Government, as is public, is concerned with the prompt study and effective resolution of the agricultural problems of the Republic. Of course I can refer to the bill, sent recently to Congress, in which powers are requested for the reorganization of the "Loan Fund for Irrigation Projects and Promotion of Agriculture," L.L.C. That initiative proposes increasing the Fund's capital, as well as the obligations that the Fund can authorize, with the guarantee of the Federal Government, to obtain foreign funds that can be used for the improvement and progress of our agriculture. In order to do so, the license of the Fund will be modified, with the intent of its operations extending to the division of land, by virtue of a partnership of the Federal Government and said Institution. Finally, it is hoped that in the event that Congress approves the cited initiative, the Fund will be able to lend greater services to irrigation and the diffusion of agricultural credit. [p. 304]

[The report goes on to detail the importance of mining, especially gold and silver, with the following brief mention of oil.]

It has not been possible to reduce to numbers data on iron, coal, and oil. The latter finds itself in the height of a period of development and offers a promising future, given that drilling wells is multiplying, in which brilliant results have been obtained, and given that various companies are proceeding to install pipelines with the goal of transporting the oil from the wells to the places where its exportation is easy. [p. 308]

* * *

[The report details imports, ending with the following.]

* * * Can we expect that in the second semester of 1911–1912, the new Government solidly established and the entire country absolutely pacified, imports present a more favorable phase? Such is, without a doubt, the vote of patriotism. In the meantime, we must not cover up that the gathered data impose upon us the obligation of proceeding with caution in making any calculation of import taxes and not expect from them an increase in product. It is undoubtable that this information, without being completely distressing, advises that the mood move away from completely enthusiastic optimism and maintain a wait and see approach.

* * *

[The report then moves on to exports. The following is from section 7, on the exportation of metals.]

Comparing the increase experienced in exportation with that which occurred in the production of gold, it is advised that, while it increased to more than $19,000,000, this only reached something more than $1,000,000. The country has then had to export a considerable quantity of gold in excess of its production. Part of this excess is constituted by money minted nationally and abroad, and the other part formed of gold bars previously possessed that in the referenced year had to be exported. For the purpose of this initiative, that which especially interests us is exportation made in monetary form, the causes of which behoove our explanation in order to understand the situation of the country in terms of commitments and obligations with foreigners; and this, with all the more reason, given that exports of minted gold had not appeared in previous years, at least in a very appreciable form. There is no doubt that the interruption of the public peace that occurred during the 1910–1911 year, determined an adverse movement of the investment of foreign capital in Mexico and even, probably, the withdrawal of some capital that was already in our country. This is a perfectly natural phenomenon: young nations like ours, when they suffer some disorder, find themselves exposed to provoke distrust in foreign capitalists, who prudently abstain from continuing to make investments, and even in those that they have made, they find a way to withdraw them. As, has been established on repeated occasions, our economic balance is settled by way of foreign capital investment, [it] is easy to understand that, when this investment is suspended for the reasons just mentioned, a scarcity of international bills of exchange will strike the market and there will be determined a stream of yellow metal exportation, that which serves as international money. The incident, then, should not surprise us: on the contrary, the observation of the way the country can stop this emigration of gold, has to serve us, in studying the condition of the balance of our accounts, to convince us once again of the economic robustness of Mexico and the confidence that, in the final analysis, inspires foreign capitalists. * * *

* * *

[In section 11, the report compares imports and exports and economic balance.]

It has been established on different occasions, and has been noted in some budget initiatives, that the surplus of exports over national imports does not cover all of the commitments that the Republic has abroad, due to imports as much as other factors that constitute what might be called negative aspects of our economic balance. In the past year, nevertheless, the effort made by this country to pay by means of exports the amount of their commitments in the greatest quantity possible, was considerably energetic and reached the highest number in our financial history. It was not enough, nevertheless, for this effort to cover the balance of our debts. The exportation of our gold coins, national as well as foreign, as was already mentioned in paragraph 7 of this initiative, demonstrates that, * * * the country had to make an awful effort represented by the extraction of a part of its gold currency, whose value reached nearly 10% of our circulating yellow metal. It was natural that it happened like this, because to the factors that constantly appear, in the sense of imposing an obligation to make payments abroad, new elements were added during this past year to those that needed to be faced, and this under difficult conditions, as is well known. These factors were determined, as was already stated, by the suspension of foreign capital investment, which is one of the favorable elements in our account balances and by the probable emigration of some national capital, all a consequence of national distrust that the revolutionary movement created abroad. Nevertheless, the emigration of gold was able to be stopped before assuming alarming proportions. The triumph of the revolution, the reestablishment of organic peace, the installation of the interim Government that rushed to offer guarantees to the whole world and dissipate fears of excess and reprisals, were returning the lost confidence in foreign capitals. Very quickly the Currency and Exchange Commission managed, in use of one of the powers that the law conferred on the institution, and duly authorized by the Secretaría de Hacienda, to celebrate two credit operations: one with the gentlemen of Speyer and Company, of New York, and the other with the German Bank of South America, the virtue of which determined an investment of $30,000,000 of foreign capital in the country. It saved, then, Mexico the difficult condition of its balance of debts by the usual process in nations that, economically, find themselves robustly constituted, that is to say, through the attraction of capital that was brought to invest in the country. The Government lent its cooperation to resolve the difficulties which are referenced, it not only authorized the Exchange Commission to execute the mentioned operations, but also gave them its guarantee. * * * The existence of part of these funds in foreign banks, on one hand, and on the other, the circumstances that the government has an amount of money in its power to establish exterior credit, just like the rebirth that has already been observed in all businesses, thoroughly guarantee that, at the very least in the near future, the difficulties alluded to in this paragraph will not be repeated. [pp. 321–323]

ALFREDO MÉNDEZ MEDINA

"The Social Question in Mexico: Orientations"

In 1891, Pope Leo XIII issued the Rerum novarum, also known as the "Rights and Duties of Capital and Labor." Medina was sent to Europe before the Revolution to study with priests in Europe and learn how to apply the Church's dictates to Social Catholicism in America. While the publication of the following document did not happen until 1913, the ideas of Social Catholicism were being discussed as the Catholic Church entered the political arena of the Mexican Revolution.

SOURCE: *Study presented at the Assembly of the National Confederation of Catholic Workers' Circles. Celebrated in Zamora, January 19–22, 1913, pp. 29–35. Available at https://babel.hathitrust.org/cgi/pt?id =uc1.31822009495417;view=1up;seq=1. Translated and adapted from the original by Stephany Slaughter and Deb Dougherty.*

PROGRAM

General Goal

To unite all our forces to promote a fundamental reform of the current economic regime, according to the principles established in the Encyclical *"Rerum Novarum."*

General Strategy

We condemn, equally, liberal and socialist tactics, rejecting both violence and bureaucratism. We do not rule out State intervention, but we maintain that it is private action that by rights must initiate this movement; official support will consist of removing obstacles to said intervention, supporting, sustaining and protecting it with prudent laws and sanctioning its legitimate aspirations.

Our public action will be loyal and openly democratic, in the sense of the Encyclical *"Graves de Communi."* We want the people to raise themselves up, that is to say, that we want advances to come from the natural and spontaneous outcome of their own efforts. We invoke, certainly, the cooperation of the so called ruling classes, but their part must not be a simple pecuniary protection, but rather a selfless provision of services, valuing the talents, studies, and personal influence of their brothers so that such progress may be easily realized.

Our Principal Demands

1st Preservation of the domestic home and family life, for which the following indispensable conditions are required:

   a) Setting in each industry by a *professional council* a minimum wage corresponding to an adult worker in normal life conditions.
   b) A rational regulation of work by women and children, tending toward the elimination of work by married women and children under 12 years old, giving firm guarantees of hygiene, morality and security to young single women.
   c) The acquisition of family property not subject to division or seizure consisting not only of the small rural farm, but also in the small urban dwelling and artisan workshop.

2nd Institutions that protect the worker against involuntary unemployment, accidents, illness, and scarcity in old age.

3rd Permanent councils for obligatory arbitration to peacefully resolve conflicts between capital and labor.

4th Ability to participate, to the degree possible, in the profits and even the ownership of the businesses that lend themselves to it, by means of stock shares or by other easily implemented methods.

5th Protection from profiteering and obvious or covert speculation that in many ways concentrates national riches in the hands of the few, taking advantage of the inexperience or needs of others.

6th Facilities for the organization and protection of the middle class, by means of independent associations of individual employees and the State, small industrialists, small businessmen, etc.

7th Effective regulation of work undertaken in the home, especially that of women and young seamstresses, with the goal of establishing, necessary social and professional protections.

8th Legal representation before authorities, of the interests of workers, by means of professional corporate delegations.

9th As for the agrarian question, we propose a separate special program, in which, taking into consideration the legitimate rights of the landowners, we offer a proposal of reforms towards ensuring for the decent and hardworking peasant, to the extent possible, possession or more stable use of sufficient land for the adequate support of his family. In said program, we will give primary importance to those institutions that at once favor the peasant economically, instruct him in his profession, and educate him against his own moral defects and errors that result in an unproductive and counter-productive economy.

Our reforms will proceed in an orderly fashion through successive stages, without abrupt transitions nor rash advances, but with consistently firm steps, they will march towards the desired goal.

* * *

WE REQUEST OF PUBLIC OFFICIALS:

In general, that they duly support the aforementioned demands.
  And especially:

1) That they recognize the juridical entity of professional unions, with rights as extensive as needed regarding real estate and other property, the right to professional authority**** over their members and the right to representation before the authorities.
2) That they recognize labor unions, trade unions, and similar private associations, the right to fix a salary tax over and above a fair and socially appropriate base salary.
3) That they enact and effectively sanction the Sunday rest law.
4) That they introduce into the Civil Code the necessary modifications in order to convert small rural or urban domains into family properties not subject to division or seizure.
5) That they subject Stock Exchanges and businesses to strong regulation.
6) That they more equitably distribute tax burdens, too heavy today for small contributors, and reform, above all, any taxes that make life more expensive, and establish in general a system of contributions such that the tax rate of the poor and that of the rich be proportionate to their relative strengths.

JOSÉ GUADALUPE POSADA

"Gaceta Callejera," 1892

The image shown here depicts mounted police dispersing anti-reelectionist protestors in Mexico City. While the document is accompanied by text, those who could not read would have focused on the image of the police versus the protestors.

SOURCE: *U.S. Library of Congress, The Elisha Whittelsey Collection, The Elisha Whittelsey Fund, 1946/Metropolitan Museum of Art.*

****Jurisdiction in strictly professional matters, in which no one better than those of the profession can competently judge [Medina's note].

GACETA CALLEJERA.

Esta hoja volante se publicará cuando los acontecimientos de sensación lo requieran.

Continuación de las manifestaciones anti-reeleccionistas.—Los acontecimientos del martes.—Las calles del Reloj y S. Ildefonso.—Alarma del comercio.

El asunto de la reelección sigue originando disturbios y escándalos que además de tener en continua sosobra á las gentes pacíficas, perjudican profundamente á los comerciantes de todos los ramos.

Más ampliamente informados sobre los sucesos ocurridos, podemos dar detalles más circunstanciados de estos acontecimientos.

En los escándalos del lunes en la noche, resultó un muerto por la calle de Tezontlale, de un balazo en la frente, recogiendo la respectiva Comisaría ese cadáver que no había podido ser identificado. Por las mismas calles fué herido el joven José Leonides Ruiz. En la esquina de las calles de Chavarría y Montealegre fué herido el gendarme José de J. Rodríguez al querer disolver un grupo de revoltosos, logrando aprehender á su heridor.

Varios gendarmes de la montada fueron heridos, pero su número no llega á diez, siendo por lo tanto exajerados los rumores que corrían de que el número de los lesionados era considerable. Entre los paisanos hubo también sus contusos pero igualmente se exajera al suponer tan grande el número de las desgracias ocurridas.

El martes 17 á las once y media de la mañana cundió la alarma sin justificado motivo y la mayor parte de los comerciantes del centro, cerraron los aparadores, y algunos hasta las puertas del despacho. Las calles se veían casi solas y la poca gente que transitaba, lo hacía demostrando el justifi-

cado temor de encontrarse repentinamente envuelta en un disturbio popular.

A las doce del día los estudiantes anti-reeleccionistas trataron de reunirse en la Alameda, pero la numerosa policía que con anticipación fué situada en aquel paseo, impidió la reunión, disolviendo los pequeños grupos que se formaban.

En la tarde el punto del escándalo fueron las calles del Reloj, S. Ildefonso y la Encarnación, en cuyo crucero se apostó un regular número de Gendarmes de la montada al mando del Coronel del Cuerpo. El General Carballeda se hallaba también en aquel sitio, lo mismo que el Sr. Cabrera, segundo jefe de las comisiones de seguridad.

Dividida la Gendarmería en grupos de ocho y diez hombres, se abrían en cruz avanzando por las calles del crucero, despejándolas hasta las banquetas donde se subían los soldados atropellando cuánto encontraban. El Sr. Cabrera siguió á un grupo de estudiantes hasta la Escuela de Jurisprudencia donde éstos se refugiaron.

No escasearon los caballazos y cintarazos propinados por los soldados y los oficiales, y hasta el fuete del coronel halló ocupación.

Numerosos individuos de la reservada y gendarmes vestidos de paisanos, se mezclaron entre los curiosos, y se nos asegura, aunque nosotros no lo vimos, que se efectuaron varias aprehensiones. Por una carta que publica "El Tiempo" suscrita por un señor Miguel Ruiz Esparza, asegura éste que el día 16 había en Belem además de él otras 22 personas detenidas por los sucesos del domingo 16.

El lunes en la noche se verificó una reunión anti-reeleccionista y los que la formaron resolvieron no retroceder en su empeño y continuar la lucha emprendida en pro de su idea. Nada de malo tiene que traten de sostener sus opiniones, siempre que lo hagan procurando evitar desórdenes y escándalos que sobre atraer perjuicios considerables á la gente pacífica y á los comerciantes, hará caer por sí sola una causa que tan malos resultados da sólo al iniciarse.

A última hora ha corrido el rumor de que por el barrio de la Palma, hubo la noche del martes un gran motín del cual resultaron varios muertos y no pocos heridos.

Igualmente se dice que por las calles de S. Francisco se renovaron los escándalos de la víspera y que en la refriega hubo heridos y entre éstos un estudiante recibió siete heridas.

Tales rumores no será estraño que resulten falsos, pues sabido es cuánto exajera la voz pública los acontecimientos que ocurren en situaciones como la actual.

La noche del martes el zócalo presentaba un aspecto muy triste. Rodeado por gendarmes de la montada, nadie podía pasar por allí, pues la gente era retirada por los soldados que no permitían el paso. Las calles de Plateros, Profesa y S. Francisco ofrecían también el más triste cuadro, pues no se veía ni una sola luz de casa de comercio abierta, y los poquísimos transeuntes que por allí pasaban lo hacían con manifiesto temor.

Procuraremos tener al público al tanto de todo lo que ocurra y que nos parezca digno de consignarse.

México.—Imp. Sta. Teresa núm. 1.

APPENDIX: ADVANCED RULES FOR USE OF POWERS

In some courses, instructors may decide to increase the complexity of the game. If they choose to proceed in this fashion, the actions provided below are available to players upon the activation of the related power.

Advanced Options for Power of Money

1. **Public Influence.** Mexicans may expend 150 pesos to buy an additional vote (that is, to invoke voter fraud). Foreigners can expend 225 pesos for the same effect (that is, to cast a vote). This represents the bribery and coercion that have been part of Mexico's history. *To Activate:* See "Public Influence" under "Power of the Press" (p. 76)

2. **Military Support.** Mexicans may expend 150 pesos to acquire the Power of Military Action (foreigners must pay 225 pesos), as explained earlier in the game book. This buys military arms for a revolutionary group. In game terms, it works exactly the same as "Overthrow/Defend the Mexican Government" (see p. 75). *It can be purchased only once per conflict and must be done before any declaration of military action.* After all, it takes time to arm and organize mercenaries. *To Activate:* see "Power of Military Action" (p. 75).

Advanced Options for Power to Arrest

Hunger Strike. Female revolutionaries were known to use hunger strikes to get themselves out of jail faster. Sentiment was more lenient on females than on males. So, *jailed female characters* may go on a hunger strike and have their jail time halved. No man would resort to such feminine means, so if you are playing a disguised woman and you go on a hunger strike you will reveal your secret. *To Activate:* Waive your red bandana and declare a hunger strike.

Advanced Options for Power of Military Action

1. **Silence a Journalist.** You can strip a member of the press of an extra vote by, for example, silencing their journal by making a speech rebutting a newspaper article created by the target. Use evidence to support your rebuttal. *To Activate:* Make a speech countering an article created by your target.

   Results: A member of the press silenced in this way must still turn in any required written articles to the GM for grading, but the articles cannot go out for mass consumption by the rest the class. In addition, that member of the press cannot use his or her Power of the Press until the end of the following Game Session (attacks on the press should happen at the end of one session so the attacked individual is silenced for a only a single Game Session).

2. **Pillage a Hacienda.** People with the Power of Military Action may attack and seize the assets, cash on hand, of wealthy landowners (foreign and domestic) in Mexico. Thus poor characters can convert this power into cash. Only characters with currency reserves can

be attacked in this way. *To Activate:* Make a speech, or publish an article with a member of the press, stating why your target should be pillaged. You must justify your action using your ideology and sources. The attack must be approved by the GM and will occur only after there has been time for the target to rally other characters with the Power of Military Action to mount a defense.

    Results: If the attack is successful, the character with currency reserves must give the attacker any *cash on hand* at the moment he or she is notified of the successful attack. This strips the target only of cash not reserves.

3. *Defense.* Anyone with the Power of Military Action may attempt to defend a journalist or other character who has currency reserves from attack. *To Activate:* Rebut the speech or article issued by the individual behind the attack. The side with the most military support wins.

    Results: If successful, the defenders prevent the attack and no money changes hands.

Advanced Options for Power of the Press

1. **Incite Military Action.** Members of the press may incite military action (offensive or defensive). If they decide to do this they can do no other press-related actions on that day. *To Activate:* Write a 250-word article justifying the action using sources and your character's ideology. This must be done before the action takes place

because getting people to organize around journalism takes time. *This cannot be used as a spur-of-the moment action.*

    Results: Your character gains access to the Power of Military Action (see p. 75 for details).

2. **Investigate Events.** Members of the press may look into an event that occurs in the game, such as an assassination. To do so, they tell the GM of their plan to dig up dirt on a particular event. The GM will then roll some dice to determine the success of the investigation. The more journalists involved in the investigative effort, the more likely it will succeed. What you do with the information you receive is up to you. *To Activate*: Write a 250-word plan justifying your actions with evidence from your character sheet or ideology.

    Results: You may find evidence uncovering who conducted an assassination or other secret event. A lot of the success in this depends on your own research and a roll of the dice. The more research you put into your plan, the more successful it is likely to be. A successful plan gives the journalists physical evidence they can use against those who orchestrated the event in question.

Advanced Options for Power of Currency Reserves

See "Advanced Options for Power of Money," p. 205.

NOTES

1. In the context of the Mexican Revolution, conservatives favored a strong central government (and some even supported the idea of a monarchy), where the interests of society as a whole took precedence over individual freedoms, and wanted the Church and the military to maintain power. Conservatism is often associated with a proclerical stance, specifically pro–Catholic Church.

2. See "The Rise of Benito Juárez" later in the game book.

3. Paul Wiseman, "Seeking soft skills: Employers want graduates who can communicate, think fast, work in teams," Associated Press, *Times-Tribune,* June 25, 2013.

4. Stephen B. Neufeld, *The Blood Contingent: The Military and the Making of Modern Mexico, 1876–1911* (Albuquerque: The University of New Mexico Press, 2017), p. 6.

5. Cynthia Radding, *Wandering Peoples: Colonialism, Ethnic Spaces, and Ecological Frontiers in Northwestern Mexico, 1700–1850* (Durham, NC: Duke University Press, 1997), p. 181.

6. Susan M. Deeds, Michael C. Meyer, and William L. Sherman, *The Course of Mexican History,* 11th ed. (Oxford: Oxford University Press, 2017), pp. 321–322.

7. Ibid., pp. 322–324.

8. Ibid., pp. 324–325.

9. Ibid.

10. Ibid., pp. 326–327, 345.

11. Ibid., pp. 338–339.

12. Ibid., pp. 340–342.

13. Susie Porter, *From Angel to Office Worker: Middle Class Identity and Female Consciousness in Mexico, 1890–1950* (Lincoln: University of Nebraska Press,

2018), pp. 2–3. Stephen Neufeld speaks of the importance of honor for both men and women in *The Blood Contingent,* p. 42.

14. Deeds., pp. 347–348.

15. Ibid., p. 349.

16. Ibid., pp. 363–364.

17. Ibid.

18. William H. Beezley, *Mexican National Identity: Memory, Innuendo, and Popular Culture* (Tucson: University of Arizona Press, 2008), pp. 87–89.

19. Armando Martín Ibarra López, "Apuntes para una historia de la telecomunicación en Mexico," *Comunicación y Sociedad* 22–23 (1994–95): p. 107.

20. Ibid., p. 109.

21. Ingrid Elliott, "Visual Arts: 1910–37, The Revolutionary Tradition," in Michael S. Werner, ed., *Encyclopedia of Mexico* (New York: Routledge, 1997), p. 2:1580.

22. Mercurio López Casillas, "Posada: Profesional de la imagen," in María Concepción Perez de Celis Herrero, ed., *Posada: El grabador mexicano* (Sevilla, Spain: Editorial RM, 2006), p. 86.

23. Pete Hamill, "The Casasola Archive," in *Mexico: The Revolution and Beyond: Photographs by Agustín Víctor Casasola 1900–1940* (New York: Aperture Foundation, 2003), p. 15.

24. Thomas Gretton, "Posada and the 'Popular': Commodities and Social Constructs in Mexico before the Revolution," *Oxford Art Journal* 17.2 (1994): p. 36; and Ron Tyler, *Posada's Mexico* (Washington, D.C.: Library of Congress, 1979), p. 60.

25. Roberto Berdecio and Stanley Appelbaum, eds., *Posada's Popular Mexican Print: 273 Cuts by José Guadalupe Posada* (New York: Dover Publications, 1972), p. xviii.

26. Robert Buffington, *A Sentimental Education for the Working Man: The Mexico City Penny Press, 1900–1910* (Durham, NC: Duke University Press, 2015).

27. John Mraz shows that many photos attributed to Casasola were taken by other photographers in his book, *Photographing the Mexican Revolution: Commitments, Testimonies, Icons* (Austin: University of Texas Press, 2012).

28. The Casasola archives include 483,993 negatives that were taken by 483 different photographers. See Hamill, "The Casasola Archive," pp. 14, 16.

29. Ibid., p. 14.

30. James Oles, *Art and Architecture in Mexico* (London: Thames & Hudson, 2013), p. 204.

31. Ibid.

32. Oles, *Art and Architecture in Mexico,* 201–205. Porfirio Díaz favored the European over the indigenous in many ways, including portraying himself as more European by wearing makeup to lighten his skin color.

33. Ibid., pp. 202–205.

34. Ibid., p. 212.

35. Ibid., p. 207.

36. Elliott, "Visual Arts," p. 1577.

37. John Holmes McDowell, "Corridos," in Michael S. Werner, ed., *Encyclopedia of Mexico* (New York: Routledge, 1997), p. 1:349.

38. John Reed, *Insurgent Mexico* (New York: International Publishers, 1969), pp. 87–89.

39. McDowell, "Corridos," p. 351.

40. Ibid.; and Ric Alviso, "What is a Corrido? Musical Analysis and Narrative Function," *Studies in Latin American Popular Culture* 29(2011): p. 60.

41. John King, "Latin American Cinema," in Leslie Bethell, ed., *The Cambridge History of Latin America*, vol. X, (New York: Cambridge University Press, 1995), p. 456.

42. Margarita deOrellana, *La Mirada circular: El cine norteamericano de la Revolución mexicana 1911–1917* (Mexico: Artes de la Mirada, 1999), p. 36. The Mutual Film Company would go on to make a deal with Pancho Villa, paying him $25,000 for exclusive filming rights.

43. Ángel Miquel, "Cine silente de la Revolución," in *Cine y Revolución: La Revolución Mexicana vista a través del cine* (Mexico: IMCINE and Cineteca Nacional, 2010), p. 33.

44. Ibid., p. 34.

45. David M. J. Wood, "Reconstruir el cine documental en el archivo de Salvador Toscano," in *Cine y Revolución: La Revolución Mexicana vista a través del cine* (Mexico: IMCINE and Cineteca Nacional, 2010), p. 42.

46. Mark Saad Saka, *For God and Revolution: Priest, Peasant, and Agrarian Socialism in the Mexican Huasteca* (Albuquerque: University of New Mexico Press, 2013), p. xv.

47. "Agrarismo," in Michael S. Werner, ed., *Encyclopedia of Mexico* (New York: Routledge, 1997), p. 1:21.

48. Raymond B. Craib, *Cartographic Mexico: A History of State Fixations and Fugitive Landscapes* (Durham NC: Duke University Press, 2004) p. 58.

49. John A. Britton, "Liberalism," in Michael S. Werner, ed., *Encyclopedia of Mexico* (New York: Routledge, 1997), p. 1:741.

50. Magón, "Class Struggle" (see p. 101 in the game book).

51. Ibid.

52. Magón, "Manifesto" (see p. 106 in the game book).

53. Ibid.

54. Magón, "Class Struggle."

55. Ibid.

56. John Mason Hart, "Anarchism and Anarchist Movements," in Michael S. Werner, ed., *Encyclopedia of Mexico* (New York: Routledge, 1997), pp. 1:48–52.

57. Stephanie J. Smith, *Gender and the Mexican Revolution: Yucatán Women and the Realities of Patriarchy* (Chapel Hill: University of North Carolina Press, 2009), p. 47. Elvia Carillo Puerto's brother Felipe would later become governor of the state of Yucatán from 1922 to 1944 and would promote women's rights legislatively.

58. Gabriela Cano, "Feminism," in Michael S. Werner, ed., *Encyclopedia of Mexico* (New York: Routledge, 1997), p. 1:480; and Martha Eva Rocha Islas, *Los rostros de la rebeldía: veteranas de la Revolución Mexicana, 1910–1939* (Mexico City: Secretaría de Cultura, Instituto National de Estudios Históricos de las Revoluciones de México, Instituto Nacional de Atropología e Historia, 2016) pp. 331–338. Some publications include *El Recreo del Hogar* (1879), *El Álbum de la Mujer* (1883–1891), *Hijas del Anáhuac* (founded by women in 1887), *La Mujer Mexicana* (1904–8; a publication that would advocate for changes to the Civil Code but not suffrage), and *La Mujer Moderna* (1915–18; a publication that signaled a change in goals of feminism as its contributors called for social and political action outside the home).

59. There were, of course, exceptions, and some women took very active roles in these organizations and advocated for women's rights. Dolores Jiménez y Muro, an active participant in anti-Díaz organizations and who participated in writing the Plan de Ayala and the Plan Social Político; and Hermila Galindo, an active member of a liberal club and fervent supporter of women's rights, are two such women.

60. Two Feminist Congresses took place in 1916 in Yucatán in January 13–16 and December. See Alaide Foppa Foppa, Alaide and Helene de Aguilar, "The First Feminist Congress in Mexico, 1916," *Signs* 5.1 (Autumn 1979), pp. 192–199; and Rocha Islas, *Los rostros de la rebeldía*, pp. 356–369.

61. Hermila Galindo not only fought for women's suffrage but also ran for office in 1918, knowing full well she wouldn't be allowed to serve, in order to draw attention to the movement for women's access to vote.

62. Cano, "Feminism," p. 480. See also Carmen Ramos Escandón, "Women and Power in Mexico: The Forgotten Heritage, 1880–1954," in Victoria Rodríguez, ed., *Women's Participation in Mexican Political Life* (Boulder, CO: Westview Press, 1998), pp. 88–89; and Anna Macias, *Against All Odds: The Feminist Movement in Mexico to 1940* (Westport, CT: Greenwood Press, 1982), pp. 13–15.

63. Macias, *Against All Odds*, p. 13.

64. Ibid., p. 15; and Ramos Escandón, "Women and Power in Mexico," p. 89.

65. Macías, *Against All Odds*, p. 15.

66. Ibid., p. 17.

67. Ibid., p. 7.

68. Kathryn Sloan, *Women's Roles in Latin America and the Caribbean* (Santa Barbara, CA: Greenwood, 2011), p. 174.

69. Other secondary schools followed in the provinces.

70. Macias, *Against All Odds*, p. 10.

71. Ibid., p. 11.

72. Susie Porter explores women's move from "Angel in the house" to working in offices in *From Angel to Office Worker: Middle-Class Identity and Female Consciousness in Mexico, 1890–1950*, (Lincoln: University of Nebraska Press, 2018).

73. Nancy LaGreca, *Rewriting Womanhood: Feminism, Subjectivity, and the Angel of the House in the Latin American Novel, 1887–1903* (University Park: Pennsylvania State University Press, 2009), p. 34.

74. Macias, *Against All Odds*, p. 12.

75. Cited in ibid., p. 55.

76. Ibid., p. 16.

77. According to Sarah Buck, "Although camp followers have supported armies throughout history, the Mexican case is perhaps exceptional for the degree to which *soldaderas* blended the 'masculine' roles of soldier with the 'female' support services." Sarah A Buck, "Rosa Torre González: *Soldadera* and Feminist," in Jeffrey M. Pilcher, ed., *The Human Tradition in Mexico* (Wilmington, DE: Scholarly Resources, 2003), p. 142.

78. Rocha Islas, *Los rostros de la rebeldía*, p. 36.

79. Neufeld, *The Blood Contingent*, p. 101

80. Ibid., 96.

81. Ibid., 99.

82. Elizabeth Salas, *Soldaderas in the Mexican Military: Myth and History* (Austin: University of Texas Press, 1990), pp. 38–39; Arce, *Mexico's Nobodies*, pp. 56–67.

83. Neufeld remarks that "the practice of stealing women from their homes, deflowering them, and eventually marrying them was long-standing and legally recognized during the Porfiriato." pp. 42.

84. Neufeld, *The Blood Contingent*, 99.

85. Joanne Hershfield, *Mexican Cinema/Mexican Woman, 1940–1950* (Tuscon: University of Arizona Press, 1996), p. 26. For roles of women in the Revolution, see chapters 3–4 of Rocha Islas, *Los rostros de rebeldía*; chapters 3 and 5 of Neufeld, *The Blood Contingent*; chapters 1–2 of B. Christine, *Arce's Mexico's Nobodies: The Cultural Legacy of the Soldadera and Afro-Mexican Women* (Albany: State University of New York Press, 2017).

86. Britton, "Liberalism," p. 1:738.

87. Recall, however, that despite liberal rhetoric, men and women were not equal.

88. Carlos Rangel, *The Latin Americans: Their Love-Hate Relationship with the United States*, trans. Ivan Kats (New Brunswick, NJ and London, UK: Transaction Publishers, 1987), p. 142.

89. See, for example, the statement from the Church issued March 20, 1857, "El clero, intolerante, amenaza a quienes juren la constitución," available at www.biblioteca.tv/artman2/publish/1857_148 /El_clero_intolerante_amenaza_a_quienes_juren _la_constituci_n.shtml.

90. Britton, "Liberalism," p. 1:740.

91. Constitution of 1857 Amendments from 1873, article 1 cited in Arthur Howard Noll, *From Empire to Republic in Mexico: The Story of the Struggle for Constitutional Government* (Chicago: A. C. McClurg & Co., 1903) p. 293.

92. In a letter to Juárez in 1858, Díaz affirmed his support of the president. See "Porfirio Díaz ratifica su adhesión a la causa liberal," available at www .biblioteca.tv/artman2/publish/1858_147/Porfirio _D_az_ratifica_su_adhesi_n_a_la_causa_liberal.shtml.

93. José Antonio Aguilar Rivera, "Liberalismo," in Javier Torres Parés and Gloria Villegas Moreno, eds., *Diccionario de la revolución Mexicana* (Mexico City: UNAM, 2010), p. 674.

94. Britton, "Liberalism," p. 1:740.

95. Aguilar Rivera, "Liberalismo," p. 675.

96. Britton, "Liberalism," p. 1:742.

97. Aguilar Rivera, "Liberalismo," p. 676.

98. Aguilar Rivera, "Liberalismo," p. 674.

99. Ibid.

100. Patricia Aceves Pastrana, "Evolución, evolucionismo," in Javier Torres Parés and Gloria Villegas Moreno, eds., *Diccionario de la revolución Mexicana* (Mexico City: UNAM, 2010), p. 655.

101. Walter Breymann, "The Científicos: Critics of the Díaz Regime, 1892–1903," *Arkansas Academy of Science* 7 (1954): pp. 23, 95.

102. Aguilar Rivera, "Liberalismo," p. 675.

103. Ibid., p. 96.

104. Margarita Vera Cusperina, "Positivism," in *Encyclopedia of Mexico*, Michael S. Werner, ed. (New York: Routledge, 1997) v. 2, pp. 1178–1180.

105. Robert E. Curley, "Social Catholicism," in Michael S. Werner, ed., *Encyclopedia of Mexico* (New York: Routledge, 1997), pp. 2:1347–1350.

106. David Espinosa, "'Restoring Christian Social Order': The Mexican Catholic Youth Association (1913–1932)," *The Americas* 59.4 (April 2003): 453–454.

107. Stephen J. C. Andes, "A Catholic Alternative to Revolution: The Survival of Social Catholicism in Postrevolutionary Mexico," *The Americas* 68.4 (April 2012): 534.

108. "Social Darwinism," *Encyclopædia Britannica* Online Academic Edition, June 2012. Available at www .britannica.com/EBchecked/topic/551058/social -Darwinism.

109. Jürgen Buchenau, "Social Darwinism," in Michael S. Werner, ed., *Encyclopedia of Mexico* (New York: Routledge, 1997), p. 2:1350.

110. Ibid., p. 1351.

111. Though this theory may seem to push past racism, many scholars have denounced this idealizing of the mestizo as erasing indigeneity.

112. Chaz Bufe, "Note," in Chaz Bufe and Mitchell Cowen Verter, eds., *Dreams of Freedom: A Ricardo Flores Magón Reader* (Oakland, CA: AK Press, 2005), p. 131.

ACKNOWLEDGMENTS

The process of writing a book is long indeed and requires constant rereading by the author(s) and friends, colleagues, and partners. Writing a game incorporates another set of people, the people who have played the game and those who have offered to run it. We have been incredibly fortunate in both regards. The process of writing *Mexico in Revolution* started in 2008 when Jon was working as an adjunct at Hamline University and the College of St. Benedict's and St. John's University. At that time it was a novel idea inspired by knowledge of Reacting to the Past, but it contained only five characters and worked in small groups. Since then it has been played at both of our home institutions— Central Michigan University (CMU) and Alma College—as well as a host of other institutions. A number of colleagues have provided incredible feedback. We wish to thank Deb Dougherty, Mary Strasma, Stephanie Mitchell, Paul Wright, Nick Proctor, Shari Orisich, Jason Dormady, David Burden, Linda Mayhew, and so many more people in the RTTP community (and their students!). In 2015, Jon had the opportunity to visit Cabrini College and meet with students who had played his game. While Jon had been brought to campus to discuss game design, the excitement of students who had played the game that semester as well as in previous years was especially edifying. We also owe a special thanks to Mark Higbee at Eastern Michigan University who has encouraged us since he first learned of the game in 2009. A brief play test of the game was conducted at Eastern Michigan during the summer of 2010, which provided us with a number of great ideas. The game also benefited from the 2012 Reacting to the Past Game Development at CMU. That conference provided many helpful ideas and allowed us to meet with Mary Jane Treacy, whose influence can be felt throughout the materials. We also wish to thank Thomas Darragh for the editorial support and comments he has provided on the game and Hugo Zayas for help locating and transcribing primary source documents. Sandy Planisek, who audited a course where the game was used, has gallantly acted as an editor for the manuscript. Additional play tests were conducted in 2014 at the regional RTTP conference held at Gustavus Adolphus College and at the 2015 Annual Reacting to the Past conference held at Barnard College. We are grateful to all of our play testers at each conference, but especially wish to acknowledge the detailed comments from Jeff Hyson and Nick Proctor.

We are also eternally grateful to our students at Alma and CMU who have played this game in a number of iterations and are even responsible for the adoption of certain characters and so many rule changes and adjustments that we had to stop counting. We also owe an especially big debt to Jon's HST 397 Colonialism, Revolution, and Dirty War class, which ran in the fall of 2012— Laci Bosquez, Nicholas Farrant, Joseph Gilbert, Benjamin Gulick, Alexandra Harkins, Benjamin Harris, Blake Mcdonald, Marie Morgan, Richard Rasmussen, Breanna Stadel, and Trent Wolf. They, more than any others, took the game on with gusto and provided a great deal of constructive criticism to help improve it. They even met and ran the game on their own for a day while Jon was at a conference—despite the fact that they could have easily have taken the day off. To our surprise, seven of them then returned to the game during the spring semester of 2013. They were not enrolled in the class, but they sat in the class for two weeks to help increase the dynamics of the game. While there, they played roles, conducted research and interacted with the students who were enrolled in the class and provided additional suggestions for improving the game.

In particular, the authors want to acknowledge and thank Benjamin Harris and Trent Wolf for their research and editorial contributions to this project. Ben wrote the "Prologue in Four Perspectives," and both he and Trent helped research and write many of the characters. While we have benefited from the support of many people, their contributions far outstripped the rest.

We also want to thank the incredibly talented team at W. W. Norton that has helped to shepherd us through the process. Justin Cahill and Rachel Taylor came to the project with a new energy and helped to make the game better. Though she arrived to the project later, Funto Omojola helped carry it over the finish line. Candace Levy's attention to detail on copy editing has made some of the more convoluted pieces better and has improved the product overall. To the rest of the team at W. W. Norton who have in one way or another touched this project, we thank you.

We have also benefitted from the outside review of William Beezley (University of Arizona), Justin Castro (Arkansas State University), Stephen Neufeld (California State University, Fullerton), and Shari Orisich (Coastal Carolina University). Thank you all for your comments, critical and supportive. You have helped to make this project better.

Last, but most importantly, we also have to thank our families (Tessa Peterson, Braeden and Kai and Victor Argueta, Ana Sofia and Alexa) who have heard no end of conversations about the Mexican Revolution, game mechanics, and how to incorporate the two. They have supported our obsession even when our conversation turned to it during official "Mexican Revolution Free Time." We thank them for their understanding, support, and feedback.

CREDITS

"Corrido of Tomochic": Republished with permission of Greenwood Publishing Group, Inc., from *Competing Voices from the Mexican Revolution: Fighting Words,* Chris Frazer, 2010; permission conveyed through Copyright Clearance Center, Inc.

Cota, José Muñoz: Republished with permission of Greenwood Publishing Group, Inc., from *Competing Voices from the Mexican Revolution: Fighting Words,* Chris Frazer, 2010; permission conveyed through Copyright Clearance Center, Inc.

Diaz, Felix: Reproduced from *Félix Díaz, the Porfirians, and the Mexican Revolution* by Peter V. N. Henderson by permission of the University of Nebraska Press. Copyright 1981 by the University of Nebraska Press.

Jiménez y Muro, Dolores: Republished with permission of Greenwood Publishing Group, Inc., from *Competing Voices from the Mexican Revolution: Fighting Words,* Chris Frazer, 2010; permission conveyed through Copyright Clearance Center, Inc.

Madero, Francisco I.: "Absolute Power in Mexico," "Are We Ready for Democracy?" and "The National Democratic Party" from *The Presidential Succession of 1910,* translated by Thomas B. Davis, Jr., pp. 148–163, 207–213, 219–221. Copyright © 1990 Peter Lang Publishing. Reprinted by permission of the Estate of Thomas B. Davis, Jr.

Magón, Ricardo Flores: "Manifesto to the Nation: The Plan of the Partido Liberal Mexicano," "1906 PLM Program," "To Women," "Class Struggle," "The Mexican People Are Suited to Communism," "Manifesto," from *Dreams of Freedom: A Ricardo Flores Magón Reader,* translated and edited by Chaz Bufe and Mitchell Cowen Verter, pp. 126–129, 131–134, 233–236, 187–190,

176–177, 138–144. Copyright © 2005 AK Press. Reprinted by permission of AK Press.

Pozas, Ricardo: From *Juan the Chamula: An Ethnological Recreation of the Life of a Mexican Indian,* translated by Lysander Kemp, © 1962 by The Regents of the University of California. Published by the University of California Press.

Rabasa, Emilio: "The Election" and "Supremacy of Legislative Power" from *Liberty in Mexico: Writings on Liberalism from the Early Republican Period to the Second Half of the Twentieth Century,* edited by José Antonio Aguilar Rivera, translated by Janet M. Burke and Ted Humphrey. © 2012 by Liberty Fund, Inc. Reprinted by permission of Liberty Fund, Inc.

Sierra, Justo: "Reservations," "Liberals and Conservatives," and "Our Battle Plan" from *Liberty in Mexico: Writings on Liberalism from the Early Republican Period to the Second Half of the Twentieth Century,* edited by José Antonio Aguilar Rivera, translated by Janet M. Burke and Ted Humphrey. © 2012 by Liberty Fund, Inc. Reprinted by permission of Liberty Fund, Inc.

"The Corrido of the Soldadera": Republished with permission of Greenwood Publishing Group, Inc., from *Competing Voices from the Mexican Revolution: Fighting Words,* Chris Frazer, 2010; permission conveyed through Copyright Clearance Center, Inc.

Womack, John, Jr.: Appendix B: The Plan de Ayala and Appendix C: The Agrarian Law from *Zapata and the Mexican Revolution* by John Womack, Jr., copyright © 1968 by John Womack, Jr. Used by permission of Alfred A. Knopf, an imprint of the Knopf Doubleday Publishing Group, a division of Penguin Random House LLC. All rights reserved.